D1073161

Teaching English as a Foreign Language in Primary School

Edited by Mary Lou McCloskey, Janet Orr, and Marlene Dolitsky

Case Studies in TESOL Practice Series

Jill Burton, Series Editor

Teachers of English to Speakers of Other Languages, Inc.

Typeset in Berkeley and Belwe
by Capitol Communication Systems, Inc., Crofton, Maryland USA
Printed by United Graphics, Inc., Mattoon, Illinois USA
Indexed by Coughlin Indexing, Annapolis, Maryland USA

Teachers of English to Speakers of Other Languages, Inc.
700 South Washington Street, Suite 200
Alexandria, Virginia 22314 USA
Tel. 703-836-0774 • Fax 703-836-6447 • E-mail info@tesol.org • http://www.tesol.org/

Publishing Manager: Carol Edwards
Copy Editor: Sarah J. Duffy
Additional Reader: Ellen Garshick
Cover Design: Capitol Communication Systems, Inc.

ISBN 193118528X
Library of Congress Control Number: 2005908946

Table of Contents

PART 3: TEACHER DEVELOPMENT FOR PRIMARY EFL

Series Editor's Preface

The Case Studies in TESOL Practice series offers innovative and effective examples of practice from the point of view of the practitioner. The series brings together from around the world communities of practitioners who have reflected and written on particular aspects of their teaching. Each volume in the series covers one specialized teaching focus.

❖ CASE STUDIES

Why a TESOL series focusing on case studies of teaching practice?

Much has been written about case studies and where they fit in a mainstream research tradition (e.g., Nunan, 1992; Stake, 1995; Yin, 1994). Perhaps more importantly, case studies also constitute a public recognition of the value of teachers' reflection on their practice and constitute a new form of teacher research—or teacher valuing. Case studies support teachers in valuing the uniqueness of their classes, learning from them, and showing how their experience and knowledge can be made accessible to other practitioners in simple, but disciplined ways. They are particularly suited to practitioners who want to understand and solve teaching problems in their own contexts.

These case studies are written by practitioners who are able to portray real experience by providing detailed descriptions of teaching practice. These qualities invest the cases with teacher credibility, and make them convincing and professionally interesting. The cases also represent multiple views and offer immediate solutions, thus providing perspective on the issues and examples of useful approaches. Informative by nature, they can provide an initial database for further, sustained research. Accessible to wider audiences than many traditional research reports, however, case studies have democratic appeal.

❖ HOW THIS SERIES CAN BE USED

The case studies lend themselves to pre- and in-service teacher education. Because the context of each case is described in detail, it is easy for readers to compare the cases with and evaluate them against their own circumstances. To respond to the wide range of language environments in which TESOL functions, cases have been selected from EFL, ESL, and bilingual education settings around the world.

The 12 or so case studies in each volume are easy to follow. Teacher writers describe their teaching context and analyze its distinctive features: the particular demands of their context, the issues they have encountered, how they have effectively addressed the issues, what they have learned. Each case study also offers readers practical suggestions—developed from teaching experience—to adapt and apply to their own teaching.

Already published or in preparation are volumes on

- academic writing programs
- action research
- assessment practices
- bilingual education
- community partnerships
- content-based language instruction
- distance learning
- English for specific purposes
- gender and language learning
- global perspectives
- grammar teaching in teacher education
- intensive English programs
- interaction and language learning
- international teaching assistants
- journal writing
- literature in language learning
- mainstreaming
- teacher education
- teaching English as a foreign language in primary schools
- technology in the classroom

◈ THIS VOLUME

Due to the increasing prominence of English as an international language, English is now taught in the early school years in many countries, resulting in teacher education challenges for teachers and planners and continuing debates on the best ages to learn an additional language. This book shows how the challenges and debates are addressed in 13 countries.

Jill Burton
University of South Australia, Adelaide

CHAPTER 1

Introduction

Mary Lou McCloskey, Janet Orr, and Marlene Dolitsky

Although there is considerable discussion—even controversy—among English language specialists about the best age for introducing English language instruction in countries where English is not usually spoken in the home (Hyltenstam & Abrahamsson, 2001; Nunan, 2003), policy changes mandating the earlier introduction of English in foreign language settings are increasingly being implemented worldwide. In this collection of case studies, language educators and program implementers from 13 countries tell their stories about programs and practices designed to support English instruction for primary-aged learners. Each program is different—the influencing factors in each country vary due to the language or languages used in students' homes, the education systems, the cultural influences on language practices, the approaches to educational administration, and each nation's history of language teaching and learning. In spite of these differences, common threads are evident in the studies.

Many of the authors of these case studies report that English has been part of the national curriculum for some time, but English has typically been introduced at the middle or secondary level. Recently, educators have been encouraged (and sometimes mandated) to rapidly implement English language education for younger learners—students 6 or 7 years of age. Often, the speed of this implementation exceeds the pace at which programs are able to prepare materials and teachers, creating questions concerning the goals of primary English language education. These cases describe models of effective instruction, effective and rapid program design and planning, methods for carrying out English language instruction with teachers who are not well prepared, techniques for rapidly improving teachers' ability to speak and teach in English, and strategies for sustaining teachers and their English as a foreign language (EFL) programs. The cases even ask questions regarding who benefits from this shift to earlier English language instruction: Does the instruction first serve the country, the politicians, the government, the ministry, the parents, or the learners?

Although most of the case studies in the collection address more than one of these issues, we have grouped the chapters in main sections according to predominant topics: approaches to primary EFL program development, primary EFL curriculum and classroom practices, and teacher development for primary EFL.

The organization of each chapter is similar. First, authors provide a brief overview and share information about the social and political context of the program or project they describe. This gives readers an opportunity to discover various sociocultural contexts, governmental policies, and historical language practices that affect the local situation. Second, authors describe their project or program, outlining the planning and implementation, describing effects of the program, and providing samples of materials developed and used. Third, authors depict distinguishing features about their project or program that make it special, notable, or universal— and perhaps worthy of replication in other countries. Fourth, authors recommend practical ideas from their program for others to use and adapt to their own contexts. Finally, authors offer conclusions regarding the accomplishments of the programs and future directions they may take.

❖ PART 1: APPROACHES TO PRIMARY EFL PROGRAM DEVELOPMENT

These first four chapters address program-level questions about teaching EFL in the primary grades.

Spain

In chapter 2, "Multilingualism in the Educational System of Valencia, Spain," Carmen Pinilla-Padilla tells how the Valencian school system met dual challenges: (1) addressing the needs of the bilingual population for instruction in their local language, Valencian, and the national language, Spanish, and (2) implementing a foreign language (English) program beginning in Grade 1 through the Enriched Bilingual Education Program (PEBE). She explains the program's use of a content-based model and how it involves a careful and progressive integration of the three languages with content instruction. Pinilla-Padilla's detailed description of how the model is implemented and scheduled in the schools highlights its operational approach.

Taiwan

English officially became one of the required subjects in elementary schools in Taiwan in 2001, starting from the fifth year, with a shift to third grade beginning in 2005. Yi-Hsuan Gloria Lo, in chapter 3, "Leading the Way in the New Millennium: An Integrated Multiage EFL Program in Taiwan," describes the Experimental English Program (EEP) at Win Wau Elementary School in Penghu County, an island of Taiwan. The program, which was implemented as a response to the new language policy, field-tested an approach to EFL education that modeled innovations in instruction, including accommodating a variety of learning styles, using groups and cooperative learning structures, fostering student autonomy through learning centers, developing English language skills and positive attitudes toward the language, promoting discussion among educators in the region about foreign language pedagogy, and initiating a partnership between the teacher training institution and the local school.

Mexico

In chapter 4, "Pass It On: English in the Primary Schools of Coahuila, Mexico," Elsa Patricia Jiménez Flores describes the process of developing and implementing El

Programa de Inglés en Primaria (English Program in Primary or PIP). The program, which originated in the state of Coahuila, is now being implemented in more than two thirds of the states in Mexico. Jiménez Flores describes the organization of the program and the pre- and in-service training in both English language and English pedagogy to prepare teachers for program implementation. She also shares how the program has successfully supported learners as well as teachers, leading to a large number of learners entering secondary schools with advanced English language skills. As a result, the design of English language instruction at the secondary level for students who completed PIP was revised.

Italy

In chapter 5, "The Long and Winding Road: A Profile of Italian Primary EFL Teachers," Lucilla Lopriore focuses on the consequences of government leadership in primary EFL program development in Italy and on the professional development of teachers for this program. As is the case with many educational programs described in this book, the rapid implementation of primary English education somewhat precedes the teacher development required for implementation. In Italy, concurrent decentralization and reform efforts have resulted in foreign language programs that serve as a specific means of implementing changes in the overall education program. Lopriore describes how these innovations are taking place in schools, how they are influenced by the *Common European Framework of Reference for Languages* (Council of Europe, 2001a), the *European Language Portfolio* (Council of Europe, 1997), and the professional development program established to enhance both English language proficiency and the pedagogy of primary English language teachers.

◈ PART 2: PRIMARY EFL CURRICULUM AND CLASSROOM PRACTICES

The case studies in Part 2 provide insights into curriculum reform initiatives at the local level in major but not capital cities in Turkey, India, Vietnam, and Bulgaria.

Turkey

Yasemin Kırkgöz begins chapter 6, "Teaching EFL at the Primary Level in Turkey," by highlighting the current state of education in Turkey, with its complex political and economic ambitions. She then describes the challenges created in the country when the introduction of EFL instruction shifted from secondary to primary schools. One challenge is to ensure that a sufficient number of skilled teachers are ready to teach in the expanding English primary program. Kirkgöz describes the multiple approaches used to prepare teachers and elaborates on the results. A second challenge is to ensure that these newly trained teachers use curriculum and instructional materials specifically designed for young learners. Kirkgöz uses a questionnaire and classroom observation protocols to collect data about actual classroom practices. This study demonstrates the appropriateness of English language instruction and the new curriculum in primary classrooms. Finally, she reports the study results based on the different types of teachers who participated in the training exercises. Kirkgöz's case study vividly illustrates how teacher training and implementation of the curriculum are integrated into primary schools in Adana, Turkey.

India

In chapter 7, "Flavoring the Salt: Teaching English in Primary Schools in India," Jayashree Mohanraj shares insights into teaching English in primary schools in Andhra Pradesh, South India, where English is one of 18 official languages. First, she provides a historical perspective of English instruction in India, with a focus on the recurring struggle to revise language instruction policy. Although English has been spoken in India for 200 years, institutional and pedagogic dimensions of English language learning are complex in this country. Mohanraj brings to light the complex nature of the massive education system in India and places the use of English in the larger multilingual context of the country. She then focuses on curriculum development and the design and production of local teaching materials, including primary textbooks. A sample lesson helps readers visualize the practical curriculum as it is implemented in primary classes.

Vietnam

Ha Van Sinh, in chapter 8, "Is Grade 3 Too Early to Teach EFL in Vietnam?" describes how English instruction was briefly started in Grade 1 in Vietnam. Then, because the community was concerned about the effects of early introduction on pupils learning to read Vietnamese, the introduction to English quickly changed to Grade 3. To examine this effect, Sinh collected and analyzed data on pupil performance in Vietnamese and English classes, parent perceptions of children's schooling, and the EFL syllabus and its implementation in the classroom. The results and analysis are insightful.

Bulgaria

In chapter 9, "A Local Approach to Global English: A Bulgarian EFL Model Based on International Children's Culture," Lilia Savova presents a three-part instructional model for teaching EFL in Bulgarian primary schools. The curriculum model applies a literacy-focused approach, a theme-oriented method, and children's culture-based techniques. Savova illustrates the model with a number of classroom activities used in Bulgarian schools and relates it to Anthony's (1963) approach-method-technique model for English language instruction.

◈ PART 3: TEACHER DEVELOPMENT FOR PRIMARY EFL

The true benefit of teaching English in primary school is its effect on the learners, who represent the future of every nation. The key aim of training programs is to address the needs of "clients." But in the case of government teacher-training programs, the stakeholders are numerous: politicians, ministries, teachers, parents, and, of course, pupils, who demand that their specific concerns be addressed. The remaining chapters in this volume address the programs that train teachers to meet the needs of these various groups.

Sri Lanka

In chapter 10, "Developing Teachers in the Developing World of Sri Lanka," David Hayes reports on a long-term training program in a country divided by regional and cultural strife, where opposing regions have different languages and where English is perceived by some as the language of colonists and by others as a language of prestige. The aim of the program was to provide teachers with needed practical training for primary instruction. Hayes describes how innovative approaches were employed to provide in-service teacher development at the primary level in state schools in Sri Lanka. Improvement in the quality of schooling is addressed through improved teacher competence. As Hayes states, it is teachers who actually decide which methodology will be used in their classrooms and who thus determine the success or failure of educational reforms. No matter how well-thought-out new methodologies are, if teachers do not buy into them, such improvements will be left by the wayside.

Egypt

In chapter 11, "The Pyramid Scheme: Implementing Activity-Based Communicative Language Teaching and Supervision With Primary Teacher Educators in Egypt," Mary Lou McCloskey, Linda New Levine, Barbara Thornton, and Zeinab El Naggar describe a project in which a multinational consultant team facilitates training for teacher educators from university faculties and ministries of education. The authors first focus on how to develop teachers' effective knowledge, skills, and attitudes about educating young learners, through consideration of such topics as child development; language development; and effective, activity-based communicative language teaching practices. Next, the authors describe how the pyramid scheme supports teacher educators in developing their own professional materials to prepare themselves and the ministry of education teacher supervisors. The principles of local ownership, cultural relevance, innovative methodologies for language teaching, technology integration, experiential and active learning, a long-term timeline, and long-term usability are applied throughout the project and result in sustainable materials and training now being used throughout Egypt.

France

Marlene Dolitsky offers suggestions for facilitating practice teaching for preservice English language teachers in chapter 12, "The French Communicative Connection: Catching Up." In the program she describes, university faculty, cooperating master teachers, and peer student teachers support and observe practice teachers as they plan and then take charge of an English class for the first time. This field experience is a reality check after the preceding theoretical training. Although the follow-up conference with the practice teachers is based on the immediate lesson, Dolitsky emphasizes the importance of readying teachers for their careers. The aim is to prepare teachers who are striving for constant self-improvement. To this end, Dolitsky presents the process used to help student teachers prepare lessons in detail and analyze their own performance in the classroom so they will learn to bring about their own personal development as in-service teachers.

Korea

In chapter 13, "EFL Teacher Training for South Korean Elementary School Teachers," Sung-Hee Park describes major teacher training initiatives in response to the introduction of English in Grade 3. Park first describes the logistical and method-ological aspects of the program and then provides information on the program's effectiveness. The aim of the program is to help primary teachers develop skills to teach English as part of the primary curriculum. The program accomplishes this aim by helping teachers understand the curriculum for elementary school English and develop appropriate teaching methods and skills, improving their ability to use English as a medium of instruction, and preparing them to teach basic communicative language skills. Park offers recommendations, based on feedback from trainees, for designing effective English language education programs for primary school teachers.

Hong Kong

Gertrude Tinker Sachs and Tony Mahon, in chapter 14, "Enabling Effective Practices in the Teaching and Learning of English in Hong Kong," describe an oral approach to primary English study and offer insight into the development of pupils' enjoyment in learning English through the adoption of a literature-based approach. In Hong Kong, English has long been part of the primary school program, albeit not always as a particularly favored subject. Tinker Sachs and Mahon describe how their team carried out a longitudinal teacher development project in shared reading. They provide a careful overview of the factors that should be considered when adopting new literacy programs, including long-term commitment in supporting teachers and careful tracking of pupils' growth in reading and writing.

These case studies highlight the global role of English as it emerges as the main foreign language in primary schools. They demonstrate how educational systems have developed policy and have planned to deal with competing demands to include English in the primary school setting. This volume describes many insightful curricular innovations and classroom success stories; we hope they provide you with insights to guide the decision-making process in the English instructional programs in your school or country.

❖ CONTRIBUTORS

Mary Lou McCloskey, past president of TESOL, is an international consultant and author of professional texts, standards, and program materials in the field of English for speakers of other languages. She has worked with teachers, teacher educators, and departments and ministries of education on five continents and in 31 of the United States.

Janet Orr was 2004–2005 chair of TESOL's Elementary Education Interest Section (EEIS) and is currently coeditor of the *EEIS E-newsletter.* Her interest lies in curriculum development and assessment of young learners in ESL and EFL settings around the world. She is currently an education specialist for the U.S. Agency for International Development in Sri Lanka.

Marlene Dolitsky is an associate professor at the University of Paris's Teacher's College (Institut Universitaire de la Formation des Maîtres). Her main mission is to train teacher learners to teach English in their future primary school classes. One of her major research interests, and the subject of her doctoral thesis, is child bilingualism.

PART 1

Approaches to Primary EFL Program Development

CHAPTER 2

Multilingualism in the Educational System in Valencia, Spain

Carmen Pinilla-Padilla

◈ INTRODUCTION

Educational authorities in Valencia, Spain, envisioned that early introduction of the teaching of English as a foreign language (EFL) would enrich bilingual education programs that were already being developed in primary schools. Because Valencia is a bilingual community with two official languages, the authorities believed that increased communicative competence would result from an integrated treatment of these two languages along with the early introduction of EFL. The educational system specific to the Valencian Community was designed with the goal that students use all three languages as means of communication in the content areas.

◈ CONTEXT

The educational system in Spain previously included teaching EFL only from the third year of primary education. Since 1998, the autonomous Ministry of Education in the Valencian Community started a plan with the ultimate goal of providing multilingual education, including one foreign language and the two official languages (Valencian and Spanish), to all children from the age of 5 onward. To maintain the time devoted to teaching other areas, the plan was devised to be developed progressively. From the beginning, teaching language has been designed according to the content-based language learning approach.

The state administration in Spain follows a decentralized model, which allows the autonomous communities[1] certain powers in the area of education, including executive and regulatory powers. The communities are responsible for implementing basic state standards and the regulation of nonfundamental aspects of the system. In the Valencian Community, the autonomous community administration has formulated its own educational administration as a councillorship (*Consellería*).

Three laws[2] constitute the basic legislative framework of the Spanish education system. The first compulsory basic educational level established is primary education,

---

[1] In Spain, the country is divided into 17 autonomous communities that have full governing autonomy except for military matters and international relationships.

[2] The Organic Law on the Right to Education (enacted in 1985), the Organic Law on the General Organization of the Education System (enacted in 1990), and the Organic Law about participation evaluation and government of teaching institutions (enacted in 1995).

TABLE 1. PRIMARY EDUCATION IN SPAIN

	Schooling Year	Students' Ages
First cycle	1	6–7
	2	7–8
Second cycle	3	8–9
	4	9–10
Third cycle	5	10–11
	6	11–12

which is divided into three 2-year cycles. The students' ages range from 6 to 12 (see Table 1).

The administration of public primary schools is the responsibility of the school council and the teachers' assembly, as collegiate bodies, and of the headmaster, head of studies, and secretary, as individual officers. In Spain, the educational coordinating bodies at the school level are the cycle teams and the pedagogical coordination commission; in Valencian Community primary schools, there are also Valencian language normalization teams, which are responsible for guaranteeing the enforcement of the law regarding the use and teaching of the two official languages. Although the educational action of the different schools is based on governmental regulations, every school has its own educational and curricular project. Therefore, different schools' syllabi, although derived from a common framework, vary from one school to another.

The teachers' assembly includes all the teachers in a school and is chaired by the headmaster. This body is responsible for planning, coordinating, and adopting all decisions regarding pedagogical and educational matters. The teachers' assembly also drafts proposals to be submitted to the school council. The school council comprises teachers, parents, and students and is the ultimate decision-making body regarding the curriculum.

The Weekly Timetable

Teaching in primary education is usually organized around twenty-five 60-minute periods per week, including a weekly maximum of 2½ hours (30 minutes per day) of break time. These class periods are usually distributed on a 5-hour-per-day schedule, Monday through Friday, although some schools have incorporated a new system increasing the class periods by 30 minutes every day to allow for a weekly in-service training afternoon. Table 2 shows the hours devoted to the core curriculum in primary education in the Valencian Community.

Languages

The 1992 constitution states that Spanish is the official language of the Spanish state and, therefore, all Spanish citizens are under the obligation to know it and have the right to use it. Some autonomous communities have a second official language, which has co-official status as stated in their autonomic statutes. These communities

TABLE 2. HOURS DEVOTED TO THE CORE CURRICULUM IN VALENCIAN PRIMARY EDUCATION

Areas of Knowledge	First Cycle	Second and Third Cycles
Knowledge of the environment (natural, social, and cultural)	175	170
Artistic education	140	105
Physical education	140	105
Spanish language and literature	350	275
Foreign language	—	170
Mathematics	175	170
Religion and social-cultural activities	105	105

Note. Based on data from Centro de Información y Documentación Educativa (n.d.).

comprise Catalonia and the Balearic (Catalonian), Galicia (Galician), Valencian Community (Valencian), the Basque Country (Euskera), and Navarra (Basque).

In the autonomous communities it is mandatory to use and study both official languages in education at levels other than university. It is compulsory to study foreign languages in the second cycle and third cycles (Grades 3–6) of primary education. Nonetheless, in almost all the autonomous communities, specific early introduction programs are being implemented in the first cycle (Grades 1–2). It should be highlighted that teaching EFL at the primary level is based on the concept of *language as a means of communication*. Through learning in other languages, pupils are introduced to other ways of perceiving reality, enhancing their cultural world, and encouraging the development of attitudes such as tolerance.

The Program

Principles Guiding Primary Education in Spain

The following principles relate directly to the introduction of EFL in primary schools:

- *Teacher training.* Primary education teachers must have general training in all subject areas except music, physical education, and foreign languages, which have to be taught by specialized teachers.

- *Teacher teams.* Every group of students is assigned a reference teacher who teaches all the subjects throughout the whole cycle (except for the specialized areas mentioned previously). The team of teachers in each cycle decides the teaching, learning, and assessment activities, which should be consistent with prior and subsequent school periods.

- *The goal.* The main goal of primary education is to favor students' social integration and the development of personal autonomy, to help them acquire a common cultural background, and to help them develop a command of oral expression, reading, writing, and arithmetic.

- *Areas of knowledge.* Learning is organized around six compulsory areas of knowledge: natural, social, and cultural environment; artistic education; physical education; Spanish language and the co-official language and literature of the respective autonomous community; foreign languages (usually English); and mathematics. General objectives are fixed for each area. The syllabus is organized around topical units (e.g., food, clothing), which provide a context for instruction and skill development targeted by the unit objectives.

Language Teaching in the Valencian Community

In the Valencian Community, there exists a bilingual situation, with households that speak both Spanish and Valencian. The use of Valencian was once rare in administrative, political, and cultural contexts, but recently the government developed a system for increasing the knowledge, use, and status of the Valencian language. It is within this system that the idea of an early introduction of EFL in primary schools was born.

In 1998, the Valencian government, through the Councillorship of Culture and Education, issued a law[3] regulating the basic requirements, criteria, and application procedures for an Enriched Bilingual Education Program (PEBE), involving the early introduction of a foreign language as a means of instruction in Grades 1 and 2 of primary education. (Similar programs exist in other communities throughout Spain, such as Catalonia or the Basque Country.) EFL was already being taught in every school starting in Grade 3, but with passage of the new law, it began to be introduced in Grades 1 and 2 in an increasing number of schools that ran the experimental program (described in more detail in the next section). In these schools, English is used as a means of communication with the intention of favoring the development of an underlying communicative competence. Because of the PEBE, a greater amount of school time than ever before is devoted to teaching both in Valencian and in English.

❖ DESCRIPTION

The very name of the program—Enriched Bilingual Education—states its main purpose: to enhance the linguistic richness of children's communicative competencies by providing an educational environment in which they can learn three languages—Spanish, Valencian, and a foreign language.[4]

The final goal of the councillorship is that the three languages be introduced in preschool education at age 3 and continue being taught until the end of compulsory education in Grade 10. For this reason, a training program for preschool education teachers from schools already participating in the PEBE was developed and began to be implemented during 2001–2002. The program approaches EFL teaching through an integrated treatment of languages (*tratamiento integrado de lenguas*). EFL is gradually introduced in the content areas. Thus, time can be devoted to building linguistic competence, without decreasing the time devoted to teaching content area material, while simultaneously providing a meaningful learning context for the

---

[3] Regulation of June 30, 1998, of the Conselleria de Cultura, Educación y Ciencia, for the establishment of basic requirements, criteria and procedures for implementation in educational centers of a program of enriched bilingual education for the inclusion of a foreign language, as a functional language, from the first cycle of primary education.

[4] Although the law refers generally to introducing a foreign language, English is actually the one chosen in every school.

language. This requires serious research, training, and coordination at every level of schooling.

This ambitious project has many facets, three of which are described in this chapter: administrative aspects and school organization, classroom implementation and methodology, and teacher training.

Administrative Aspects and School Organization

Before the PEBE, Valencian schools had three types of linguistic programs for teaching Valencian and Spanish, which differed from one another in the number of hours devoted to Valencian. Through the collegiate bodies mentioned earlier, every school had to decide which program to use as a guide for its activities. The three programs are Program of Progressive Incorporation (Programa de Incorporación Progresiva, or PIP), Program of Linguistic Immersion (Programa de Inmersión Lingüística, or PIL), and Program of Teaching in Valencian (Programa de Enseñanza en Valenciano, or PEV). In 1998 the PEBE appeared as a fourth possibility for schools. The appendix shows the number of hours dedicated to Valencian, English, and Spanish in Valencian primary schools, as well as the distribution across content areas for these languages.

If a school elects the PEBE, the whole school must undertake it as a collegiate project and parents must fully agree with this choice. Schools that want to participate in the PEBE have to fulfill a number of requirements[5] concerning the following organizational and pedagogical aspects:

- Both state-funded schools and private schools can participate in the PEBE.

- Schools that participate in the program have to develop their own project consisting of an adaptation of their linguistic program based on the suggested outlines. It is very important that the amount of time devoted to the foreign language does not reduce the amount of time devoted to other areas as stated in the law. Thus, the foreign language has to be introduced through nonlinguistic areas, so that the law[6] regarding time-tables is respected. To date, the amount of time devoted to English in the first cycle of primary education never exceeds a maximum of 30 minutes per day.

- The whole school community has to be involved in the project.

- The program must be approved by the school council.

- Collegiate bodies must agree on participating and state their commitment to the development of the program.

- All families have to give their written consent to the implementation of the program at Level 1.

- The school must have enough human resources to fulfill the needs related to program implementation; no additional teachers or personnel will be assigned to schools. There must be enough English language

---

[5] Regulated by the Orden of June 30, 1998, published as DOGV, July 14, 1998.
[6] Regulated by the Orden of May 12, 1994, published as DOGV, July 19, 1994.

teachers working at the school on a permanent basis to guarantee program implementation throughout all the schooling years.

- The school must state its commitment both to contribute to the self-training of the teachers and to send teachers to training activities organized by the councillorship.

- After fulfilling all the requirements, the school must send its project to the councillorship. The project can be started once the councillorship approves it.

Classroom Implementation and Methodology

Teaching English at the primary level (Grades 1–6) has as its main objective the practice of communication so as to establish the basis for language learning and an underlying communicative competence. In the Valencian Community, the early teaching of English rests on the following principles: acquisition of communicative competence, learning through exposure, and an integrative approach to instruction.

Communicative Competence

When studying the mother tongue, or a second or foreign language, a person acquires certain interconnected skills and competencies that constitute communicative competence. In the Valencian Community, teaching is grounded on the idea that all speakers have a certain communicative competence, which includes components that are common to speakers of all languages. According to such a principle, language teaching has to be organized from an integrative point of view, incorporating such elements as

- *grammatical competence,* the ability to choose from a system of lexical, morphological, syntactic, and phonological rules

- *sociolinguistic competence,* the capacity to adapt language output to different types of discourse

- *discourse competence,* the ability to produce different types of discourse

- *illocutionary competence* (conveyance of the speaker's intended meaning), the ability to organize messages around the negotiation of meanings

- *cultural competence,* the skill necessary to interpret nonlinguistic elements derived from cultural realities and transmitted by language

Learning Through Exposure

Children learn language through exposure to comprehensible input and opportunities to use the language in different situations and for different purposes. A language is more easily learned when children are exposed to it outside the school context, where they can put their learning into practice. In the Valencian Community, non-Valencian-speaking children have opportunities to interact and be exposed to the Valencian language through the media or by interacting with Valencian speakers outside the school, but opportunities to use English are extremely rare as English is not a second language but a foreign language in Spain. Therefore, teachers try to create multiple and varied situations, organized around nonlinguistic areas, to expose children to English. This exposure occurs in content area experiences, and learners are prompted to use English for those studies. The content areas chosen vary from one school to another, but all schools choose areas that require active involvement of children. Music education, art education, new technologies, and physical education are frequently chosen because they offer greater opportunities for providing both comprehensible input and student output. In these subject areas, it is easier for children to produce language because of the limited vocabulary and active involvement required of learners. Nonetheless, some experiences are beginning to be carried out in other areas such as science and mathematics. In the case of science, a high amount of active experimentation helps children to infer and deduct meanings. Mathematics, on the other hand, makes use of an international code that gives clear hints to help children understand and produce utterances in the target language.

Integrative Approach

It becomes every teacher's responsibility to teach the language(s) of instruction, and it is necessary to do so from an integrative point of view. Teachers agree on the methodology they will use, the content they will teach in every language, the metalanguage or linguistic terms they will use when explanations are needed, and the linguistic reflection that they will favor (how to focus children's attention on the metalanguage). Teachers work together to organize the teaching activities, so the various areas of learning are interconnected in a way that allows for mutual reinforcement and an integrated approach. Teachers meet weekly to review and reorganize their teaching.

Primary schools' teaching processes are required to include the means not only to help students learn how to learn, but also to help them develop effective learning strategies. Therefore, activities tend to be student oriented so that children's innate motivation to learn is exploited. It is in this respect that recreational activities with an educational aim provide a particularly suitable learning mechanism; the activities and materials prepared in the schools all are intended to be enjoyable. Teachers use storytelling, songs, rhymes, riddles, guessing and other games, and movement and support materials such as realia, pictures, and flashcards.

It is nearly impossible to find a pure application of one type of methodology in schools in Valencia. Teachers in the PEBE practice teaching strategies from the communicative approach while they use language as a means of communication for content-based teaching. In sum, they try to manage an integrated treatment of languages.

Teacher Training

In these new multilingual programs, teachers in the Valencian Community are confronted with having to learn to cope with a new reality and a new situation. The introduction of English requires a greater degree of coordination among all teachers in a school and the development of a culture of cooperation that has not always been present.

Training needs derived from the implementation of the PEBE are twofold. First, teachers need to be trained in the methodological aspects of teaching and of collaborative work. Second, teachers need language training. Content areas taught in English are taught by language specialists because teachers who are not language specialists do not have the necessary language competence.

The councillorship has made efforts to see that teachers involved in the program are trained in its basic aspects. Teacher training is a core task for any innovation as well as for research in the classroom, and it may take various forms, from traditional training to action research. In the case of the Valencian Community, courses have been organized combining these approaches to teacher training. Although training activities started at the beginning of the program, because the program was so new, both teachers and teacher trainers have been learning through experimentation. They have been conducting action research into different methodological approaches and are actually learning as new methods are tried, revised, and reformulated. (Table 3 shows the progression and evolution of the content of the PEBE teacher training activities.)

In addition, there is a need to develop new materials that can be used with younger children who are learning content in English. At present, publishers generally develop content materials with native speakers in mind as the potential market.

⬦ DISTINGUISHING FEATURES

There are two distinguishing features of the Valencian language program in primary schools. First and most distinctive is the linguistic situation, in which two official languages coexist, requiring integration of the treatment and teaching of languages into the general curriculum. Through simultaneously teaching three languages, the program seeks the development not of children's competence but of their *multicompetence.*

Second, in the PEBE, languages are not the explicit object of study. Rather, children learn things through the languages. English, Spanish, and Valencian are taught through the content areas, so they are learned as tools that are necessary for communication. The program is collegial, and coordination and cooperation are core values for its implementation.

⬦ PRACTICAL IDEAS

Although each setting has its distinctive characteristics, the following suggestions, which derive from successes in Valencian classrooms, may be useful for other primary school settings.

Maintain Close Working Relationships Among All Teachers

Close relationships help to guarantee coordination and continuity. Coordination is crucial because of the fragility of language acquisition at these early stages.

Be Flexible Regarding Methodology

Teaching must be adapted to the needs of the students, not only because every teaching situation is different, but also because this particular situation is so new.

TABLE 3. SUMMARY OF PEBE TEACHER TRAINING ACTIVITIES FROM 1998 TO 2001

1998–1999	• Seminars were offered to teachers who worked at schools near one another. • Training activities were organized around the revision of existing materials and resources. • Training was conducted, dependent on time availability and goodwill of the staff involved. Given that everything was new, the exchange of feelings and opinions as well as materials and experiences played an important role.
1999–2000	The first 50-hour PEBE training course was organized. The specialized part dealt with the following: • methodology for teaching English to young learners • communicative approach • task-based learning • topic-centered learning vs. task-based learning • theoretical aspects of course design; how to develop didactic units • field experiences in classrooms At the same time, several seminars for in-service teacher training action were developed.
2000–2001	• The second PEBE course was organized; it dealt with didactic units. In the course model, didactic units were provided by the trainers. • The new didactic challenge was for teachers not only to add a new language to the curriculum, but also to coordinate with other teachers for working in an integrated way with all the languages of the syllabus. • The working procedure was again that of action research: each school chose one of the didactic units to further develop. • In their schools, teachers coordinated and revised their syllabus to adapt it to the multilingual treatment. The school team adapted, rebuilt, or remade the unit. • The unit was put into practice and evaluated, then was revised and reshaped. • The results were shared with the other teachers participating in the course, and materials were exchanged.
2001–2002	Preschool teachers were incorporated to the training process. Training activities were divided into • courses for newcomers to the program • courses for experienced teachers
2002–2003 2003–2004	• Training activities for primary teachers were conducted: courses and school seminars where teachers put into practice and evaluated didactic units. • Preschool teachers continued working and experimenting with materials, didactic units, and methodology related to teaching languages to very young learners.

Carry Out Ongoing Evaluations

Evaluate classroom activities, materials, and methodology. One useful idea is to keep a class log of experiences during the implementation of the program. Having clearly articulated objectives and taking notes about what has been done to achieve them make it much easier to continue implementing the program and to evaluate it. Teacher evaluations can be undertaken through a collegiate system in which evaluation is internal and teachers help one another perform self-evaluations.

Use the Teaching Portfolio

Some teachers in the program organize their teaching portfolios and share them with their colleagues so that everyone can benefit from them. The portfolios can also be a facet of the aforementioned internal collegiate self-evaluation system.

Use Meaningful Activities

The evaluations already carried out have demonstrated the importance of preparing activities that are meaningful to the children and that are always developed in a context recognizable to the children.

Teach in Short Segments

Use short activities that last for a limited time period every day. Children have to put so much energy into participating in language activities that they can easily get tired and lose focus.

Involve Families

It is important to have family involvement. When family members are aware of what is going on at school, they may better reinforce it.

Teach Language Through Content

Content-based learning allows children to better infer meanings and to understand the reason for using English in the classroom.

Make Learning Activities Enjoyable

No matter which language the children are learning and using, they always participate more and are more willing to learn if they can enjoy themselves at the same time.

◈ CONCLUSION

There is not yet evidence showing that this particular adaptation of an integrated treatment of language is successful in its aim to develop a greater underlying communicative competence. As has already been explained, the areas chosen for the introduction of English require a higher level of manipulative activity, for example, music education, art education, new technologies, physical education, and other nonlinguistic areas. The need to constantly switch from linguistic goals to curricular goals, however, presents the danger of losing instructional focus.

It is important to reinforce the teaching of the less frequently spoken languages and local languages. In the case of the Valencian Community, it is precisely this situation that initially gave birth to the PEBE and has offered the possibility of further developing it. Nonetheless, participating in the program implies a greater number of hours devoted to Valencian teaching. Not all schools are willing to go along with this change—some schools decide not to introduce English at the early levels because they would be required to teach Valencian as well.

When a new program is started, there is a greater need for energy, time, and money to implement it. If the program is initiated by the educational administration, that administration has to provide the means for the effective in-service training of teachers and an adequate budget for investment in more human and material resources. So far, the councillorship has provided means for program implementation and teacher training, but great effort is still required of those involved directly with the program.

Although more research on the results of the program remains to be done, the case of the Valencian Community shows that teacher training in both linguistic and methodological aspects is a major step toward the effective implementation of any program for teaching English to young children. Valencian teachers are to be commended for their attitudes toward training. They have shown a strong willingness to work, demonstrated excitement about improving their practice, and made great efforts to become competent teachers and to update their knowledge about newly emerging methodologies and practices.

◈ CONTRIBUTOR

Carmen Pinilla-Padilla has taught English from elementary school to university levels. She currently works as director of the Centro de Formación, Innovación y Recursos Educativos in Torrent (Valencia) for the Valencian Councillorship.

APPENDIX: COURSE SCHEDULES FOR FOREIGN LANGUAGE PROGRAMS IN THE VALENCIAN COMMUNITY

TABLE A1. SCHEDULE FOR THE EARLY TEACHING OF A FOREIGN LANGUAGE IN THE PROGRAM OF PROGRESSIVE INCORPORATION (PIP)

	Cycle	Teaching of Valencian	Content-Based Teaching and Usage of Valencian and Spanish in Nonlinguistic Areas		Content-Based Teaching and Usage of Foreign Language (FL)	Teaching of Spanish
Pre-school	Second	Not established	Contents in Spanish			Systematic working on reading and writing in Spanish 4 hours
Primary Education	First	4 hours	Valencian 3 hours (knowledge of the environment)	Spanish 10 hours (nonlinguistic areas)	FL 1.5 hours	3 hours
Primary Education	Second	3 hours	Valencian 4 hours (knowledge of the environment) 1.5 hours (nonlinguistic areas)	Spanish 8.5 hours (nonlinguistic areas)	FL 2.5 hours	3 hours
Primary Education	Third	3 hours	Valencian 4 hours (knowledge of the environment) 2 hours (nonlinguistic areas)	Spanish 6 hours (nonlinguistic areas)	FL 4 hours	3 hours

TABLE A2. SCHEDULE FOR THE EARLY TEACHING OF A FOREIGN LANGUAGE IN THE PROGRAM OF TEACHING IN VALENCIAN (PEV)

	Cycle	Teaching of Valencian	Content-Based Teaching and Usage of Valencian and Spanish in Nonlinguistic Areas	Content-Based Teaching and Usage of Foreign Language (FL)	Teaching of Spanish
Pre-school	Second	Systematic working on reading and writing in Valencian 4 hours	Contents in Valencian	(hatched)	Spanish
Primary Education	First	3 hours	Valencian 13 hours (nonlinguistic areas)	FL 1.5 hours	Intensive review of reading and writing in Spanish 4 hours
	Second	3 hours	Valencian 12.5 hours (nonlinguistic areas) / Spanish 1.5 hours (nonlinguistic areas)	FL 2.5 hours	3 hours
	Third	3 hours	Valencian 10.5 hours (nonlinguistic areas) / Spanish 2 hours (nonlinguistic areas)	FL 4 hours	3 hours

TABLE A3. SCHEDULE FOR THE EARLY TEACHING OF A FOREIGN LANGUAGE IN THE PROGRAM OF LINGUISTIC IMMERSION (PIL), OPTION A

	Cycle	Teaching of Valencian	Content-Based Teaching and Usage of Valencian and Spanish in Nonlinguistic Areas	Content-Based Teaching and Usage of Foreign Language (FL)	Teaching of Spanish
Pre-school	Second	Systematic working on reading and writing in Valencian 5 hours	Contents in Valencian	///	///
Primary Education	First	4 hours	Valencian 16 hours (nonlinguistic areas)	FL 1.5 hours	
			Valencian 14 hours (nonlinguistic areas)		Intensive review of reading and writing in Spanish 3 hours
	Second	3 hours	Valencian 9.5 hours (nonlinguistic areas) / Spanish 4.5 hours (nonlinguistic areas)	FL 2.5 hours	Spanish 3 hours
	Third	3 hours	Valencian 8.5 hours (nonlinguistic areas) / Spanish 4 hours (nonlinguistic areas)	FL 4 hours	Spanish 3 hours

Table A4. Schedule for the Early Teaching of a Foreign Language in the Program of Linguistic Immersion (PIL), Option B

	Cycle	Teaching of Valencian	Content-Based Teaching and Usage of Valencian and Spanish in Nonlinguistic Areas	Content-Based Teaching and Usage of Foreign Language (FL)	Teaching of Spanish
Pre-school	Second	Systematic working on reading and writing in Valencian 5 hours	All contents in Valencian		
Primary Education	First		Valencian 16 hours (nonlinguistic areas)	FL 1.5 hours	Intensive review of reading and writing in Spanish 4 hours
	Second	3 hours	Valencian 8 hours (nonlinguistic areas) Spanish 5 hours (nonlinguistic areas)	FL 2.5 hours	
	Third	3 hours	Valencian 7 hours (nonlinguistic areas) Spanish 4.5 hours (nonlinguistic areas)	FL 4 hours	Spanish 3 hours

TABLE A5: SCHEDULE FOR THE EARLY TEACHING OF A FOREIGN LANGUAGE IN THE ENRICHED BILINGUAL EDUCATION PROGRAM (PEBE)

	Cycle	Teaching of Valencian	Content-Based Teaching and Usage of Valencian and Spanish in Nonlinguistic Areas	Content-Based Teaching and Usage of Foreign Language (FL)	Teaching of Spanish
Pre-school	Second	Valencian	Contents in Spanish		Systematic working on reading and writing in Spanish 4 hours
Primary Education	First	4 hours	Valencian 0.75 hours (nonlinguistic areas) / Spanish 12.25 hours (nonlinguistic areas)	FL 1.5 hours	
Primary Education	Second	3 hours	Valencian 1.5 hours (nonlinguistic areas) / Spanish 12.5 hours (nonlinguistic areas)	FL 2.5 hours	3 hours
Primary Education	Third	3 hours	Valencian 4 hours (knowledge of the environment) 2 hours (nonlinguistic areas) / Spanish 6 hours (nonlinguistic areas)	FL 4 hours	3 hours

CHAPTER 3

Leading the Way in the New Millennium: An Integrated Multiage EFL Program in Taiwan

Yi-Hsuan Gloria Lo

◈ INTRODUCTION

English officially became one of the required subjects in elementary schools in Taiwan in 2001, starting from the fifth grade onward. The latest English as a foreign language (EFL) policy in 2005 requires that young children take the subject of English starting in the third grade. The Experimental English Program (EEP) was developed in the late 1990s in anticipation of these language policies. The EEP took place at an elementary school in Penghu County, an island of Taiwan. Twenty elementary school children, ranging from Grades 2 to 6, participated in the program in the 1998–1999 academic year. The intent of EEP was to serve as a starting point for all stakeholders—the Bureau of Education, administrators, teachers, students, and parents. It was designed to be a springboard for discussions about the implementation of EFL education in elementary schools. The EEP also provided an alternative approach for EFL instruction in elementary schools in Taiwan in the new century.

◈ CONTEXT

Knowledge of English is perceived as one of the most important tools for establishing Taiwan as the Asian-Pacific center of transportation management, technology, and humanities. The purpose of the foreign language policy enacted in 2001 was to meet the increasing demands of the information technology era and the global nature of the 21st century. Although the policy was not officially implemented until 2001, school administrators, English language educators, parents, and students had been anticipating and preparing for this milestone of English language education in Taiwan. The EEP was a response to the trend made official by the 2001 language policy. With the latest EFL policy in 2005, the program has been transformed and reshaped; however, the fundamental principles that characterized the EEP have remained the same. Rather than coming to the program on a weekly basis, students throughout Penghu County participate in an English summer camp program developed and implemented by an EFL professional learning community, which I direct and which also serves to meet the objectives set for the EEP. In the past two summers, about 750 students in Grades 2–8 participated in 20 multiage English classrooms in 15 schools.

EEP began after several meetings I had with the principal of Win Wau Elementary School. This school served about 250 pupils and was one of 42 elementary schools in Penghu County, which is located on an island off the Taiwan Strait and is nicknamed "The Hawaii of Taiwan." As a former EFL teacher in Penghu County schools and an English instructor in the only college on Penghu Island, National Penghu Institute of Technology, I initiated the program. I believed it was my responsibility to get involved in the preparation for the 2001 language policy; I felt that the island needed to start preparing for EFL instruction in elementary schools before the implementation of the 2001 policy. The principal of Win Wau Elementary strongly supported my ideas. He wanted to offer an experimental EFL program in his school to initiate an alternative approach for EFL education and to open discussions among all the elementary schools in Penghu County.

For the second semester, I developed extra support for the program through a community partnership with members of a student club at National Penghu Institute of Technology. I served as a mentor for the club, which was called Learning Cultures Through Watching Movies, and I invited club members to participate in EEP. Funded by Taiwan's Ministry of Education and sponsored by my college, the community partnership program was added in the second half of the EEP. Funds were used to purchase the materials, furniture, and equipment needed for this experimental innovation. The students from the club helped set up the classroom and create an English-rich environment by creating learning opportunities inside and outside the classroom.

❧ DESCRIPTION

EEP was the first EFL program developed for elementary children in public school in Penghu County. The objectives of EEP were as follows:

- provide an alternative pedagogical methodology that is developmentally, cognitively, and emotionally appropriate for elementary school children
- foster autonomy of learning, appreciation for cooperative learning, and a respect for different learning styles, paces, and paths from those of different age groups
- create an English-rich environment by developing learning centers inside the classroom and learning activities outside the classroom
- enhance inner motivation and develop positive attitudes toward English language learning
- develop basic listening, speaking, reading, and writing skills
- offer a public space for those involved in EFL education in 2001 in county elementary schools and engage in discussions

The Learners

EEP was a multiage program. Twenty volunteer students participated in the program: 6 boys and 14 girls, ranging from second to sixth grade. About half of them came from Grades 2–3, and half came from Grades 4–6. Six of the 20, all fourth, fifth, and sixth graders, had learned English outside of the school system (at so-called cram schools in Taiwan). They had received 6 months to 2 years of English instruction before joining the EEP. One student who had studied English for 2 years knew how to say his English name and how to greet people in English, and he knew a fair amount of everyday vocabulary, such as *milk, desk, book,* and so on. Those who had 6 months of instruction could identify almost all the letters of the alphabet in both upper and lower cases. However, most students in the program were beginning-level

TABLE 1. OUTLINE OF THE PROGRAM FOR EACH SEMESTER

Week	Themes	Stories/Plays	Rhymes	Songs
		First Semester		
1	Greetings	Goldilocks and the Three Bears	Number 1–5	"How Are You?"
2	Numbers	Goldilocks and the Three Bears	Number 1–5	"This Is a Nice Song"
3	Colors	Goldilocks and the Three Bears	Teddy Bear	"This Is a Nice Song"
4	Colors	Goldilocks and the Three Bears	Teddy Bear	"The Alphabet Song"
5	School	Goldilocks and the Three Bears	Bees!	"The Alphabet Song"
6	School	Goldilocks and the Three Bears	Bees!	"This Is the Way"
7	Places	Goldilocks and the Three Bears	Review	"This Is the Way"
8	Places	The Gingerbread Man	Lost and Found!	Review
9	Vehicles	The Gingerbread Man	Lost and Found!	"When You Are Happy"
10	Vehicles	The Gingerbread Man	Review	"When You are Happy"
		Second Semester		
11	Animals	The Gingerbread Man	The Zoo Is Fun!	"See You Later, Alligator!"
12	Animals	The Gingerbread Man	The Zoo Is Fun!	"See You Later, Alligator!"
13	Food	The Three Little Pigs	Peanut Butter and Jelly	"The Salt and Pepper"
14	Food	The Three Little Pigs	Peanut Butter and Jelly	"The Salt and Pepper"
15	Home	The Three Little Pigs	Review	Review
16	Home	The Three Little Pigs	Home Sweet Home!	Review
17	Parts of Body	The Three Little Pigs	Home Sweet Home!	"The Body Song"
18	Parts of Body	The Three Little Pigs	Stamp Your Feet!	"The Body Song"
19	Clothes	The Three Little Pigs	Stamp Your Feet!	"This Is the Way I Wear"

Note. Most of the materials used for the whole-group curriculum (e.g., stories, rhymes, songs) were from either *Kids 1* (Walker, 1989) or *Let's Go* (1993).

learners who had never attended English classes, with no experience reading or speaking English. After being introduced to various media in the learning centers in the classroom, the students were divided into five heterogeneous groups based on gender and age. Each group had at least one child from an upper grade, one from a lower grade, and one boy and one girl.

Course Intensity and Length

This project lasted throughout the 1998–1999 academic year. As their teacher, I met with the learners for two 40-minute periods each week. The students also learned English from eight college students (three male and five female), who were members of the Learning Cultures Through Watching Movies club. The college students were interested in English instruction and therefore were willing to spend 2 hours every other week with the elementary students.

Program Outlines

The program was organized according to thematic units (see Table 1). The students and I selected five themes for each semester. The first semester's themes were numbers, colors, school, places, and vehicles; the second semester dealt with animals, food, home, parts of the body, and clothes. Rhymes, songs, and learning tasks in each learning center were chosen to engage learners in a particular thematic unit. In addition, each week the students were exposed to storytelling; they were encouraged to make props for the stories and to act them out by the end of the semester.

The Five Learning Centers

One of the key components of this program was the learning centers in the classroom. Learning centers, also known as learning stations, learning laboratories (labs), or learning areas (Ingraham, 1997, p. 15), are areas "where students can explore the English language in a variety of ways by working cooperatively in small groups or independently" (Lo, 2000, p. 3). That is, learners, alone or with others, complete learning tasks by engaging in multisensory activities that encourage speaking, listening, writing, and reading using materials provided in learning centers (McClay, 1996).

Five learning centers were designed: a computer center, a video center, a reading center, a listening center, and a writing center. Table 2 shows the equipment and materials used in each center.

Activities in the centers were as follows:

- *Computer center.* Two computer stations were available for the students to use. Students in each group (two at each computer) worked together to complete the tasks designated on interactive CD-ROMs. These tasks included coloring, calculating, playing games, listening, differentiating and categorizing objects, and practicing oral skills.

- *Video center.* This center used two sets of theme-based videos with different language levels. Prior to viewing, each learner was given a worksheet explaining the theme of the week and the task to be completed after watching the video. Learners watched the videos at least three

TABLE 2. EQUIPMENT AND MATERIALS FOR EACH CENTER

Centers	Equipment	Materials
Computer center	2 computers (monitors, key boards, microphones, speakers) 1 bookshelf	Theme-based multimedia CD-ROMs (12) Activity books Teachers guides
Video center	1 VCR 1 TV 1 TV cabinet 5 sets of headphones	Theme-based videos (21) Activity books Teacher's guides
Reading center	2 bookshelves 1 big carpet 5 pillows	Big books (13) Trade books (47) Flash cards (200)
Listening center	5 portable cassette players 5 sets of headphones 5 pillows	Alphabet books with tapes (27) Leveled story books with tapes (71)
Writing center	1 table 5 pillows 1 large bulletin board	Crayons, paper, scissors, glue, clay, and so forth

Note. The numbers in parentheses indicate the number of items required.

times: once with Chinese subtitles, once with English subtitles, and once without any captions.

- *Reading center.* It is difficult for beginning learners to read without acquiring sufficient vocabulary. Beginning learners were therefore first exposed to pictures and puzzles in the reading center. Then they were given children's literature, mainly picture books, from a variety of publishing companies. As the program progressed and the learners developed a fair amount of vocabulary, they were gradually encouraged to read children's literature with more English words and to try to make sense of the stories.

- *Listening center.* The same principles of the reading center applied to the listening center. Because it was difficult for beginners to comprehend spoken texts at the beginning of the program, richly illustrated storybooks were chosen. In addition, the groups were encouraged to take risks to guess the meaning of words on the audiotape based on a book's illustrations.

- *Writing center.* Although reading and listening are difficult tasks for beginning English language learners, writing is without a doubt the most difficult. Learners in the writing center not only had access to a variety of tools (stationery supplies), but they also were invited to use alternative media (e.g., clay, paper, crayons) to make meaning. For instance, before the beginners spelled the names of different animals, they might use clay to portray the animals or paper to create two-dimensional pictures of animals. Flash cards were also useful resources in the writing center.

Different sets of flash cards (e.g., animals, vegetables, vehicles, clothes) were used to help beginners spell the words in written form. Figure 1 shows how the classroom was organized into different learning centers.

A Thematic Approach

A thematic unit approach is one of the most effective ways to develop curricula for learning centers (Schurr, Lewis, LaMorte, & Shewey, 1996). A thematic approach means that the goals and activities for the different learning centers are based on the same learning theme (see Figure 2). For example, if the learning theme for a week is "home," then learners in the computer center might play a computer game that requires learners to click on the correct buttons when different family members are introduced. Learners in the video center might watch a film such as *The Family* (Qkids, 1999) to find out what each member of the family does from morning until night. Learners in the reading center might read *Are You My Mother?* (Eastman & Eastman, 1976) and learn to identify different family members in English. Learners in the listening center might listen to *Three Little Pigs* (Hillert & Wilde, 1984) and learn to pronounce the names for different members in a family. In the writing center, learners might draw a family tree and write the text in English. For an example of a lesson plan, see the appendix.

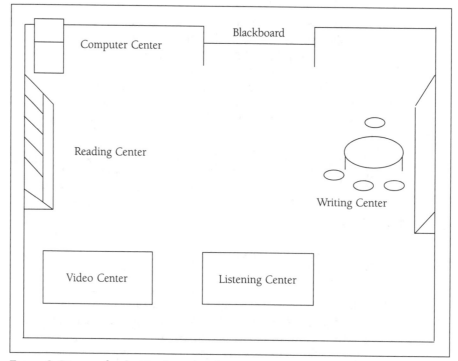

FIGURE 1. Diagram for the Five Learning Centers

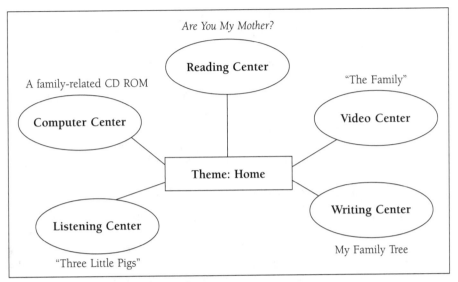

FIGURE 2. A Thematic Unit Approach

◈ DISTINGUISHING FEATURES

There are several features that made this program innovative and different from most elementary EFL programs in Taiwan.

A Multiage Class

A prevalent practice in education in Taiwan is to place children of the same age in a class. This practice seems to suggest that children of the same age are developmentally and cognitively at the same stage. However, every learner is unique: Each child has his or her own learning pace and path and therefore should not be grouped simply by age. According to Gardner (1993), learners have multiple intelligences: verbal/linguistic, musical/rhythmic, logical/mathematical, visual/spatial, bodily/kinesthetic, and interpersonal/intrapersonal. The existence of these different intelligences results in different learning styles and different needs (Chapman & Freeman, 1996). Some of the EEP students were better listeners or speakers, and others were better at reading or writing. They came together to benefit from each other's strengths and to develop their weaker areas. The appreciation and respect for differences among the multiage learners in this program built a nurturing environment for children who were at different developmental and cognitive stages (Nye, Cain, Zaharias, Tollett, & Fulton, 1995).

A Language-Rich Environment

The environment in which learners are surrounded is critical to meaning making. Grounded in Gardner's (1993) theory of multiple intelligences, a multisensory and multimedia learning environment was created both inside the classroom, through the five learning centers, and outside the classroom, through the community partnership program. As a result, different sensory modes and intelligences were enhanced in these 20 children.

All the materials in the learning centers were chosen based on three criteria. First, the materials had to address the themes chosen for the program. Second, the materials had to be highly motivating, interactive, and authentic (Froese, 1991a). Third, the materials had to be developmentally appropriate for elementary school children (Watson, 1994).

In addition, the classroom setup played an important role in the learning environment (see Figure 1). Instead of cultivating competition by placing students in rows for individual work, the physical environment of the program (e.g., carpet, pillows, bookshelves, flowers, plants, posters) cultivated a sense of respect and care that enhanced group dynamics and promoted language learning (Kagan, 1995).

A Community Partnership Program

The college students' participation added another positive element to this program in terms of learners' high motivation and positive attitude toward the English language. As mentioned earlier, eight college students from the same school district took part in the program twice a month on Saturdays. They brought more excitement to the learning and shared the workload with me. Consequently, not only did the children learn English with me inside the classroom, but they also had opportunities to interact in English with college students both inside the classroom in the learning centers and outside the classroom in the activities designed and implemented by the college students. Based on the results of a survey taken at the end of the program, 18 of the 20 students indicated that they loved to learn English with the "big brothers" and "big sisters." Almost all of them said that they enjoyed participating in the theme-based learning activities designed by the college students.

Authentic Use of the Four Skills

As stated earlier, the program employed a thematic approach that incorporated the five learning centers in the classroom and learning activities outside the classroom. This approach was selected because research shows that children learn to use every aspect of language, not simply writing, to make meaning (Edelsky, Altwerger, & Flores, 1991). The theme-based pedagogy fostered integrated language learning, which did not break language into pieces. Learners improved their language skills by using them in a meaningful and functional way. They learned about reading and writing while listening and speaking, they learned about writing from reading, and they gained insights about reading from writing (Newman, 1991). The cueing systems of language (e.g., phonology, orthography, morphology, syntax, semantics, pragmatics) were always present and part of every instance of language use (Altwerger, Edelsky, & Flores, 1989), both inside and outside of the classroom.

Autonomy and Cooperation

Traditionally in Taiwan, teachers are perceived as the major, if not the only, source of knowledge. This unexamined assumption especially holds true in EFL environments, where the English teacher is often considered the only person in the classroom who knows the language and hence the only person responsible for passing the language down to the learners. Cultivating learners' sense of autonomy was an essential part of the EEP. Students gained ownership of their learning by discussing with me which thematic units would be included in the curricula. Even the beginning-level students were given opportunities to take initiative in their learning at the learning centers and were encouraged to approach problems in their own way without my involvement.

Although independent learning was emphasized, cooperative learning (Balkcom, 1992; Coelho, 1992; Stahl, 1994) among group members was another factor that made this program unique. Language is socially constructed (Edelsky et al., 1991); therefore, language learning should be social. The learning centers enhanced cooperative learning. In addition to interaction with me, the learners acquired the four language skills by working with group members in learning centers. Collaboration among peers created an interactive atmosphere in the classroom that cultivated a socially constructive and emotionally supportive learning environment (McDonell, 1992).

Open Discussions and Open Classroom

Public and extensive discussions between the Bureau of Education and the principals, administrators, and teachers also contributed greatly to the EEP. During the program's implementation, several workshops were held for local teachers. In these workshops, teachers discussed how to find qualified EFL teachers for the program, how to promote EFL teacher development, and how to design the education of future EFL teachers in Penghu County. They also discussed appropriate methodology to use in elementary EFL classrooms.

The EEP was intended to offer an alternative approach to EFL education in elementary schools in Taiwan, and many features of the program were innovative. This program served as an open and welcoming place for interested visitors. Throughout the year and almost every week, one to five guests could be seen sitting in the class observing the students and me. During recess, the guests and I discussed the teaching approach, methodology, techniques, skills, and materials as well as the implementation of the program. We also exchanged ideas about the challenges we faced in our EFL classrooms and discussed strategies to cope with them.

The EEP was effective in many aspects. The majority of students indicated in interviews that they would be very willing to participate in the program again if it were offered the next year. Students indicated that they were extremely motivated in learning English through cooperative learning at learning centers and through the thematic approach, both inside and outside the classroom. They also developed positive attitudes toward learning English. Rarely did they cut class with no reason, even though the program was not part of their schoolwork. They seemed to really look forward to the class. Each week the students arrived at the classroom much earlier than they needed to. Through my observations, I concluded that they loved to learn and work with their classmates and the college students. A culminating 40-minute presentation, along with classroom work (e.g., drawings, clay sculptures) and portfolios, demonstrated that the students learned to speak, sing, listen, read, rhyme, act out, and write in English because of the program.

Parents were encouraged to attend and learn English with their children in the classroom and participate in the weekend learning activities. The parents who came to our program told me they appreciated that their children could learn English in an interactive and interesting way that motivated their children.

In addition, all of the stakeholders' discussions in the workshops and in the classroom were valuable and insightful. Because of this program, the school became the center of EFL education in Penghu County and has continued to be dedicated to EFL education. Various features (e.g., thematic approach, multiple assessment methods, cooperative learning, interdisciplinary approach) that characterize the program have been greatly emphasized in EFL education in Taiwan since 2001. Along with the latest language policy in 2005, the characteristics and impact of the EEP can still be clearly observed in the latest development of the EFL program in Penghu County.

◈ PRACTICAL IDEAS

This section includes some practical ideas to consider before incorporating learning centers into an EFL curriculum.

Identify Planning Steps Before Getting Started

Step 1: Who Are My Target Students?

- What level are my students?
- What do my students need in terms of language development?
- How many students do I have?
- How many students would I like to have in a group?
- How will I organize the students into groups (e.g., by gender, age, interests)?

Step 2: What Are My Resources?

- How many and which types of learning centers are necessary?
- What do I need to prepare for each center?
- What resources are available to me?
- What additional materials and equipment do I need?
- Where can I get what I need (e.g., school budget, outside funding, student donations)?

Step 3: How Do I Organize Learning Centers in the Classroom?

- How much space do I have in the classroom?
- What is the most appropriate location for each center (considering, e.g., electrical outlets, lighting)?
- Which centers should be next to each other (considering noise activity levels)?

Step 4: How Do I Incorporate Learning Centers Into My Curricula?

- When do I want to incorporate learning centers into the curriculum (in the first or second semester)?
- How many minutes do I want students to spend in each center?
- Would a thematic approach work? If not, what other approach would be effective?

Develop Management Strategies for Learning Centers

Creating learning centers is time consuming and requires serious planning. Both the teacher and the children need time and experience to adjust to the approach. Developing and managing too many learning centers at the same time can be overwhelming. I suggest that teachers start with the centers that they feel most confident managing; more centers can be added gradually when teachers are more confident. Strategies for managing learning centers are critical to the success of a curriculum that uses them, particularly with elementary school students. The following are three helpful strategies (Bagby, Basile, McClay, & Wallace, 1996; McClay, 1996):

- *Charts.* I designed a chart and put it on the chalkboard before assigning groups to centers (see Table 3). This allowed me to encourage the students to take responsibility for who was going to which learning center each week. Students could quickly look at the chart and know in which group and center they were to work. The chart also helped

TABLE 3. A ROTATING CHART FOR THE FIVE LEARNING CENTERS

Number	Names	Computer Center	Video Center	Reading Center	Listening Center	Writing Center
1	May	🖥				
1	John	🖥				
1	Sarah	🖥				
1	Anna	🖥				
2	Katie		☺			
2	Peter		☺			
2	Julie		☺			
2	Amy		☺			
3	Larry			📖		
3	Lisa			📖		
3	Jill			📖		
3	Judy			📖		
4	Monica				🎧	
4	Natalie				🎧	
4	Roger				🎧	
4	Laura				🎧	
5	Vickie					✏
5	Jerry					✏
5	Pearl					✏
5	Echo					✏

Note. The names used here are pseudonyms.

expedite rotation among learning centers—for instance, from computer center, to video center, to reading center. All I had to do was shift magnets on the chart (e.g., move the magnets from computer center to video center) every week until each group had worked in at least three different learning centers. Depending on the time and the curriculum, each group could work in all five centers to explore the same theme.

- *Music.* Instead of spending time giving instructions, I introduced students to different musical rhythms for different purposes. For example, a certain rhythm was played for learning center work and another for cleanup time. Music is a powerful tool that adds to the learning atmosphere of the classroom (Ingraham, 1997).

- *Portfolios.* Assessment was collaborative, contextualized, complex, multidimensional, informal, direct, diagnostic, and continuous (Froese, 1991b; Goodman, 1989). Portfolios allowed each group to save artifacts created both individually and collaboratively. I looked at portfolio collections and assessed how all of the students were doing, individually as well as in groups (Farr & Tone, 1998). I used the portfolios to ask questions of and give suggestions to students. Both the students and I monitored their language development over time.

Form a Support Group

The development of learning centers requires a tremendous amount of time. It takes work and energy to communicate and coordinate with others; to plan for, search for, and select materials and equipment; and, finally, to develop lesson plans. To reduce the teacher's workload, dividing the work among others is highly recommended.

A community partnership with college students is one way to share the burden of the workload. An alternative is to form a support group with colleagues and teachers in the same district. A support group can serve various purposes. Members can get together regularly to discuss which materials are needed and which teaching strategies will be used. They can share information on where to find equipment, furniture, and materials. Some members of the group can work as material finders and some as activity designers for each center. Some can work as administrative officers to coordinate different issues concerning the development of learning centers in the school district. Most important, the group can form a network of teachers that support each other.

◈ CONCLUSION

EEP was initiated by local educators in Taiwan. It provided an alternative EFL approach that was developmentally appropriate for elementary students in Grades 2–6. By incorporating learning centers in the classroom, and learning activities outside the classroom, this program created an English-rich environment that encouraged the authentic use of the four language areas. It fostered autonomy for learning, appreciation for collaboration among peers, and respect for different intelligences and paces of learning. As a result, the learners' basic speaking, listening, reading, and writing skills were developed; motivation was enhanced; interests were nurtured; and a positive attitude toward English was cultivated. Most important, EEP offered an open classroom for further discussion among future EFL teachers on the island. It provided a starting point for all stakeholders to prepare for the nationwide initiative in EFL elementary education in Taiwan.

❧ CONTRIBUTOR

Yi-Hsuan Gloria Lo is an associate professor in the Department of Applied Foreign Languages at National Penghu University in Taiwan. She currently works with local EFL teacher educators and teachers to create a model for EFL professional development through learning communities. Her research interests include the use of the learning community as a model for professional development and the analysis of competing systems of knowledge about EFL, EFL teaching, and EFL learning through discourse analysis.

❧ APPENDIX

This appendix contains a typical lesson plan for a two-period (80-minute) elementary English class. In the first period, the learners and the teacher work together in a big group. In the second period, the students work in groups in learning centers to complete their assigned tasks. The example described here corresponds to the animals theme.

First Period (40 minutes)

Warm Up (10 minutes)

1. Review words, sentence patterns, rhymes, and songs learned in the previous weeks.

Introduction of the Theme of the Week: Animals (10 minutes)

2. Play the rhyme "The Zoo is Fun" three times with body language to imitate the characteristics of the eight animals.

> One one, the zoo is fun!
> Two two, see the kangaroo.
> Three three, see a chimpanzee.
> Four four, hear the lions roar.
> Five five, see the seals dive.
> Six six, the monkey does the tricks.
> Seven seven, elephants eleven.
> Eight eight, the tiger is great!
> Nine nine, giraffes in a line.
> Ten ten, let's come again!

3. Ask the learners to recite the rhyme along with the tape three times. Meanwhile, the teacher shows them the flash cards with the eight animals introduced in the rhyme.

4. The learners and the teacher recite the rhyme together while making body movements mimicking each animal.

5. Teach the students sentence patterns, such as "Where is (an animal that the student intends to find)?" and "Do you have (name of animal)?" before the following game.

Animal Hunt Game (5 minutes)

6. Eight learners are randomly assigned to sit on one of the eight flash cards, each showing an animal they learned in the rhyme.

7. One learner is designated as a hunter and remains outside while the whole group decides which animal they want the hunter to find.

8. When the hunter comes in, the whole class asks, "Where is the (name of animal for hunter to find)?"

9. The hunter is given three opportunities to locate the chosen animal. Each time the hunter walks to one of the students and asks, "Do you have the (name of animal)?"

10. The class answers the hunter by saying "Yes" (if the hunter finds the chosen animal) or "No" (if the hunter does not locate the animal).

Favorite Animals Discussion (5 minutes)

11. The teacher displays the animal flash cards on the blackboard or wall.

12. The teacher asks the learners to identify their favorite animals.

> T: Which animal do you like?
> L: I like (name of animal).

13. The learners ask each other which animals they like.

Song (5 minutes)

14. The teacher plays the song "See You Later, Alligator!" (Bradman & Hawkins, 1986) three times.

15. The teacher asks the learners to sing along with the tape several times until they are familiar with the melody and lyrics.

Storytelling (5 minutes)

16. The teacher plays "The Three Little Pigs" (Hillert & Wilde, 1984), acting out the different parts with various voices.

17. The teacher asks the whole class to read the story along with her in a big storybook.

18. The teacher asks the learners to tell her, in Mandarin, what happens in the story.

Second Period (40 minutes)

Getting Ready (10 minutes)

1. The teacher explains what is to be accomplished in each center:

   - *Computer center:* Learners play a computer game that requires the learners to click on the buttons of the animals as their name is heard.

   - *Video center:* Learners watch a film and identify the animals they see.

   - *Reading center:* Learners read a picture book and write down all the animals mentioned in the book.

   - *Listening center:* Learners listen to a tape containing sounds of animals and identify each animal heard.

   - *Writing center:* Learners draw their favorite animals and write their English names.

2. The teacher assigns the groups to different learning centers.

Working in the Five Learning Centers (20 minutes)

3. Each group has 15 minutes to complete the center task.

4. The teacher acts as a facilitator and answers learners' questions, solves potential equipment problems, observes each group's work, keeps anecdotal records, assesses each group and individual, and keeps time. When 5 minutes are left, the teacher reminds each group of the time and asks them to finish their tasks.

5. The learners put away all the materials and equipment at their last center. The students put their work with their findings ("answers") into their own group's portfolio and submit the portfolios to the teacher.

Large-Group Review (10 minutes)

6. The teacher and the learners spend the last 10 minutes in large-group instruction. The teacher reviews the tasks to be completed at each center by asking the class questions and eliciting responses. Then, the teacher shares the "answers" from their group work in the portfolios.

7. The teacher reviews the major content of the week.

8. The class sings "See You Later, Alligator!" at dismissal.

CHAPTER 4

Pass It On: English in the Primary Schools of Coahuila, Mexico

Elsa Patricia Jiménez Flores

In a sixth-grade English class at the Escuela Coahuila in Saltillo, the student leading an activity handed a marker to a classmate seated in the first row. "Pass it on, pass it on, pass it on," he said to his classmates as they handed the marker down the rows. "Stop," he called at various points. The student holding the marker then described the plastic dinosaur the student leader was holding.

◈ INTRODUCTION

This is impressive work after 6 years of English, yet not unusual for the public school students in Coahuila. "Pass it on," the student said, and just so, English is being passed on in the state and the nation through El Programa de Inglés en Primaria (English Program in Primary, or PIP) for children in public primary schools.

One of Mexico's greatest priorities at present is to increase the level of education of its people. The government of Mexico is convinced that the growth and development of the country will be enhanced as its people's education improves. Since Mexico signed different trade agreements with the United States, Canada, and other countries, the teaching of foreign languages, especially English, has been of increasing interest. Several innovations have been added to the National System of Education, particularly in the state of Coahuila where, since 1995, PIP has been implemented and expanded, along with pre- and in-service training programs for teachers of English.

I served as principal planner, creator, and organizer of Coahuila's primary English program and supervised its creation, design, and publication. Coahuila also implemented other English programs to support and enrich PIP, including centers for English learning (for children, adolescents, and adults), training and specialization programs for teachers of English, and teacher resource centers. The support program for students includes the establishment of English learning centers for children, adolescents, and adults. These centers represent an alternative for children who do not have an English program at their school but who wish to learn the language.

The training and specialization program for English as a foreign language (EFL) teachers is offered to prepare qualified personnel for bilingual programs. In addition, Coahuila offers alternative support to teachers through self-access resource centers for language and materials development. These centers offer alternative options for professional growth that respond to the needs of the program and the teachers.

◈ CONTEXT

The development of PIP was influenced by the status of education of children and teachers in Mexico and in Coahuila, the support from the Secretariat of Education and Culture in Coahuila (SEC), Coahuila's location in the country, and the methods of English instruction and teacher development in the state.

In Mexico, basic education offered throughout the republic follows the National Study Plan and Programs guidelines (Secretaría de Educación Publica [SEP], 1993). All programs of study in the 32 federal entities conform to this plan. Each state must provide evidence that it follows the National Study Plan and accompanying programs to the best of its ability, ensuring not only that the plan is well implemented and that the results are well documented but also that the needs of the children are being adequately met. Basic education (preschool, primary, and secondary, i.e., pre-K–9) in Mexico is free and compulsory. Coahuila is the third largest state in the Mexican Republic. It has 5,248 schools, 4,630 of which are for basic education. There are 330,565 students in primary school and 133,573 in secondary school.

An important factor in the implementation and success of the English program has been the support of the state government and the Secretariat of Education and Culture in Coahuila. The government has wholeheartedly supported and, in some cases, actively promoted PIP and its various constituent elements, including the Centers for Learning English, which serve citizens who do not have the resources to attend other English classes.

Situated in northeastern Mexico (see Figure 1), Coahuila is bordered by the United States to the north. Because of its proximity to the United States, foreign investment and participation in Coahuila has been strong, and the state's industrial growth is considered one of the most prominent nationwide. These facts point to the reasons that English is important in the state.

Nationwide, English teaching starts in secondary school (Grades 7–9) as part of the National Study Plan. Secondary school students study English for 45 to 50 minutes, 3 days per week. Nevertheless, after a 1991 analysis of the results of this program, conducted by the state and federal departments of education, experts concluded that students could not achieve the goal of written and oral communication in a foreign language in these three years. In addition, research indicates that students make more progress in a foreign language if they start at an earlier age (Brumfit, Moon, & Tongue, 1991).

Mexico has specialized schools for teachers at each level (kindergarten, primary, and secondary). In these university-level normal schools, English teacher candidates learn how to teach the different subjects included in each level of the National Study Plan for the secondary level. However, because English is not included in the National Study Plan at the primary level, there is no specific training for English teachers of primary-age children. Therefore, before the nationwide implementation of any English program at the primary level, training courses for these teachers must be designed and implemented.

Rationale for English Language Teaching in the Primary Schools

For the previously mentioned reasons, and because of the 1992 decentralization of authority that permits each state to offer compensatory or support programs to its

FIGURE 1. Location of the Five Regions of the State of Coahuila in the Mexican Republic

students, the state government, through the SEC, started PIP in selected public schools throughout the state of Coahuila in the 1995–1996 school year.

❖ DESCRIPTION

This section describes the initial planning and implementation of PIP, including its growth and future plans, components, and critical elements.

Planning and Implementation

Prior to implementation of the program, I spent a year planning and organizing the initial start-up. The principal point to consider was the objectives, which were either general, language related, or formative (those that produce a well-rounded student). Other factors included the number and length of classes, the number of schools in which to start the program and their distribution within each region, and the schedule (either during or after school). I also had to consider what materials to use, as well as their acquisition and development; the organization of the program; the administrative structure, including the duties of the technical and administration teams; and, most important, the follow-up and evaluation.

Based on the context of education in Mexico and the particular needs of the citizens of Coahuila, two overall objectives became the program's guiding principles:

- to give the students knowledge, practice, and enrichment in the four English language skills (reading, writing, listening, speaking)

- to train and update teachers in both the English language and English language teaching techniques

In addition, the National Study Plan from the federal Secretaría de Educación Pública provides the following objectives for learning a foreign language:

- to encourage appropriate development of students, with the purpose of giving them autonomy, analytic abilities, and the desire to participate and to be creative, independent, and self-assured

- to ensure that students have an education that will give them the knowledge and the capacity to increase their level and quality of life

- to enrich the intellectual development of the student

- to reinforce students' knowledge of their own culture and customs in order to strengthen their national identity (Secretaría de Educación Pública, 1993, p. 133)

Furthermore, because of the formative nature of primary schooling, by learning a foreign language, PIP would help primary students to be able to

- develop learning strategies that will allow them to reflect and to discover appropriate techniques for their learning

- interact with the group, the school, and the community, increasing their respect for the ideas of others and their responsibility toward their jobs

- actively participate in their own learning through opportunities for communication, which promote creativity

After the objectives were identified, the program was implemented in the first grade in 100 public primary schools. In 1995–1996, 59 teachers taught 7,100 pupils in the program, and it was administered by a state coordinator, an administrative assistant, and five regional technical advisors, one for each of the five regions in the state. These five regional technical advisors were each assisted by a head teacher. The program has been so successful that, 11 years after its implementation, 500 schools and more than 148,000 children in Grades 1–6 are learning English from 700 teachers in all 30 districts and cities in the state. Table 1 shows the growth of the program from its initiation in 1995 through 2006.

Most important, in 2001–2002 more than 42,000 adolescents began their first year of secondary school. Of these adolescents, 7,000 entered at an advanced level of English. To accommodate students who graduated from PIP, the technical specialists of the English Coordination Team designed and developed an advanced secondary workbook and accompanying teacher's guide for Grades 7–9 (see Figure 2).

For students who started their secondary education without prior knowledge of English, a separate basic secondary workbook and teacher's guide based on the official SEP program were also designed and developed for the three grade levels. The English Coordination Team evaluates the progress and development of both teachers and students, and it continues to revise existing materials and develop new materials for both the basic and advanced levels in Grades 7–9.

In 2005–2006, 50 new schools were added to PIP. The program plans to add 25 schools each year, although more schools can be added if enough qualified teachers are found. The goal is to implement PIP in all urban schools in the next 3–4 years.

FIGURE 2. Workbooks and Registers 7th, 8th, and 9th – Basic Level

PIP and Its Components

The program has several components: PIP, which is the focus and core; a training program for teachers; Centers for Learning English for Children, Adolescents, and Adults; and Self-Access and Materials Development Centers for Teachers, which focus on language and material development.

The program has nine levels: six grades in primary school and three in secondary. It begins in first grade with children 6–7 years of age. The curriculum in each grade consists of nine units that are covered in 120 hours throughout the academic year. English classes are scheduled three times a week for 50 minutes. The classes occur within the normal school schedule, in the morning and afternoon. The majority of these classes are taught by teachers who have specialized in the English language and who receive continuous training and guidance throughout the school year. The program emphasizes this continuing education of teachers, in part, to ensure that the objectives of the program are being met.

The purpose of the teacher training program is to offer teachers the opportunity to learn and to improve their English, as well as to understand and develop

TABLE 1. NUMBER OF TEACHERS, SCHOOLS, AND STUDENTS IN PIP FROM 1995 TO 2006

School Year	Teachers	Schools	Students
1995–1996	59	100	7,100
1996–1997	172	250	22,238
1997–1998	300	300	39,881
1998–1999	370	350	61,490
1999–2000	468	375	83,945
2000–2001	667	400	106,449
2001–2002	800	425	125,000
2002–2003	670	400	130,155
2003–2004	700	450	136,763
2004–2005	700	450	142,471
2005–2006	700	500	148,000

techniques that will strengthen the teaching process. In cooperation with the English Coordination Team, training courses are designed and implemented by different international institutions, as well as internal and external consultants. In addition, as part of the reference materials given to teachers, a series of manuals titled *On the Road to Excellence* was designed by the English Coordination Team through the state government in conjunction with the Secretariat of Education and Culture of the State. These materials help teachers attain a higher level of teaching ability and simplify their daily work in the classroom. Titles of these manuals include *Lesson Planning and Grammar, Methods and Techniques, Evaluation, Celebrations, Idioms, Materials Development, Am I Teaching Well?,* and *Grammar and The Five Basic Skills* (Secretaría de Educación Pública, 1993).

The purpose of the Centers for Learning English for Children, Adolescents, and Adults is to offer English classes to children who do not have PIP in their schools and to help children who joined the program in the upper levels and therefore do not have basic knowledge of English. The centers also give students from the secondary level the opportunity to learn and reinforce the English they study in school to facilitate their development. Centers are also available to adults, and many parents attend to be able to help their children with their homework (and, often, to do homework together!) as well as for their own benefit. One of the goals of the centers is to help instill a sense of dignity and pride in the family. By raising the educational level of parents—particularly mothers—the educational level of children can also be increased. In these centers, English classes are held twice a week for 1.5 hours. The academic program for primary-age children is the same as in PIP. The program offered to adolescents and adults is based on their knowledge of the language and their needs.

Since the beginning of PIP, the demand from teachers to learn and to improve themselves has increased considerably. Offering training courses was not enough. It became necessary to design and implement another means to meet their needs. Thus, in July 1997, Self-Access and Materials Development Centers for Teachers were opened. These centers have computers, televisions, video recorders, tape recorders, cassette copying machines, as well as various teaching and reference materials for teachers, including textbooks, novels, and storybooks. Nine centers have been opened in the state-run Institutes for Teacher Learning and Development (IECAM) and three in the normal schools (teacher training institutions). They were opened in these places to take advantage of teachers' current use of the IECAMs as well as normal school students' need for extra help in English and in materials development for English instruction.

Critical elements of the success of PIP include the methodology used in classes, the materials that it provides, and ongoing supervision and evaluation. The teacher education program is based on a methodology that addresses the development of students' communicative language abilities, use of learning strategies, and cognitive abilities in accordance with the National Study Plan of education. For the teaching of a foreign language, the methodological focus that the national SEP proposes is a communicative approach, which takes into account teaching practice and various theories about foreign language acquisition (including cognitive as well as affective aspects; SEP, 1993, p. 139). It is this same focus that PIP offers. The main objective is to develop communicative competence—that is, the ability for speakers to send and receive messages, to negotiate meaning, and to speak appropriately in a specific context (Brown, 2000). Students use language as an instrument of communication to acquire knowledge; to express and comprehend ideas, feelings, and experiences; and to share the responsibility for the educational process. It is important to note that, with this focus, grammar is deemphasized.

To communicate in a foreign language, it is not necessary that the grammar be perfect. The message still can be understood even if errors occur. From this communicative point of view, the four language skills (oral comprehension, oral expression, written comprehension, and written expression) are developed equally (SEP, 1993).

The National Study Plan establishes the conditions for students to learn rules regarding language and its usage, which they do through experimentation and discovery (i.e., students analyze what they know how to say, develop hypotheses about how language works, test these hypotheses, and modify them as necessary). This process encourages students to reflect and, through specific oral and written exercises provided by the teacher, infer the rules that they need at that moment. Students make the language their own by practicing situations proposed by the teacher or themselves. Students become motivated to learn in situations that have authentic interest for them, and they soon gain the capacity to speak the language in a more efficient and practical way.

The contents of PIP are based on language functions. Grammar and vocabulary that arise naturally from certain functions, situations, and roles are integrated into the program. The teacher's role is that of facilitator. The teacher is the organizer of the classroom activities. The student is the center of the educational process through which the relationships between teacher and students and the student environment are reinforced. The students, as mentioned earlier, share responsibility for the educational process. To ensure this, and owing to the large number of students in the classes, students are frequently organized into working teams. This type of organization develops the following important aspects that align with the goals of PIP and the National Study Plan:

- respect for the ideas of others
- ability to help others
- experience in collaborative work
- self-control
- self-confidence
- responsibility

Program materials are designed and written by the technical specialists of the English Coordination Team. Besides the acquisition of a foreign language, the purpose of PIP is to reinforce the development of the student as a whole. Because English is taught within the normal school schedule, the English Coordination Team designed and developed a student workbook based on the official SEP study plan. The team also provides materials to teachers: a scope and sequence, daily activities, a planning book, a grade book, and other support materials such as stamps, scissors, crayons, pronunciation cassettes, posters, flashcards, videos, and puppets.

The workbooks developed by the team reinforce the objectives of the course and stress the four abilities to develop in the language. Also included are commemorative dates, patriotic symbols, and traditions to strengthen students' understanding of

Mexican culture as well as other cultures. One reason for including these materials in the program was the notion that, as students become more proficient in English, they become cultural ambassadors and, when talking with English speakers, they will need to know and be able to talk about their own country in the context of other cultures. The other reason was that, because English classes were incorporated into the regular school day, time for other subjects had to be shortened. Therefore, the workbook supports and reinforces skills taught in the official program.

The workbooks contain four types of activities: unit-based activities, songs and chants, reading, and celebrations. The unit activity pages support the learning concepts based on language functions stipulated in the National Study Plan. The activities also take into consideration different learning styles and intelligences. For example, in the fourth-grade workbook, students make digital clocks and practice telling time (see Figure 3). Other types of activities include puzzles, construction of mural sentence strips to generate storytelling, and memory games.

To further reinforce concepts and give students valuable practice in learning phrases and proper intonation, PIP uses songs and chants. For example, the jump-rope chant "Teddy Bear, Teddy Bear" is used with the My Toys unit in first grade. The Reading Corner section of the workbook includes rhymes, poems, and short stories for students to read. However, once again, students are not passive learners; they are actively involved in dramatizing, making posters and books, developing story maps, and so on. These activities help them develop reading skills. For example, before students read the nursery rhyme "The Three Little Kittens," they color, cut out, and glue finger puppets. These puppets are then used to dramatize the story as students

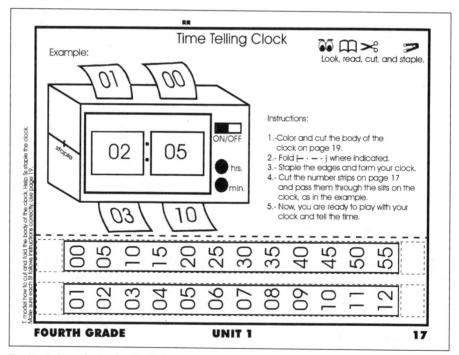

FIGURE 3. Fourth-Grade Clock Activity

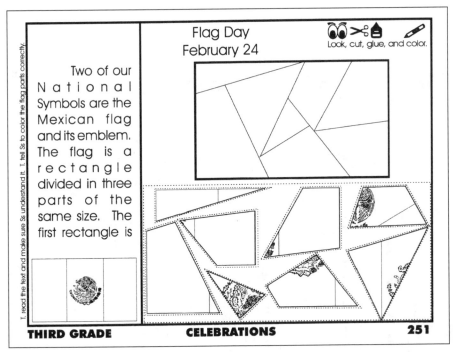

Flag Day
February 24

Look, cut, glue, and color.

Two of our National Symbols are the Mexican flag and its emblem. The flag is a rectangle divided in three parts of the same size. The first rectangle is

T. read the text and make sure Ss understand it. T. tell Ss to color the flag parts correctly.

THIRD GRADE   **CELEBRATIONS**   **251**

FIGURE 4. Third-Grade "Celebrations" Activity: Flag Day

read it. Another section of the workbook, Celebrations, provides activities that relate to various international holidays and traditions that occur throughout the year. Again, students are actively engaged. For example, in the third grade, students read about the Mexican flag, make a flag from a puzzle, and color it (see Figure 4).

An important addition to the student workbook is the temporary report card. Completed monthly, this record provides parents with a concrete means to evaluate their children's progress in English class. This temporary report card is replaced by the official report card at the end of the school year (see Figure 5).

The technical specialists of the English Coordination Team also designed a teacher's register for every grade, which provides teachers with a resource for planning and evaluating and an overview of each unit. The first part of the register consists of a blank schedule for teachers to fill in; a yearly calendar and schedule of events and holidays; and a list of suggested classroom rules and commands. These commands come complete with graphics that can be enlarged and used as posters in the classroom. Commands include "Open your book," "Raise your hand," and "Please be quiet" and are used throughout the school year and in all grades. A materials page lists all nine units and required materials, such as posters, realia, storybooks, songs, and chants that relate to the unit and are available for all teachers at the regional office. The second part of the teacher's register addresses each of the nine units to be covered during the year. Each unit contains setup information, a scope and sequence, unit objectives, vocabulary, grammatical structures, activities, assessment methods, and materials and motivational ideas (see Figure 6).

Another page shows each unit divided into 12 working sessions, which cover

Coahuila
El Gobierno de la Gente
Secretaría de Educación
y Cultura

SECRETARÍA DE EDUCACIÓN Y CULTURA
DEL ESTADO DE COAHUILA

PROGRAMA DE INGLÉS EN PRIMARIA

BOLETA DE EVALUACIÓN

ESCUELA: _____

CLAVE SEGÚN CATÁLOGO DE CENTROS DE TRABAJO

ALUMNO: _____

NOMBRE

PRIMER APELLIDO   SEGUNDO APELLIDO

C.U.R.P.   GRADO   GRUPO   TURNO

NOMBRE Y FIRMA DEL MAESTRO

NOMBRE Y FIRMA DEL DIRECTOR

LUGAR DE EXPEDICIÓN

FECHA DE EXPEDICIÓN

DÍA   MES   AÑO

SELLO

AL PADRE DE FAMILIA O TUTOR:

Para facilitar la comprensión en la evaluación del idioma Inglés, a continuación se desglosan las cuatro habilidades que el alumno(a) desarrollará a lo largo del curso, las cuales se tomarán en cuenta para su calificación:

1.- COMPRENSIÓN AUDITIVA (LISTENING)

- Atiende indicaciones y órdenes.
- Comprende lo que se dice.
- Sintetiza la información.
- Interpreta y realiza la actividad.

2.- EXPRESIÓN ORAL (SPEAKING)

- Se expresa de forma coherente.
- Pronuncia correctamente.
- Domina e integra las palabras del vocabulario básico.
- Participa y expresa sus pensamientos.

3.- LECTURA (READING)

- Decodifica con facilidad.
- Entona correctamente.
- Comprende globalmente un texto.
- Capta la idea central.

4.- EXPRESIÓN ESCRITA (WRITING)

- Entiende lo que quiere expresar y lo hace ordenadamente.
- Utiliza vocabulario adecuado a su edad.
- Domina la ortografía natural.
- Tiene buen dominio del trazo.

*MONTHLY AVERAGE-PROMEDIO MENSUAL
*FINAL AVERAGE-PROMEDIO FINAL.

TEACHER'S COMMENTS (COMENTARIOS DEL MAESTRO)	UNIT
	1
	2
	3
	4
	5
	6
	7
	8
	9

UNIT MONTH	MONTHLY AVERAGE (PROMEDIO MENSUAL)	ABSENCES (INASISTENCIAS)	PARENT'S SIGNATURE (FIRMA DEL PADRE O TUTOR)
UNIT 1			
UNIT 2			
UNIT 3			
UNIT 4			
UNIT 5			
UNIT 6			
UNIT 7			
UNIT 8			
UNIT 9			
FINAL AVERAGE (PROMEDIO FINAL)			

FIGURE 5. Report Card

SCOPE AND SEQUENCE	📖 1 My Activities		WORKBOOK: SEPC 4TH GRADE	4th grade
OBJECTIVES	**LANG STRUCTURES / VOC.**	**ACTIVITIES**	**ASSESSMENT**	**MATERIAL / MOTIVATIONAL IDEAS**
COMMUNICATION: - To use classroom language - To identify the sequence of activities and daily activities - To tell time by the hour, half hour, and quarter hour, to tell about daily activities - To tell when one does activities - To review numbers to 60 **LANGUAGE SKILLS:** - To answer questions with HOW MANY - To ask questions with WHAT and WHAT TIME - To pronounce /u/ /ew/ /or/, /al/, and /v/ - To use the simple present tense - To use before and after - To identify and use "s" **LEARNING STRATEGIES AND THINKING SKILLS:** - To compare and contrast - To listen for detail - To organize information - To sequence - To use charts - To use prior knowledge **READING AND WRITING SKILLS:** - To reread for details and self-assessment - To set a purpose for reading **WORKBOOK:** - To work on pp 1-23 - Songs and Chants: p 185	- Hello, N, good morning (afternoon), (evening). - How do you do? - How are you? I'm just fine/grand. - Shake my hand. I get up at - I get dressed after/before breakfast - Do you get dressed before school or after school? (David) gets up at (7:00). (He) gets dressed (before) (after) breakfast. - What time is it, please? It's - Whose clock is this? It's (Maria's). - What time do you go to school? - What time do you eat breakfast/lunch? - What time do you go to sleep? - (Sara) eats breakfast at (7:30) everyday. **VOCABULARY:** read, breakfast, dinner, lunch, after, before everyday, fifteen, forty-five, o'clock, thirty, how many what, what time, who, go ahead (one) space, go back (two) spaces, routine **T.P.R. VOCABULARY:** brush (my) teeth, comb (my) hair, do (my) homework, eat (breakfast/lunch), get dressed, get up, go to bed, go to school, go to sleep play soccer, take the bus, watch TV, go to the board, raise your hand, stand up, open your book, get your markers **BORDER VOCABULARY:** bed, toothbrush, toothpaste, comb, bike TV, school bus, soccer ball, alarm clock, clock wristwatch	**WARM UPS:** - Use TPR to review classroom vocabulary. - Draw a sun in the sky, a partial sun above the horizon, and a moon on the Bb. Have Ss match good morning, good afternoon, and good evening to the appropriate pictures. - Write numbers at random on Bb. Have Ss call out numbers as they point to them. Have Ss put the numbers in order. **ACTIVITIES OR PRESENTATIONS:** - Show video. - Have Ss work in pairs to mime actions. - Encourage Ss to read, and tell about their day. - Have Ss draw and write about activities they do every day. - Encourage Ss to read, say, and match clocks and times. - Have Ss listen and circle the clock, make a clock, listen and sing the song. - Encourage Ss to read and write "before/after." Have Ss make a chart. - Have Ss read a story. - Have Ss summarize a story. **REACHING ALL STUDENTS:** - Focus Ss attention on border pictures. - Have Ss write charts, draw action flashcards; draw diagrams with differences and similarities.; have Ss work in groups; play guessing games. - Encourage Ss to use possessive ('s). - Have Ss recycle terms by working in pairs. - Have Ss write interviews after using the chart. - Challenge Ss to make the longest "action chain" using before and after. or - Have Ss discuss ways people get food.	**Oral:** - Sing songs, charts, and rhymes to check pronunciation, rhythm, and stress. - Use pair and small group work to check oral production through short dialogues. - Have students speak out, call out vocabulary. - Practice reading aloud (words, sentences, paragraphs). **Comprehension:** - Check comprehension by giving directions and doing "show me" acts. - Check listening comprehension through drawing, coloring, cutting, gluing, and counting activities. - Evaluate Ss knowledge using realia, flashcards, vocabulary, and sentence strips. - Check reading comprehension by asking Wh questions, by summarizing and retelling the story. **Written:** - Include writing activities such as spelling bee, speaking out, fill in the blanks, scrambled words and sentences, crossword puzzles, hangman, parallel writing, descriptive paragraph, summaries, riddles, etc. - Include reading acts such as reading aloud (words, sentences, paragraphs), silent reading, skimming, scanning, reading comprehension, etc. - Use delayed reading and delayed copying techniques (see daily plan). - Check wb pp 4,5,11,12 and 15. - Grade Ss dictation p 21 and homework p 23.	- cassette/ CD - video and video guide - posters - scissors - different colored markers - game pieces such as coins, erasers or paper clips - erasers or paper clips. - workbook - T's own material, and reading books **OPTIONAL:** - index cards - paper for murals or poster paper - cardboard **Motivational idea:** *Compliment students on everything they do well.*
OBSERVATIONS	Vocabulary: Pronunciation:	Spelling:	Grammar:	
Note Problems in the following areas.		Others:		

14

FIGURE 6. Fourth-Grade Unit Scope and Sequence Page: My Activities

the planned objectives and include suggested activities and exercises. Lesson plan forms are also presented. Lesson plans include five elements: warm-up, presentation, guided practice, independent practice, and assessment. Finally, a suggested end-of-unit test is provided, along with the teacher's instruction sheet.

The teacher's register also includes a practical grading chart, which entirely eliminates the need to use a calculator; an instruction manual for using the teacher's grade book; the original format of the teacher's schedule; and because all materials are in continuous review, questionnaires for the teacher to evaluate the student workbook and the register. These questionnaires help the team of technical specialists improve these resources.

The Coahuila state government, through SEC, has enriched PIP by providing scissors, crayons, motivational stamps, flashcards, and posters. The first two items are used by the students, the others by teachers. The motivational stamps include sayings such as "Good job," "Well done," "Excellent," and "Good reader."

Cassettes accompany each unit. The students can listen to unit vocabulary, oral readings for activities that include a reading component, songs and chants, and the items in the Reading Corner—all spoken by a native English speaker. Other cassettes serve as pronunciation and intonation support for the Mexican English-speaking teachers. These cassettes are not meant to be used with the children.

The English Coordination Team has acquired reading books, which are housed in the teaching resource centers located in the five regions of the state. These regional centers ensure that teachers have easy access to materials as they need them, instead of having to rely on a central facility in the capital city. These additional reading materials enable students to improve reading habits, in both oral and written comprehension. Using such authentic materials can introduce into the classroom a very rich image of the outside world from a cultural point of view.

Students' learning and abilities are evaluated during each school year through a variety of means. The evaluation criteria mandate participation in the form of teacher-student and student-student interactions, holistic assessment of all four language abilities (listening, reading, writing, speaking), and continuous assessments throughout the year. It is therefore possible to evaluate and modify lessons and activities continually, making the program constantly relevant for the learner. The objective is to detect anything the student does well or, in the case of any mistakes, to make immediate corrections. Previously, students were evaluated only at the end of the school year, making it impossible to make changes in the program to fit the needs of the students or to give students constant and immediate feedback.

The grade given at the end of each thematic unit is based on a written test (40%); individual oral participation (20%); whole-group participation (10%); and exercises or homework, or both (30%). The minimum passing grade is 6 on a scale from 5 (lowest grade) to 10 (highest grade). The English Coordination Team prepares nine suggested written exams for each level, which are included in a booklet for students. These booklets are given to teachers, one per student, eliminating the need to reproduce booklets. Additionally, each student is given an oral evaluation at some point throughout the unit. At present, no semester or end-of-year exam is given.

◈ DISTINGUISHING FEATURES

As discussed in the previous section, several key elements have made it possible for PIP to be a success: the organization of the technical and administrative teams; the development and acquisition of the teaching material; and the continuous evaluation process. In this section, the administrative organization and the technical personnel are discussed.

Administrative and Technical Organization

Because English in primary grades is not part of the national curriculum, there was no entity within SEC that could supervise the program. Therefore, an office had to be created to oversee all aspects of the program, including the hiring of personnel, development and acquisition of materials, and continuous monitoring and evaluation of the program.

At present, the team at the state level consists of the state coordinator, technical advisors and specialists, administrative personnel, and a team of graphic designers. The state coordinator, who oversees the program, gives general instructions regarding innovating, planning, implementing, and controlling all English projects within the state. Each of the five technical advisors is responsible for one region. These advisors direct and provide follow-up on program implementation in their respective regions and support the work done by the regional technical and administrative liaisons. The administrative liaisons monitor and control all accounts and logistics regarding the program. They keep in constant communication with the five technical advisors and make suggestions about areas of excellence and improvement. The graphic designers support the technical specialists in the design of materials, workbooks, and registers.

There is a similar administrative structure at the regional level. Currently, 21 technical liaisons supervise the work of the 35–45 teachers under their charge. The 10 administrative liaisons keep track of the logistics related to the program. These regional team members report to their respective technical advisor. The teachers are, of course, the backbone of the program. Because of teachers' dedication both in teaching the children and in improving themselves as English speakers and as teachers, the program is a success.

Hiring, Training, and Supervising Teachers

Program staff prioritize working effectively with the teaching staff. To ensure that the best possible teachers are hired, the staff has set several criteria regarding candidates' level of English and knowledge of teaching. Because it is generally difficult to find qualified teachers in an EFL environment, the state coordination implemented a training program for teachers before starting the program. Various international centers throughout the state provide both English language and teacher training courses for our teachers. SEC has supported the programs by providing scholarships for teachers to attend English language courses at these international centers. So far, about 4,000 teachers have participated in various support programs for English language development.

To become a PIP teacher, candidates have to take both an oral and a written exam to ensure that they have mastered the necessary level of English. They also have to demonstrate teaching knowledge, either through previous experience (a minimum of 3 years) or enrollment in teacher training courses at an international center. After candidates are deemed qualified, they sign a contract for a school year. The salary of PIP teachers is similar to that of teachers in secondary schools, and they also receive some of the benefits given to each of the workers in SEC. Throughout the year, teachers need to demonstrate their abilities and performance to continue working in the program.

Training is extremely important because 80% of the teachers who work in the program do not have a degree in teaching from the state normal school (teacher training institution). Therefore, in-service training for the teachers is a priority. In their own region, the teachers attend nine training sessions. Materials development workshops are also occasionally part of these sessions. The training sessions are organized entirely by the English Coordination Team, but the program for each session is suggested by the teachers in accordance with their needs and those of their region. Additional support for the teachers is provided through scholarships offered by the SEC, which allow teachers to attend various training and specialization courses as well as to pursue a higher level of education.

In addition to the training sessions, teachers receive continuous training and support by their technical advisor or the liaison. Teachers are supervised at least six times during the school year and receive a written evaluation of their accomplishments as well as their areas for improvement. During the 2000–2001 school year, a format for self-evaluation was implemented. In this format, teachers analyze their work and establish short- and long-term goals and objectives. Afterward, teachers attend a feedback session with their technical advisor or the liaison to discuss work and goals. The main objectives of these supervision, self-evaluation, and feedback sessions are to give teachers additional tools to become more effective and to monitor the progress of the program.

◈ PRACTICAL IDEAS

Based on my personal experience in implementing PIP in primary schools, I offer the following advice to readers who are planning to initiate such programs:

- Determine objectives and goals to achieve as well as the extent and structure of the program.

- Make sure that the teachers who work in the program have sufficient knowledge of the English language.

- Consider the teaching qualifications necessary for the personnel. Take into account the experience of those who will work directly with the children—for example, a candidate must have at least 3 years of teaching experience.

- Select materials carefully in accordance with the age of the children, the length of the program, its objectives, and the fact that English is being taught in an EFL environment.

Furthermore, design support materials for teachers and students with the specific necessities of your country in mind. Include references to important historical dates and holidays to reinforce the students' culture and customs. Strengthening the students' national identity is very important.

- Provide initial and ongoing training for the administrative, technical, and teaching staff.
- Structure the operational aspects for the program.
- Follow up and evaluate the program throughout the entire school year.
- Provide materials in sufficient quantities so the teachers can do their work well and productively.
- Have an open mind about change. Expect day-to-day innovations. Perfect and improve on the successes already achieved.
- Suggest or provide means that allow teachers to upgrade their level of English without any cost to them. For example, in Coahuila, we provide teachers with Self-Access and Materials Development Centers.
- Present alternative environments in which to learn English. In Coahuila, a very practical and functional alternative is the network of Centers for Learning English for Children, Adolescents, and Adults. These centers do not represent a great investment but do represent an opportunity for those who do not have access to English through any other means.

◈ CONCLUSION

I have presented relevant aspects of the structure and function of the English Program in Primary in Coahuila, with the purpose of offering my experience to those who are piloting or are planning to start a similar program in their own country. Teacher training, follow-up and evaluation of the program, and acquisition and elaboration of support material are key points that should be considered when planning to provide a strong English language program. Equally important is the design of the academic program.

In the case of PIP, the support and financial resources given to the program have contributed to its success. The program recently received recognition as the state's most successful innovative and educational practice. SEC also received the Recognition of Excellence award for the program. PIP points to Coahuila as the nationwide leader in the field.

The teachers and students are "passing it on"—they are increasing access to English for the citizens of the state of Coahuila. But new challenges await; teachers and administrators need to maintain the quality achieved in the program or, better still, increase it for all children. The goal is to surpass the achievements obtained during the past 11 years. For more information about our program and especially information for teachers, visit our Web site www.seycc.gob.mx.

◈ ACKNOWLEDGMENTS

On behalf of the Secretariat of Education and Culture in Coahuila, I wish to recognize the work of the Public Diplomacy Section of the American Consulate in Monterrey, Mexico, for its continuing support of the Programa de Inglés en Primaria.

In particular, I offer my sincerest appreciation to the late Dr. Kathryn Z. Weed, who, through her talent and experience in writing, was of immeasurable support and help to me, not only in the writing of this chapter but also in the work she did with the teachers of the program.

❖ CONTRIBUTOR

Elsa Patricia Jiménez Flores, who has 17 years of teaching experience as a primary and secondary teacher, holds a master's degree in education from the Universidad Iberoamericana. She was principal planner and organizer for Coahuila's English program. She works as the English coordinator for the Secretariat of Education and Culture of Coahuila and as national coordinator of the Binational Migrant Education Program.

CHAPTER 5

The Long and Winding Road: A Profile of Italian Primary EFL Teachers

Lucilla Lopriore

◈ INTRODUCTION

The teaching of foreign languages in Italy during the past 25 years has been characterized by specific innovations introduced by the Italian Ministry of Education[1] either at a national level or through several local experimental projects, which have subsequently led to major curriculum renewals. The ministry interventions in this field have always been accompanied by ad hoc teacher education projects for teachers involved in the innovations. Thus, foreign language teaching in Italy has always been sustained by specific training interventions aimed at successfully implementing the initiatives undertaken both at the experimental stage and during the first steps of curriculum implementation.

The idea of introducing foreign languages in the primary curriculum in Italy dates back to the early experimental projects carried out in several Italian schools in the late 1970s with the ILLSE Project (Italian Ministry of Education, 1985). This was later followed by the official introduction of the study of one foreign language from the age of 8 years (third year) with the 1985 *New National Primary Curriculum*[2] (Italian Ministry of Education, Legislative Decree n. 59/2004). More recently, English has been introduced in the first year and, in many cases, also at kindergarten level with the New School Reform (Italian Ministry of Education, Legislative Decree n. 53/2003).

Among the most debated issues of the past 25 years are the choice of teacher (i.e., who is most suited to teach foreign languages at the primary level), the type of training needed and offered, and the number of hours per week to be devoted to the study of foreign languages. This chapter focuses specifically on these three issues, given their relevance in terms of government policies, long-term teacher professional development, and learning benefits for children.

---

[1] The Italian Ministry of Education was formerly called Ministero della Pubblica Istruzione (MPI); in 2001 it was renamed Ministero dell'Istruzione dell'Università e della Ricerca (MIUR).

[2] Italian primary school lasts 5 years. According to the most recent educational reforms, children start at $5\frac{1}{2}$ years of age. Kindergarten starts at the age of 3.

◈ CONTEXT

The teaching and learning of foreign languages at the primary level cannot be fully understood unless it is seen in the more general context of Italian foreign language education policies. This section describes the framework for the case study: the general foreign language curricula in Italian schools. Some of the reasons for and the policies behind the present condition might sound familiar to language educators from other countries, but the choices made are in some ways unique to the Italian context and might help the reader better focus on similarities and differences.

The languages most commonly taught in Italian schools are English (now compulsory at all school and university levels), French, German, and Spanish. German is widely spoken in some areas (e.g., in tourist areas in the northern bilingual region of Trentino-Alto Adige). Arabic is being taught in several schools in Sicily, where many immigrants from Arabic-speaking countries reside. Bilingual education and, in some cases, trilingual education is carried out in the northern regions of Trentino-Alto Adige (German and Italian, in addition to Ladino, which is spoken in parts of the region) and Valle d'Aosta (French and Italian), and is encouraged in Friuli Venezia Giulia (Slovenian, Italian), where there is widespread use of Friulano at home and at school.

Foreign language education in Italy has undergone several important changes in the past few years because of its close connection with the major innovations occurring in education. Before the mid-1990s, foreign language education in Italian state schools was, compared with other subjects, a privileged area of special intervention because it was the only subject area with a specific in-service program, the Progetto Speciale Lingue Straniere, from 1978 to 1994 (Lopriore, 1998). Other contributing factors included the innovative foreign language curriculum guidelines of the middle school reform in 1979 and the experimental ones partly implemented at the high school level between 1991 and 1993 (Programmi Brocca), the extension of foreign language teaching at the primary level in 1991 (Italian Ministry of Education, 1994; Sanzo, 1993), and recent national training projects.

In the past 15 years, several innovations at all school levels have occurred, including the development of autonomy for the state schools (Italian Decree Law 440, 1997),[3] emphasis on continuity of methodology and approach throughout all school levels (Italian Ministry of Education, CM 339, 16.11.1992), introduction of preservice teacher education postgraduate courses (Scuole di Specializzazione all'Insegnamento Secondario, 1999), the new graduate courses for primary school teachers (Corsi di laurea in Scienza della formazione primaria, 1998), and the new school system reform (Law 53/2003; Riforma, 2003). Some of these innovations have helped sustain the professional development of Italian foreign language teachers who formerly entered the profession without any specific training. The Ministry of Education, the business world, parents, and the media are currently paying more attention to the issue of foreign language learning, particularly of English, which is perceived as an asset for Italian students.

---

[3] State schools are autonomous in terms of the internal organization of the school curriculum within the Ministry of Education national guidelines and the regional education authority's framework. This status allows each school to create independent action plans in terms of foreign language teaching and certification initiatives.

The most important innovative factor in foreign language teaching has been the diffusion of the Council of Europe documents about language teaching and learning between 1997 and 2000. To adjust the Italian school system to the required European standards in education and to the European language policies as outlined by the Council of Europe (2001), specific financial investments in education and some innovative projects have been offered recently. These projects include the experimental introduction of foreign language teaching in kindergarten, the addition of a second foreign language (besides English) in middle school, the primary use of the *Progetto Lingue 2000* (Italian Ministry of Education, 2001; Implementation Decree n. 197, 6 August 1999, of the Decree Law n. 440/1997) in teaching English in the first year of the new primary school in 2003, and the implementation of distance training programs for primary foreign language teachers. (For additional information, see Appendix A.)

◈ DESCRIPTION

The most recent national education reforms have expanded opportunities to learn foreign languages throughout the primary cycle. At the same time, they promote a shift of responsibility for teacher education from the national education ministry administration to local regional education authorities. These reforms have created the need to adjust to a new type of organization in which national curriculum policy is outlined by the ministry but is autonomously designed, structured, and implemented at the regional level. As for recruitment, previous preservice teacher education programs (instituted in 1999) had ensured a certain degree of homogeneity in the teachers' background preparation, but recent education reforms have resulted in regionally controlled in-service language improvement or methodology courses for primary teachers, which local education authorities delegate either to freelance tutors or to private language schools, thus providing a wide variety of services but also heterogeneity of input. In some regions, such as Piedmont, Lombardia, Liguria, and Veneto, where the regional education authorities have been more active and more directly involved in teacher education issues, primary school teachers have benefited more than others from several strong initiatives and training projects.

In the past 2 years the Ministry of Education Scientific Committee has developed a plan for English language courses at the national level to be attended by all primary school teachers who will thus have the opportunity to learn English and to reach a level (B1) that should enable them to teach English in their classrooms (Cerini & Gianferrari, 2005; Italian Institute for Pedagogical Research and Documentation based in Florence [INDIRE], 2004, 2005).

Societal Conditions

Besides the institutional factors, several other societal conditions have played a role in the recent policy choices that have been—and are currently being—made regarding foreign language teaching at the primary level. These include the different historic and socioeconomic conditions of the northern and southern Italian regions, the large immigration flow of the past 15 years, and the influence of dialects on first and second language learning. Italian as a national language reached the highest percentage of the population during the 1960s through the broadcasting of television programs nationwide, which helped people use Italian instead of or in addition to regional dialects (De Mauro, 1963). However, within the family context, local dialects have played and still play an important role in the acquisition of Italian as a first language, as well as in the learning of a foreign language at school.

In addition, the increasing presence of children of immigrants with many diverse language and cultural backgrounds has posed new and challenging problems for foreign language syllabus design, while also enriching the sociocultural stimuli within the classroom. One of the most interesting consequences of the immigration phenomenon has been the increase in studies of these populations, including methodological research about teaching Italian as a second language. These studies have provided new perspectives to the teachers of Italian as a core subject and to programs educating teachers of Italian as a second language at all school levels.

The widespread diffusion of information technology[4] in Italy has also played a relevant role in syllabus development and the organization of foreign language teacher education courses, particularly for kindergarten and primary school teachers. More teachers regularly use computers for their professional development, and in the past few years, most Italian primary teachers of English have regularly and successfully attended online in-service courses conducted by the Ministry of Education.

Foreign language teachers' professional development has largely been influenced by the demands of the work market for foreign language competencies, the status and consideration of teachers in Italian society, the need to adjust to European standards, and the role played by foreign language teachers' professional associations as well as by foreign cultural institutions. The British Council for English, the Alliance Française for French, the Goethe Institut for German, and the Instituto Cervantes for Spanish have all been highly influential and directly involved in the development of the Ministry of Education national curriculum and its teacher education guidelines in the past two decades.

Figure 1 summarizes most actions and innovations that have led to the present context in Italy. Appendix B provides a detailed account of the main innovations and reforms in the foreign language curriculum in Italy.

Focus on Primary Education

The foreign language teaching and learning initiatives undertaken by the Ministry of Education in the past 2 years at the national level focus mainly on primary school, making changes in both the overall organization of the school curriculum and in the

---

[4] In the past decade, most average Italian families have become more familiar with information technologies; there is almost one computer per house, and nearly 30% of the Italian population used computers in 2001. Although this has inevitably affected people's habits and improved their familiarity with international communications, it is important to note that most users live in northern Italy. Less than 20% of them live in the southern regions and the islands, where economic inequality has always determined different educational perspectives on topics including foreign language competencies. Media and films have played a minor role in the diffusion of foreign languages in Italian society, mainly because of the lack of films in the original language with subtitles and the release of dubbed-only films. The recent availability of films on DVD has, however, contributed to the diffusion of foreign languages, as has the use of satellite channels that connect more people to international networks.

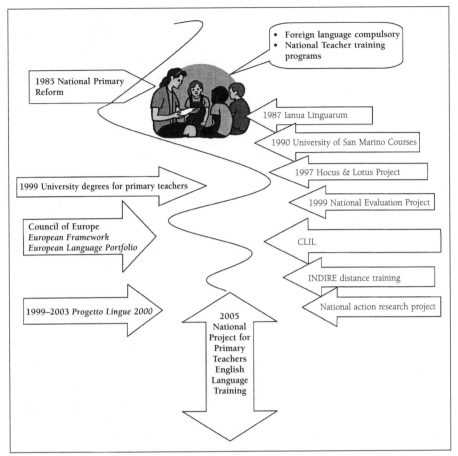

FIGURE 1. History of Foreign Language Reforms and Innovations in Italy

teacher training and language improvement opportunities offered to teachers. Primary education has become a specific means to implement the new school reform, and the teaching of foreign languages at the primary level has become pivotal for most of the actions undertaken at the national level. Introducing the study of a foreign language at such an early stage was first—almost 25 years ago—justified as a way to provide children with an additional learning tool, a way to enhance their cognitive development as well as their understanding of other people and cultures. Recently, the emphasis on early foreign language learning has been justified mostly by the importance of knowing English in a global society. The shift to this focus on adjusting to the requirements of a global society has not, however, affected the core of the many initiatives undertaken so far.

One among several noticeable changes in the ministerial documents and actions involves the language to be taught at the primary level. The *Teaching Programs for Primary School* (Italian Ministry of Education 1985a) guidelines made very clear that the main aim for introducing foreign languages at the primary level was to "provide children with yet another tool to organize their thoughts and knowledge" (p. 15).

Although this permitted the introduction of any foreign language, in the more recent ministry documents, English is the only foreign language mentioned both in the new foreign language syllabus recommendations and in all distance training courses so far promoted and directly geared to training teachers of English. Justification for this focus can be found in the policy of the current government, which has set four priorities in its plan: computer science, industry, and English, as well as an increasingly wider diffusion of English as the internationally acknowledged additional language of communication.

Foreign languages at the primary level were first officially introduced in Italy in 1991 (Italian Ministry of Education, DM 28/06/91) as a direct implementation of the 1985 primary school reform (Italian Ministry of Education, DPR 104, 1985; Italian Ministry of Education, 1985b). Originally, the foreign language—English, French, German, or Spanish—could be chosen by children's parents, provided not only that the chosen language was one in which teachers were specialists but also that the language was offered in the children's school. In most cases, the available teachers are specialists in English, which has inevitably led to a shift in the general policies that now promote English as the main, if not the only, foreign language taught in Italian schools.

The Teachers

Italian primary and kindergarten teachers have a longstanding tradition of high-quality professionalism that has been acknowledged internationally. This was the main reason the ministry asked them to be in charge of teaching foreign languages in Italian primary schools from the onset of the reform. Primary teachers know best how to teach children, they know how to develop language skills and can better enhance language education, and they are the ones who are most aware of the different degrees of cognitive and affective difficulties that children may experience in primary school. Because learning a new language means developing a new form of understanding and communication, teachers must be aware of how to best handle and enhance children's communicative growth. The major training problem that the Ministry of Education faced was the primary teachers' foreign language competence, which often was very low. The teachers eventually selected as foreign language teachers were primary teachers who either had attended the ministry's special training courses or already had a qualification in foreign language teaching. Therefore, for most primary teachers of foreign languages, the specific training courses developed since 1991 have included approximately 50 hours of specific methodology components and 500 hours of a language improvement component. The language component was emphasized because, although the primary language teachers were to teach material at a beginning level, they needed to be confident with and have a good command of the foreign language. Narrating a story in a foreign language to a group of children, for example, requires more than perfunctory English proficiency. Foreign language teachers at the primary level are well aware that the language tasks they need to perform are specific and peculiar to their context.

There have so far been two types of primary foreign language teachers in Italy. One, *specializzato* (specialized), can teach the foreign language as well as another subject area (e.g., mathematics) for one or two classes per day. The other, *specialista* (specialist), can teach only the foreign language in approximately six classes per day.

Using both types of teachers helped the ministry use fewer teachers for more classes when first implementing foreign language teaching in primary school. The situation is now gradually changing because of the many training courses and the arrival of newly graduated teachers specializing in a foreign language.

Starting Age and Weekly Timetable

From 1991 to 2003, Italian children began studying a foreign language at the age of 8 (in the third year of primary school) for an average of 3 hours per week, except in some primary schools where foreign languages were experimentally introduced earlier (in the first or second year) or those kindergarten classes where different types of foreign language experimental teaching were carried out (Benvenuto & Lopriore, 2000; Taeschner, 1993). However, the recently published ministerial guidelines for implementation of the school reform (Italy Implementation Decree n. 59, Decree Law n. 53/2003) have reduced English teaching from 3 to 2 hours per week. The Ministry of Education justified this choice by the anticipated introduction of English starting in the first year. Several Italian professional associations of teachers have strongly criticized this current ministerial policy as well as the established foreign language syllabus.

Approach and Syllabus

Primary English teachers usually use a learner-centered approach, with a theme- or topic-based modular syllabus and the inclusion of communicative games. Aural-oral skills are emphasized, as are interdisciplinary links because foreign language teachers also teach other subjects besides English, and the English lesson is inevitably influenced by what children learn in other content areas. This weighting, given its connection with the other subjects, is the most interesting feature of the foreign language syllabus. Because foreign language and Italian have common cognitive objectives, there are several opportunities for foreign language in the primary school curriculum to have a cross-curricular learning function (Titone, 1990). Connections between the foreign language and other subjects exist not only through content but also through the teaching strategies developed for these subjects. The ministry guidelines and objectives for foreign language (MIUR Italy Decree Law n. 53/2003, Implementation Decree n. 59, 2004) include the following meaningful links to the teaching of other subjects:

- In mathematics, teachers are encouraged to use "concepts, methods, attitudes in order to develop the ability to order, quantify and measure real facts and phenomena and develop the ability to critically interpret reality."

- In science, students "develop a closer connection between doing and thinking."

- In history, geography, and social studies, teachers should "develop and stimulate the passage from a culture lived and absorbed directly from life to a culture that is an intellectual artifact."

- In image education, students should "be able to decode the adopted codes and to understand the communicative context."

- In music and sound education, learners should be able "to perceive sound reality as a whole, to understand it and to produce it."
- In physical education, the subject "regards movement as another language, totally integrated in the development of one's own autonomy." (pp. 13–20)

One way or another, language education comes into the primary school curriculum, and foreign language study underlies all subjects. The quality of foreign language learning lies in its communicative nature, which allows learners to enhance the knowledge they acquire from other subjects and thus to deepen their understanding of communication and of language as a system. Figure 2 provides an interdisciplinary syllabus developed in an Italian primary third-year class (Olimpieri, in Benvenuto & Lopriore, 2000). Lessons or units are usually organized according to the sequence suggested by the 1985 ministerial guidelines (Italian Ministry of Education, 1985): Comprehension → Assimilation → Production.

Aims and Objectives
• To understand that there are community rules and that a class is a community where everybody should respect the rules
• To understand the expressions in Italian and in English that regulate classroom life
• To understand basic Italian and English commands for movement activities
• To acquire basic body awareness through the learning of body vocabulary in Italian and in English

Activities	Subjects Integrated
1. Basic activities are aimed at understanding the concept of community and the need for community rules.	Italian, history, social studies, religion
2. Specific roles and tasks to be fulfilled in the class. Each student narrates his or her experience.	Italian, foreign language, history, social studies
3. Each task has a specific deadline and turnover; it has to be regularly registered in a class historic memory log.	Italian, foreign language, history, social studies, logic
4. Each student is given a specific seat and a visual representation of the classroom with each seat. The student describes the classroom from his or her position.	Italian, foreign language, logic, mathematics, geography, image education
5. Understand and practice everyday expressions and commands during routine class activities (e.g., homework correction, break, classroom change).	Italian and foreign language
6. Use movement commands related to parts of the body and actions (e.g., vocabulary, picture drawing, movements).	Italian, foreign language, science, physical education, image education
7. Use movement and sound association activities (e.g., rhythm, song animation, dance execution).	Foreign language, musical education, physical education

FIGURE 2. Interdisciplinary Third-Year Syllabus

Warm-up and review	Conduct routine activities such as a song to introduce the lesson and create a unique climate. A review of previously learned vocabulary or functions with flashcards or other materials follows.
Introduction	Present the day's activities and objectives.
Presentation	Introduce new language (e.g., vocabulary, functions).
Controlled practice	Conduct teacher-supervised activities based on the new language introduced.
Production	Play a game, role-play, or engage in dialogue. Use the language and try out what has been learned.
Review	Review what has been learned. Assess students by providing activities with the goal of finding out what needs to be reinforced.

FIGURE 3. Typical Lesson Sequence

Figure 3 provides an example of the sequence of traditional learning phases; each phase can take place in a different sequence or can be repeated as time constraints allow or specific teaching needs require. In each lesson, teachers try to vary the type of activities presented (e.g., problem solving, problem posing, drama, songs, games, role-play, picture dictation), use different types of interactions (teacher–class, teacher–learner, student–student, group–learner), and engage children in different skills at different times.

◈ DISTINGUISHING FEATURES

Language Awareness

The ministerial guidelines (Italian Ministry of Education, 1985a) specifically recommend focusing children's attention on certain contrasts between their native language and the foreign language. Teachers point out simple contrastive features—such as differences in sentence building, tenses, and time expressions—and linguistic choices in the performance of language functions in celebrations. Recently, some specific metalinguistic and grammar awareness activities in the native language have become more common (Titone, 1993).

Textbooks and Teaching Materials

Italian and international publishers alike have found a fast-growing market in the field of foreign language teaching at the primary level. Use of textbooks is compulsory, and texts are usually written specifically for the Italian market and comply with the ministry guidelines and the Council of Europe descriptors. They are selected by teachers and sold by publishers at a special price.[5] They generally include a teacher's guide, a student's book for each school year, and an audiocassette for the listening component. Schools usually purchase accompanying videotapes and CDs,

---

[5] Except for specific materials, textbooks in elementary schools are usually provided for free. Foreign language textbooks are specially reduced in price to meet ministry regulations.

which are used in a designated foreign language classroom, if there is one available in the school building.

The *European Language Portfolio* (Council of Europe, 1997) is recommended for learners of a foreign language in Europe and is meant to record the learner's competencies and learning progress in one or more foreign languages. Italian versions of the *European Language Portfolio* booklets have recently been adopted at all school levels, even at the primary level, where the Ministry of Education has introduced the use of a learner portfolio for all subjects. Teachers are developing more self-assessment activities to help their students learn how to monitor their own progress in the foreign language.

Computers and multimedia products are widely used for children's language learning projects. Primary school teachers have been offered specific training in the use of multimedia resources for teaching purposes and in using the Internet (*Progetto Lingue 2000*; Italian Ministry of Education, 2001). The Internet may offer teachers more opportunities for exposure to the foreign language and thereby help them gain self-confidence. Teachers have been specifically trained in the use of language learning software materials, such as hypertext and video games; in the exploitation of foreign language teaching Web sites; and in the regular use of language labs. They have also been encouraged to develop syllabi incorporating the use of information technologies.

Foreign Languages in Kindergarten and the Issue of Continuity

Foreign languages have also been introduced in kindergarten through several experimental projects launched at the national and European levels (Blondin et al., 1998). One example is the FORMAT approach (Taeschner, 1993), introduced through the education ministry's experimental project, *The Adventures of Hocus and Lotus* (Taeschner et al., 1997), which was carried out in 114 kindergarten schools nationwide between 1994 and 1997 (Italian Ministry of Education, 1994). Other examples are the initiatives within *Progetto Lingue 2000* (Italian Ministry of Education, 2001) since 1999 for primary and kindergarten teachers.

Future training will address sustaining continuity in content while preventing learning plateaus that create a general dissatisfaction with foreign language learning. The training opportunities and the courses in the *Progetto Lingue 2000* (Italian Ministry of Education, 2001) were in many cases organized with teachers from different school levels. This training gave teachers the opportunity to share experiences and learn about each other and the differences in school levels. In many cases, kindergarten, primary, and middle school teachers had the opportunity to start moving together toward foreign language curriculum continuity.

Assessment and Results

As a country that belongs to the European Union, Italy has had to adjust to European education regulations. Recently, the Council of Europe's language policies and publications, such as the *Common European Framework* (2001) and the *European Language Portfolio* (1997), have become more influential in the Italian school system. Until 2003, the official Ministry of Education documents used the descriptors of competence levels in foreign languages as outlined in the *Common European Framework* currently used by schools, publishers, and teachers as a standard for the school exit levels. For the primary school exit levels, the descriptors used have so far been the ones defined at the A1 level, also called Breakthrough. The middle school exit levels are those described in the A2 level, or Waystage. Figure 4 summarizes the European descriptors for the two levels and for each language skill.

A1	A2
Understanding	
I can *recognize familiar* words and *very basic phrases* concerning myself, my family and *immediate concrete* surroundings when people speak *slowly* and *clearly*.	I can *understand* phrases and the *highest frequency vocabulary* related to areas of most immediate *personal relevance* (e.g., very basic personal and family information, shopping, local geography, employment).
	I can *catch* the *main point* in *short, clear, simple* messages and announcements.
Reading	
I can *understand familiar* names, words and *very simple sentences,* for example on notices and posters or in catalogues.	I can *read* very short, simple texts.
	I can *find* specific, *predictable* information in *simple, everyday material* such as advertisements, prospectuses, menus and timetables and I can *understand* short, simple personal letters.
Spoken Interaction	
I can *interact* in a *simple* way provided *the other person* is prepared to repeat or rephrase things at a *slower rate* of speech and help me formulate what I'm trying to say.	I can *communicate* in *simple* and *routine* tasks requiring a *simple* and *direct* exchange of information on *familiar* topics and activities.
I can *ask and answer simple* questions in areas of *immediate need* or on *very familiar* topics.	I can *handle* very short *social* exchanges, even though I *can't* usually *understand enough* to keep the conversation going myself.
Spoken Production	
I can *use simple phrases* and *sentences* to *describe* where I live and people I know.	I can *use a series* of *phrases* and *sentences* to *describe* in *simple* terms my family and other people, living conditions, my educational background and my present or most recent job.
Writing	
I can *write a short, simple* postcard, for example sending holiday greetings.	I can *write short, simple* notes and messages relating to matters in areas of *immediate need.*
I can *fill in forms* with personal details, for example entering my name, nationality, and address on a hotel registration form.	I can *write a very simple* personal letter, for example thanking someone for something.

FIGURE 4. Descriptors From the *Common European Framework* for Levels A1 and A2

In 2000, the Ministry of Education and the Department of Education of the University of Rome (La Sapienza) carried out a national evaluation project regarding foreign language competences of children leaving primary school with 3 years of foreign language learning. The results of the tests administered for English and French to almost 3,000 fifth-year primary students throughout Italy were positive. Questionnaires were also administered to teachers and students, the purpose of which was to find out more about teaching practices as viewed by both groups. Students with higher results described best teaching practices in the questionnaires. Thus, there was a significant correlation between results and teaching practices. In a subsequent test administration carried out by the ministry in 2002, the results of approximately 250 students of English were well above the A1 level of the *Common European Framework* (Council of Europe, 2001).

The forms of assessment most commonly used by primary teachers are objective tests of listening and reading, including multiple-choice, true-false, completion, and matching questions. Speaking is assessed through descriptions or pair interviews. Writing, however, is not assessed. Most teachers use tests provided with their textbooks or create tests modeled after those used by International Certifications (e.g., for English, the *Movers and Starters* tests developed by the University of Cambridge, n.d.).

Teacher Training Experience

The most controversial issue in introducing foreign languages at the primary level has been the foreign language competence of primary teachers who had never specifically studied foreign languages before. Most in-service courses offered by the education ministry since 1991 have devoted much content to language improvement, creating the opportunity for teachers to develop their English language skills and enhance their self-confidence.

The ministry's in-service teacher training courses have always been characterized by quality input from trainers and a strong professional commitment from primary teachers. In Italy, primary teachers usually teach an average of 32 hours per week, have classes with up to 30 children, and attend courses in their free time. Attending the language training courses was certainly more difficult for teachers who had to start learning a foreign language from a low level, with the knowledge that they would later be required to teach the language. This issue has been the subject of many debates, but asking primary teachers to teach the foreign language has proved so far to be the right choice. They have learned how to cope with the few resources available to them and have responded on feedback forms that their training courses provided them with opportunities to develop professionally (Benvenuto & Lopriore, 1999). Still, there is quite a bit to do. Learning a foreign language is a lifelong process that implies constant exposure to the foreign language. For some people, this idea is very difficult to grasp. Offering one language improvement course, even a 300-hour one, is certainly not enough. Getting an international certification might provide a good long-term objective, but again, this is not enough. What teachers need, after specifically working on language ability, is the opportunity to continuously sustain their competence in the foreign language, through discussion groups, training options, time in a native-speaking country, or online courses. Recently, there have been two good examples of sustained professional development for primary school teachers:

1. the Ministry of Education Action Research Project, between 2000 and 2002, whose main aims were to

   - improve and broaden the study of foreign languages, both curricular and within the *Progetto Lingue 2000,* with a special focus on the languages spoken in the European Union

   - ensure cooperation in implementing such actions between the ministry and associations

   - develop and activate educational opportunities for teachers and teacher trainers to focus and reflect on methodology and pedagogical aspects

   - provide the basis for a national foreign language curriculum

2. specific courses for primary teachers, run jointly by the Ministry of Education and INDIRE, whose purpose was to provide distance training in the 2003–2004 school reforms at a national level to primary teachers of different subjects (INDIRE, 2005)

Both training projects have interesting features that are worth looking at for several reasons:

- The 2000–2002 courses were based on an action research approach in which the teachers, together with colleagues, investigated their own classroom practice (Kemmis & McTaggart, 1982).

- The ministry-INDIRE courses have undergone an experimental stage, offered to a group of only 200 schools throughout Italy. Courses selected to be part of the experimental implementation of the New School Reform are now offered at the national level.

- The ministry-INDIRE courses were offered partly as distance courses and partly as classroom courses.

- The ideas used in the courses and the teachers' positive reactions have been the starting point for a national training project accompanying all of the foreign language primary school teachers involved in the reform beginning in 2003.

The experimental ministry-INDIRE training courses were officially run by INDIRE, using a distance training platform for the online component, and by a group of 40 tutors for the classroom courses. On the INDIRE Web site, primary teachers could access the following training opportunities:

- a language improvement course

- a language learning course, with samples of communicative language activities for primary learners

- an orientation about the new reform

- methodology training

- an online discussion group

The methodology training component was a set of theme-based courses prepared by experts in the field of teaching language to young learners. Each component included an open forum where the experts discussed the theme and answered specific theme-related questions asked by primary teachers. The themes included children's cognitive development, early foreign language learning, teaching methodology, information technologies in early language learning, profiling at the primary level, portfolio use, and principles of second language acquisition.

The online discussion group addressed a wide variety of issues and offered primary teachers the opportunity to read downloadable documents and publications from the INDIRE Web site; to share ideas, experiences, and suggestions with other colleagues; to ask questions of and get advice from academics and experts belonging to professional associations; and to develop teaching plans and classroom activities and post them on the Web site.

Primary teachers were also offered the opportunity to regularly attend off-line seminars conducted by tutors. These seminars enabled teachers to work with a group of colleagues on the themes discussed in online courses. Among the topics most frequently addressed by the experts, required by primary teachers and discussed during the off-line seminars, were assessment and evaluation of young learners, syllabus design, the use of the *European Language Portfolio* (Council of Europe, 1997), and the use of new technologies.

Specific language improvement courses and some methodology seminars were conducted at the same time on an educational TV channel (RAI Educational) to reinforce primary teachers' learning and to provide feedback from teachers. The Italian national TV network (RAI) also provides specific language courses online (Il Divertinglese) for young learners to access at school and at home.

The whole INDIRE training experience lasted from January to June of 2003 and received positive feedback from the participants. During the 2003–2004 school year, a new INDIRE training project was set up by a scientific committee created by the Ministry of Education to support teachers at primary and middle school levels as they implement the reforms.

Feedback so far indicates the need for a specific teacher training project that would prepare foreign language primary teachers with a more clearly defined set of competencies. Following are some of the major components of the foreign language primary teacher profile emerging from the debate that started informally among the experts of the scientific committee and that still remains to be officially defined:

Competencies and Foreign Language Teacher Education

Language competence: at least at level B1 of the *Common European Framework*

Teaching competence: A FL [foreign language] primary school teacher should be able to

Professionalism/Dispositions
- regard FL teaching as a whole experience where both the native language and the FL are aimed at developing communication and the understanding of other cultures
- teach the FL as an integrated part of everyday teaching in an interdisciplinary perspective
- work together with other colleagues from his/her school level and from other school levels

- promote intercultural and language mediation activities in order to develop children's understanding of other cultures

Language
- continuously update his/her FL competence and learn about new teaching concepts and ideas either individually or within a course

Instruction
- know about and use multimodal and multiple sense approaches in FL teaching
- know about and use Information and Communication Technology for FL teaching
- plan interdisciplinary projects and learning paths as well as specific content-based activities and meaningful experiences with the use of the FL as in Content Language Integrated Learning (CLIL). CLIL refers to any dual-focused educational context in which an additional language, thus not usually the first language of the learners involved, is used as a medium in the teaching and learning of non-language content
- lead learning groups directly in the FL
- involve and motivate children's curiosity and interest in using the FL
- develop specific activities for those children who have not achieved the foreseen results
- use and exploit specific drama, mime and music activities
- use a variety of materials, realia and teaching resources

Assessment
- plan specific learning paths and assessment and self-assessment procedures with the objectives of developing the student's Language Portfolio and of promoting continuity to the following school levels
- develop and monitor the implementation of Individual Learning and Study Plans
- value children's experiences and competencies gained outside the school environment and insert them into the children's profile and Learning Portfolio (INDIRE memo, July 4, 2004)

Introducing foreign language teaching in Italian primary schools has been characterized by features that derive from the longstanding high-quality tradition of Italian primary schools, the foreign language practical experience carried out at the school level, and the numerous foreign language teacher training courses. Figure 5 summarizes some of these features. The competencies should be the outcome of specific teacher training courses, with principles as outlined in Figure 6.

❧ PRACTICAL IDEAS

The experience of early foreign language learning in the Italian context has proved very positive overall. In particular, what has been done so far in the implementation of foreign language teaching in primary schools may be the starting point for gradually building and sustaining continuity in language teaching and learning across all school levels.

Foreign Language Learning

- is part of a whole cognitive and affective learning experience in which the foreign language is one of the learning tools, another opportunity to further enhance children's cognitive and affective development
- is much more meaningful and productive if carried out with an interdisciplinary perspective and a content-, theme-, or topic-based approach
- is much more significant for children if it is carried out through motivating and entertaining activities, such as storytelling, songs, drama, and mime
- is part of language education because it is based on communication and language awareness
- is also aimed at non-language-specific objectives, such as multicultural and intercultural comprehension and understanding
- is a powerful tool to overcome racial prejudices and barriers
- primarily focuses on the development of aural and oral skills within an integrated skills approach
- is facilitated by establishing meaningful connections with other subjects
- is enhanced through self-assessment procedures
- is enhanced by the use of multimodal and multisensory approaches

Foreign Language Teaching

- offers a variety of input, activities, and materials
- uses different input sources and resorts to information technologies
- uses tools such as the *European Language Portfolio* (Council of Europe, 1997) to help learners value language learning as a self-development experience and as part of lifelong learning

FIGURE 5. Principles of High-Quality Foreign Language Learning and Teaching

Almost all of the foreign language training projects for Italian primary teachers during the past decade have been characterized by features that make the process highly innovative. I regard the following features as pivotal in developing future foreign language programs for young learners:

Trust Primary Teachers to Be English Teachers

As I have already stated, trusting the teachers' pedagogical competence and teaching experience with a particular age level provides the drive to improve teachers' language competence. The recent Ministry of Education and INDIRE initiatives aimed at offering teachers opportunities for ongoing language improvement courses are ways of sustaining professional development in an area where primary teachers often feel less confident.

Promote Language Through Content, Content Through Language

Teachers use foreign language as a way to strengthen children's cognitive development and help them learn other subjects. Using the language to learn the language

- A language improvement component is always an indispensable opportunity for primary teachers. It should have specific learning objectives and offer opportunities for continuous improvement. Teachers should be offered the opportunity to spend some time in another country to have direct exposure to the foreign language and culture. Opportunities for international school visits or exchanges could be offered through specific agreements with foreign cultural institutions.

- Both language improvement and methodology courses should be based on an action research approach that allows teachers to regularly observe, monitor, and reflect on the implementation of new ideas in their classes.

- Courses should include a specific component on the use of computers, the Internet, and Web sites for foreign language teaching.

- Courses should alternate plenary sessions with workshops and small-group discussions. Primary teachers are very good at working in groups and appreciate discussing their teaching ideas and problems with their peers as well as with their tutors.

- Courses should be based on a variety of input, such as sessions conducted by experts, videos, individual readings, and group planning.

- Online courses should allow for face-to-face meetings as well as open discussion forums.

- Teachers should be encouraged to produce their own teaching plans and teaching materials.

- Teachers should be encouraged and guided in setting specific foreign language learning standards and developing assessment procedures.

- Primary teachers' background knowledge and experience should be acknowledged and used throughout the course, particularly when developing language awareness and interdisciplinary activities or projects.

FIGURE 6. Principles of High-Quality Foreign Language Teacher Training

while learning literacy skills has always been the first and most relevant learning principle maintained throughout all levels.

Focus on the Learner

The learner-centered approach emphasizes that the language learning process starts with young learners' interests as well as their cognitive and affective needs. This approach also enhances the motivation and drive for learning.

Share Common Objectives

The widespread use of the language competence descriptors of the *Common European Framework* (Council of Europe, 2001) for planning language activities, as well as use of the *European Language Portfolio* (Council of Europe, 1997) for younger learners, is the sign of a shared approach and language among foreign language teachers at all levels. By sharing common objectives and encouraging students to use language portfolios, Italian teachers are gradually building and sustaining continuity in language learning, thus overcoming a diffused feeling of dissatisfaction among foreign language students who have often complained of being forced to "start all over again" when moved from one school level to another. Using European guidelines is also a step toward better and more effective collaboration and exchanges of teachers and groups of students among European countries.

◈ CONCLUSION

The Council of Europe language policies have highlighted the importance for European citizens to know at least two other languages besides their native language, thus enhancing a truly multilingual and multicultural society. The long and winding road of the foreign language curriculum for young Italian learners, with its gradual changes and innovations, can be considered a healthy and productive response to the European vision, one that centrally includes English as a foreign language.

◈ CONTRIBUTOR

Lucilla Lopriore is a teacher, teacher trainer, and textbook writer and has taught in Italian high schools for more than 25 years. She is currently a research fellow in English linguistics at the University of Cassino in Italy. She has a master's degree in teaching English as a foreign language from the University of Reading and a doctorate in Italian as a foreign language from the University for Foreigners in Siena. She was president of TESOL Italy (1996–1998) and a member of the TESOL board of directors (2001–2004).

◈ APPENDIX A: BACKGROUND ON FACTORS IN FOREIGN LANGUAGE INNOVATION

The Common European Framework of Modern Languages

An official document issued by the Council of Europe, the *Common European Framework* (2001) was first formally introduced in Italy via the *Progetto Lingue 2000*, and it is having a major impact on foreign language teaching in the country. More foreign language teachers are now familiar at least with the framework's descriptors of the levels of competence. At the beginning, it was not easy for many teachers who were unaccustomed to developing language competencies to adjust to a system based on "can do" statements. It was and still is difficult to grasp the concept of competencies and implement a teaching path with a detailed description of the students' progress and skills. Slowly, but gradually, Italian teachers are becoming familiar with the overall approach underlying the framework, and they are beginning to see the advantages of developing a different way to organize the syllabus in their contexts. One of the main issues raised by use of the framework is the concept of working toward the achievement of specific levels of competence. In an educational system like Italy's, where there has so far been very limited understanding and use of standards, where the foreign language syllabus has for a long time been described only in terms of language content rather than competencies to be achieved, and where an evaluation culture has only recently begun to be diffused, the impact of the framework will be slow but long-term.

The European Language Portfolio

The *European Language Portfolio* (Council of Europe, 1997) is a self-assessment document completed by the learner. It provides information about foreign language experiences, cultural experiences, and school certificates as well as evidence of competence in the use of one or more foreign languages. The portfolio comprises the learner's passport, biography, and dossier—a collection of the most significant projects and activities to document the learner's language competence and progress. The learner decides which projects to include in the dossier, which looks like a folder or file. The learner may include, for example, any significant homework or class work, a copy of a test, an oral activity recording, an individual or team project (e.g., booklet, CD-ROM, photo of a poster), or a copy of any language certificate.

Progetto Lingue 2000

The *Progetto Lingue 2000* (Italian Ministry of Education, 2001), the most recent and important innovation in the development of schools' autonomy and the renewal of Italian foreign language curriculum, outlines the optional introduction of the study of a second (in some cases, first) European foreign language outside the national curriculum at all school levels from kindergarten to high school. The project responds to the emerging language needs of students and to one of the distinctive features of the Italian context: the role of multilingual foreign language learning. The project also responds to the autonomous organization of individual schools that are offered a way to broaden and enrich their school curriculum. Teachers recruited for the project are either state teachers specifically hired for this position with a separate contract, or freelance teachers with qualifications for the job. Specific ad hoc in-service training courses for the teachers involved in the project, which focused on the major methodological implications, were conducted between 1999 and 2002. The two most important aspects of the project in terms of innovation are its approach and its monitoring system. The methodology suggested by the project guidelines focuses on a few extremely significant factors: use of the *Common European Framework* (Council of Europe, 2001) levels and guidelines, modular organization of teaching, small learning groups (maximum 15 students), use of new information technologies for language learning, use of autonomously created teaching materials, use of local teacher resource centers, and optional use of international certifications as an opportunity for student assessment.

The Modular Curriculum

A modular organization of the curriculum allows teachers to work within a flexible structure where objectives are established in terms of competencies to be achieved, based on those previously acquired. A modular system allows students to monitor their own learning process and acquisition, to become more aware of their individual learning styles, and to start planning their own learning paths. Modules are short and meaningful learning paths, whereby students' competencies can be assessed and certified. The difference between a unit-by-unit syllabus and a modular one lies in the multidimensional framework of the latter. Modules contain sets of different learning segments that can interact at several stages of the module and in different ways. Modules should mirror the way a student's brain organizes learning and at the same time provide the possibility for both students and teachers to track the competencies acquired and taught. Modules are an attempt to provide a different way of organizing knowledge and competencies around self-contained segments of learning, in which topics, language functions, and language structures interact. At the beginning of each module, students are told what they will learn, in terms of language as well as competencies. At the end, they are asked to check whether or not they learned to measure their progress.

Professional Associations of Foreign Language Teachers in Italy

A significant role in the professional development of Italian foreign language teachers has been played by some of the professional associations of teachers, which through the years have organized local or national conventions, conducted seminars or teacher training courses, diffused journals and publications, published books and materials, and sustained teachers in various other ways. There are five main associations: Associazione Ispanisti Italiani (AISPI, the association of teachers of Spanish), Associazione Docenti Italiani di Lingua Tedesca (ADILT, the association of teachers of German), Associazione Nazionale Insegnanti Lingue Straniere and Lingua e Nuova Didattica (ANILS and LEND, two associations of teachers of all foreign languages), and TESOL Italy (the association of teachers of English). These associations have in many cases provided the type of sustained development teachers need, have often led the debate about foreign language teaching and learning in their journals and at their national conventions, have organized local symposia (ANILS, LEND, TESOL), and in the case of LEND, have specialized in specific publications. Two years ago all of the professional associations were officially acknowledged by the Italian Ministry of Education as authorized teacher training entities (i.e., the courses conducted by the associations could be recognized as official training courses by the educational authorities).

◈ APPENDIX B: MAJOR FOREIGN LANGUAGE REFORMS AND INNOVATIONS IN ITALY

Dates	Reforms, Projects, and Innovations	Description
1977–1989	ILSSE Project	Experimental project in several Italian towns: 550 classes at the end of 1981 (Italian Ministry of Education, 1985b; Porcelli & Balboni, 1985)
		Languages: English, French, or German, taught from the third year. The choice was made according to the teachers' availability and the context-specific needs.
		Principle: Any language can help develop children's minds.
		Teachers: Primary teachers in their classrooms
		Aims:
		• to broaden children's communication
		• to enrich children's cognitive development through different linguistic stimuli
		• to broaden children's contact with international experiences

Dates	Reforms, Projects, and Innovations	Description
		• to sustain children's understanding of other cultures and peoples
		Teaching methodology:
		• emphasis on aural-oral skills at the beginning, later introduction to reading and some writing
		• reference to the notional-functional approach
		• use of games
		• central role of lexis
		• time: 30 minutes daily
		Teacher training: Courses with two components: language and methodology
1985	National Primary Reform	Foreign language as one of the eight compulsory curricular subjects at the national level officially starting in the 1992–1993 school year (Italian Ministry of Education, 1994). In spite of most recent innovations, the 1985 programs are still valid in terms of general guidelines.
		Aims:
		• *Cognitive:* to foster children's cognitive development through another knowledge-organizing tool
		• *Communicative:* to facilitate children's communication with others through another language
		• *Multicultural:* to guide children's understanding of other cultures and people through the medium of another language
		Languages: English, French, German, or Spanish (The choice is irrelevant because of such aims, but the international status of English as a vehicular language gives it a special role.)
		Teaching methodology: Same as for the ILLSE Project, but there are no clearly specified syllabus guidelines that one would expect in a national curriculum. Class time required equals 3 hours per week on different days, staring in the third or sometimes second year.
		Teacher: Primary teachers, but because of the lack of teachers with specific foreign language competence, the easiest solution was to use two types of teachers: a specialist teacher, who only teaches the foreign language in six classes, and a specialized teacher, who teaches the foreign language as well as other subjects in one class.
		Teacher training: Three phases of training:
		1. initially (in 1990), special methodology courses for primary teachers who already had foreign language competence (100 hours)
		2. a language improvement component (50 to 200 hours according to the language level) together with a

Dates	Reforms, Projects, and Innovations	Description
		methodology course for those who did not have any foreign language qualification
		3. Besides these courses, a specific training project (DIRELEM-LISE) was devoted to training all teachers still in need of training in all primary schools (1991–1995). Features of this last phase were the structure of the training components (language improvement, up to 400 hours; language teaching methodology, 30 hours; specific language activities, 70 hours) and monitoring and assessment of the achieved language competency.
		The trainers of methodology were specifically qualified teacher trainers. The language component was run by private language schools, university language centers, or foreign cultural institutions (Pavan De Gregorio, 1999).
1987–1994	Ianua Linguarum Project	An experimental project promoted and carried out in the Veneto region by the regional education authorities, its purpose was to develop curricular guidelines and implement the foreign language component of the primary reform and investigate its effectiveness. The results of this project helped better define the implementation of the primary curriculum (Balboni, 1993).
1990–1993	University of San Marino Specialist Training Course	Specialist international teacher training courses were offered to foreign language primary teachers, with two summer modules and a research classroom project based on action research. Models of primary foreign language syllabi were developed (Brumfit et al., 1991). Many of the Italian teachers who attended the course have now become teacher trainers in the Primary Training Schemes.
1990–2000	Foreign cultural institution scholarships and grants programs	The Ministry of Education and foreign cultural institutions, such as the British Council, regularly offered Italian foreign language primary teachers a certain number of grants to attend summer primary teacher training courses internationally.
1997–1999	FORMAT Hocus & Lotus Project	The Ministry of Education launched an experimental national teacher training program for 120 kindergarten teachers with the FORMAT narrative approach (Blondin et al., 1998; Taeschner, 1993).
1999	National Evaluation Project	In 1997, the Ministry of Education asked the Department of Education of Rome University to evaluate the results of introducing foreign language in primary school. The project consisted of a set of tests of listening and reading comprehension and of lexical competence in French and English, a set of tests of metalinguistic competence in Italian, and two parallel questionnaires for primary teachers and students, which were administered—on the basis of a

Dates	Reforms, Projects, and Innovations	Description
		national sample—to almost 2,500 students of English and 400 students of French at the end of their last year of primary school in June 1999. The results were positive and validated the type of approach undertaken by the ministry at the primary level, while acknowledging striking differences geographically (Benvenuto & Lopriore, 1999; Lopriore, 1997, 2001).
1999–2003	Progetto Lingue 2000	With Progetto Lingue 2000 (Italian Ministry of Education, 2001), the in-service scenario was partly modified: Specific trainer training and teacher training courses at all school levels were organized, conducted, and monitored for the four foreign languages. Between 1998 and 1999, a specific task force of 320 trainers for middle and high school was prepared with the aim of introducing Italian teachers to the fundamental concepts underlying Progetto Lingue 2000. In June 2000, 115 new trainers were trained for kindergarten and primary school, and another group of 58 for middle and high school. The in-service courses, averaging 30 hours, were conducted constantly for all school levels. At the moment, the goal of the project has been achieved, and the initiative of continuing this form of training is in the hands of individual head teachers and their school staff. The most important features for the foreign primary teachers in this specific training project were the emphasis on the role of new technologies in language education, the use of the Common European Framework descriptors of levels, and the optional use of the international language certifications.
1999–present	Preservice university training for primary teachers	In 1999, the first university degrees for primary teachers were started. In each course, a foreign language course and a foreign language methodology course are part of the curriculum. Until 1999 an Italian primary teacher did not need a university degree, only a passing score on a specific post-high-school teaching exam.
1999–present	The CLIL Experience	An important innovation, CLIL is slowly beginning to influence the foreign language curriculum and the language policies of the Italian school system. It uses a foreign language as the medium of instruction (i.e., content-based instruction of a non-foreign-language subject). There is a new trend toward the diffusion of CLIL in several schools throughout Italy, particularly in those regions where bilingualism is encouraged. Several primary and middle schools are implementing this type of instruction because the new law for school autonomy allows schools to try experimental projects like this (Marsh & Langé, 1999).
2000–2002	National Action Research Project	This joint project of the Ministry of Education and the main foreign language professional associations had the overall goals of investigating the students' results at all school levels and for all foreign languages, identifying the most common

Dates	Reforms, Projects, and Innovations	Description
		teaching practices used in Italian classes, and defining and aligning the descriptors of the competencies at each exit level to the results emerging from national research.* Some primary classes were involved. The tests administered in those classes have shown results well above the expected level (A1).
2002–2003	New School Reform and the distance training program for primary teachers	Within the New School Reform law, a specific distance training program was started for primary teachers of English by the Ministry of Education in collaboration with INDIRE and professional associations.
2003–2004	Ministry of Education guidelines for language and methodology training of primary teachers	In July 2003, the Ministry of Education set up a scientific committee to develop training guidelines for all primary teachers of English for a project to be started in the following school year. In 2004, a pilot project for language and methodology training of primary teachers was launched.
2005	Ministry of Education decree for the implementation of nationwide training in language and methodology	A scientific committee was established to provide specific guidelines for primary teachers training in foreign language teaching and a TV language teaching program for children was developed (INDIRE, 2005). In the 2005–2006 school year, all Italian primary school teachers were offered specific training in English language (to reach Level B1) and foreign language teaching methodology (Cerini & Gianferrari, 2005). All the new guidelines have been published on the Italian Ministry of Education Web site.

* The project used three main research tools: a set of tests for all language skills developed by a group of language teacher trainers selected by the professional associations, a number of teacher training courses based on the action research approach and conducted throughout Italy for each language and at each level, and a set of classroom research tools (e.g., questionnaires, observation grids, diaries) used during the teacher training courses and administered—together with the tests—by the teachers attending the courses in their own classes. The report on the results of the research, which involved thousands of students, will be published by the Ministry of Education. The partial results emerging from this important project already show a great interest from teachers in their classroom practices and in the action research approach as well as in the search for new forms of assessment for evaluating their students' results.

PART 2

Primary EFL Curriculum and Classroom Practices

CHAPTER 6

Teaching EFL at the Primary Level in Turkey

Yasemin Kırkgöz

◈ INTRODUCTION

Since the 1980s, many countries have witnessed a marked increase in the teaching of English as a foreign language (EFL) at the primary level of education (Rixon, 1992a). The introduction of EFL in Turkish primary education took place in 1997, when the Turkish Ministry of National Education (MNE) initiated a major reform in English language teaching. This initiative introduced a distinct change—it increased the duration of all primary education from 5 to 8 years of instruction. As a consequence, English began to be taught at the primary level in Grades 4 and 5 to young learners as a compulsory school subject, nationwide. Before this educational reform, however, English was taught from Grade 6 onward.

◈ CONTEXT

In Turkey, basic education constitutes the foundation of the national education system. It is compulsory for every Turkish citizen between the ages of 6 and 14 years. The official language of instruction is Turkish, the mother tongue. In this non-English-speaking environment, English has the status of EFL because it is part of the school curriculum. The major motivating forces underlying the decision to introduce English to young learners are the status of the English language and Turkey's political and economic ambitions to keep up its relations with foreign countries using English. It is also believed that lowering the starting age provides longer exposure to the foreign language and broadens children's cultural horizons (see MEB, 2001). In the Turkish education system, primary education currently lasts 8 years, from Grade 1 through Grade 8. In this chapter, the term *young learners of English* means all learners who study EFL within the framework of Turkish primary education, particularly those in Grades 4 and 5, because this is when the learners in state-owned primary schools begin learning English.

The introduction of English into the primary school curriculum presents complex problems across the country, placing a great strain on human, financial, and organizational resources. A nationwide debate focused on how to provide enough teachers with appropriate skills in a relatively short time. Some new sources for teacher education were established because teaching staff responsible for teaching English to young learners would require appropriate theoretical and practical training. To compensate for the existing shortage of teachers, the MNE set up an initial training program specifically for teachers who may not have taught a foreign language previously but were already involved with young learners of English in state primary schools. These training programs aimed to provide concrete support while giving teachers the opportunity to obtain the special expertise necessary to instruct this student population. Many shorter courses were established to encourage former adult education EFL teachers to broaden their experience. In addition, non-English-language teachers (e.g., graduates of the business college) attended short training courses on methodology and English language to teach young learners (Bada, 1999).

Despite the current popularity of early foreign language teaching, there is still insufficient empirical research to demonstrate the extent to which young learners can acquire a new language effectively. Anecdotal evidence points to the existence of several factors that affect results, such as the shortage of English language teachers and teachers' lack of experience in teaching young learners. To address the fact that programs for young learners are quite a recent phenomenon in the Turkish education system and that a shortage of research exists in this context, this chapter offers new insights into the process of teaching young learners.

Language Learning Characteristics of Young Learners

Teaching young learners requires a major difference in approach from teaching adults. One of the most obvious differences between these groups is motivation, that is, the purpose for which each group is studying the language and factors that keep their interest alive. It has been suggested that gaining an understanding of young learners' needs, interests, and developmental processes takes precedence over other considerations that might weigh more heavily in teaching English to adult learners (Cameron, 2001; Moon, 2000; Rixon, 1992b). Young learners are enthusiastic and thrive on praise for their actions to sustain their enthusiasm (Scott & Ytreberg, 2001). Therefore, it is imperative that learning a foreign language be pleasant and that the child's initial motivation never be allowed to disappear (Wright, 1989).

Another difference between teaching young learners and adults lies in the cognitive and affective domains. Differences have been observed in how young learners of English process foreign language, and it has been pointed out that language acquisition is affected by differing mental processors of children versus adults (Harley, 1986; Krashen, Scarcella, & Long, 1982). Halliwell (2000) raises two issues in the language development of children: the need to communicate and the child's capacity for indirect learning. She suggests that children need to be provided with occasions in which to communicate. For this purpose, setting up tasks and games is particularly beneficial because they are enjoyable and create a desire to communicate. Through continuous exposure to language tasks, children can pick up and internalize new language items without intentionally being taught by the teacher, as they do when acquiring their first language (L1). It is therefore suggested that in the classroom children need to be provided with a breadth of indirect learning focused on making meaning.

Attention span, or lack thereof, resulting from the age of the learner is another major difference between adults and children. Because young learners have a relatively shorter attention span than adults (Fisher, 1990; Wood, 1988), teaching methods must change rapidly to hold the children's shorter attention to a task. The pace at which new material is introduced, and the expected time required for assimilating it, can differ significantly with young learners. Activities such as role-plays, games, songs, poems, and stories are suggested as more conducive to learning (Murphey, 1992; Toth, 1995; Wright, 1995). As a result of these differences, curricula required for young learners of English must be tailored to the age of the students.

English Language Curriculum

In Turkey, the English language curriculum and the syllabi for primary schools are centrally administered by the MNE. The entire curriculum for primary education for Grades 4–8 lays the English language foundation for secondary education. The main goals of English language teaching (ELT) in primary education (Grades 4–5) are to

- raise students' awareness of a foreign language
- increase students' interest in and motivation toward the English language
- encourage students' use of the target language in daily communication
- help students develop appropriate strategies
- create a positive attitude toward learning English (Kocaoluk & Kocaoluk, 2001)

The ELT approach advocated by the MNE is predominantly communicative, with elements of the cognitive approach. Priority is given to students' acquisition of basic communicative skills for daily communication at a basic level for Grades 4–5. The MNE emphasizes that in these grades English should be taught within the context of games so that students enjoy learning the language.

The MNE also makes clear that subjects such as physical sciences, in which the goal is to convey information, are different from the ELT curriculum, which focuses on communication. The role of the teacher is that of guide and facilitator of the learning process, addressing students' different learning styles. Students are expected to take an active part in the learning process through various activities orchestrated by the teacher (see Kocaoluk & Kocaoluk, 2001).

The syllabus of Grades 6–8 is more complex. The function of English instruction for these grades is to expand basic communicative skills that students have gained through the integration of the four communication skills (listening, speaking, reading, and writing). It is also aimed at broadening the basic communicative skills that students previously acquired at the sentence level to the paragraph level and expanding literacy with short texts.

The MNE objectives are made concrete in the syllabus. Within the broad category of goals, a list of behavioral objectives is specified. The MNE syllabus is explicit and instructive; it contains comprehensive guidelines for teachers concerning management of the learning process, information on how to use teaching aids, and a set of activities for the development of communicative skills. Within this broad framework, each school draws up its own syllabus of English language instruction to fulfill MNE objectives. A short extract from the MNE syllabus for primary Grade 4 is shown in Table 1. A sample Grade 4 English syllabus designed for a school is shown in Table 2.

The objective of promoting young learners' communicative competence is made concrete through the course books, which are aligned with the specified objectives. Since the educational reform in 1997, the content and quality of the course books

TABLE 1. EXTRACT FROM THE MNE SYLLABUS FOR PRIMARY GRADE 4

Function	Structure	Vocabulary
A. Greetings Teaching personal pronouns Present form of verb *to be*	Hello! Good morning-good afternoon. I'm Mr., Mrs. . . . How are you? Fine thanks, and you? I'm fine, thank you. A SONG AND A GAME	*Hello. Hi.* *Morning, afternoon* *I, you, he, she, it, we, they*
B. Introducing oneself or someone else	What is your name? My name is Bilge. Her name is Zeynep. His name is Mert.	*My, your, his, her, its*

Source. Kocaoluk, F., & Kocaoluk, M. Ş. (2001). *İlköğretim Okulu Programı 1999–2000* [Primary Education Curriculum 1999–2000], p. 903. Istanbul, Turkey: Author. Copyright 2005 by F. Kocaoluk and M. Ş. Kocaoluk. Reprinted with permission.

prepared for young learners of English have increased. The course books used by state-owned primary schools are locally prepared and approved by the MNE. The books specifically produced for primary Grades 4–5 are written within a clear lexical and structural framework. They are planned very carefully; contain simple language; and use large, colored print with minimal text. They are beautifully illustrated, using a variety of formats. There is a conscious attempt to appeal to boys and girls through the inclusion of topics such as family, home, and school for Grade 4 and weather,

TABLE 2. EXTRACT FROM THE GRADE 4 ENGLISH SYLLABUS OF A PRIMARY SCHOOL

Timing		Subjects			Methods and	Teaching
Month	Week	Function	Structure	Objectives	Techniques	Aids
Sept.	2	Greetings, introducing oneself/someone	Present form of verb *to be*	1. Acquiring accurate pronunciation of new words	Grammar translation Direct method	Course books Grammar books
	3	Asking/saying where someone is from Asking for/ giving personal info	Personal pronouns Imperatives	2. Understanding structures of simple sentences and using imperatives	Audiolingual	Videocassettes *Note.* From Bayram Karadağ Primary School.
	4	Giving classroom instructions: sit down, stand up, come here		3. Understanding and using imperatives		

shopping, and relatives for Grade 5. The syllabus is topic based; students learn language functions in different situations. Books produced for Grades 6–8 contain more complex language, fewer illustrations, more text, and longer dialogues. Because older children already have more familiarity with a second language (L2) and expanded L2 literacy skills, their reading themes demand greater maturity.

Each student book is accompanied by a practice book, an audiocassette, and a teacher's book. An inspection of the teacher's books produced for each grade shows a series of recommendations that focus on management of the teaching and learning process, instructions for both communicative and noncommunicative activities, teaching aids, and detailed methodological guidelines on how to use the student and practice books.

Another interesting feature of the books is their extensive use of Turkish culture, which is apparent in a statement in the teacher's guide: "The object of the course is to draw on the students' own culture as well as to introduce them gradually to the differences between their own and those of other nations" (Dede & Emre, 2002, p. 11). The lessons make references to Turkish architects and statesmen with whom young Turkish children are familiar.

The goal is to achieve communicative competence; however, formal aspects of the language that need practice are also dealt with through a wide range of structural drills in the practice book. As noted by Dede and Emre (2002) in the teacher's book, "The main purpose of the course is to enable the students to communicate effectively in English. To achieve this goal a variety of communicative activities and manipulative drills have been combined in a well-balanced manner" (p. 11).

In state primary schools, two lessons per week are allocated to teaching English in primary Grades 4–5 (each lesson is 40 minutes), and five lessons to Grades 6–8. Before the start of the school year, the list of MNE-approved books is officially issued, and teachers are required to choose locally prepared course books that are approved by the MNE. Each school creates its own syllabus, as illustrated in Table 2, and teachers are responsible for preparing their own lesson plans. Figure 1 shows a sample lesson plan for Grade 4 students, which was shared by a primary teacher. Assessment is an important part of the curriculum. Students in Grades 4–5 are required to take two written tests each term, and upper grades are required to take more than 2 hours of assessment per term, as recommended by the MNE. The number of oral tests to be given is determined by the teachers. The passing grade is 2 points out of 5.

The current assessment focuses on testing young learners' knowledge of English. Teachers check whether learning has taken place based on specified learning input using various types of questions. The results are concrete and expressed qualitatively as a score. Because testing is a required part of the curriculum, teachers are often faced with the dichotomy between facilitating learning and meeting demands to demonstrate students' levels of achievement to parents and school officials. Assessment, however, is an attempt to analyze the learning that a child has achieved over a period of time as a result of classroom instruction and the learning situation. Therefore, it would be ideal, as suggested by Smith (1999), for the language learning outcome of young learners of English to be assessed in both a formal and an informal way.

Because assessment is an important part of the curriculum of young learners' programs, I believe that the current assessment can complement other types of

Lesson: English Language

Date: 17.04.2003

Class: 4-A

Subject: Adjectives

Objectives:

1. Students (Ss) will learn new vocabulary consisting of adjectives.

2. Ss will be able to recognize these adjectives while reading and listening.

3. Ss will be able to use adjectives in their sentences.

4. Ss will be able to describe people and objects using these adjectives.

Activities:

1. Teacher shows pictures of different people and objects and asks Ss to describe them in Turkish. Then, she presents the English version. She writes the words on the chalkboard, showing the related pictures, and asks students to repeat the adjectives for correct pronunciation (15 min.).

2. After having Ss write the new vocabulary, the teacher asks them to find the right picture for each adjective (10 min.).

3. Ss read the sentences in the book and try to write similar sentences that describe their friends (5 min.).

4. Ss work in pairs to write sentences describing their teachers (10 min.).

5. The teacher asks questions about the objects in the classroom (e.g., "Is the table big?" "Are these pencils heavy?") (5 min.).

6. Ss work in pairs to prepare similar questions to ask their friends. Each correct question-and-answer pair is rewarded by a "plus" (15 min.).

7. The teacher explains the homework. Ss are to write 10 sentences that describe their family members (5 min.).

8. Ss play a game. One student chooses another in the class and describes him or her without giving the name. Other students try to guess this person. Each student can only guess once. The student who makes the correct guess tries to describe another student and is rewarded with a plus (15 min.).

FIGURE 1. Sample Grade 4 Lesson Plan

assessment. Although portfolio assessment is not currently in use in Turkish primary education, it could be used to obtain a more realistic assessment of young learners' performance. Portfolio assessment allows samples of written and spoken English to be included so that student growth in all skills can be recorded. Thus, the learning outcome does not need to be expressed by a mark, particularly for Grades 4–5; it may include (subjective) teacher comments on the child's achievement in terms of participation as well as cognitive and physical development relative to the child's progress based on his or her starting point and abilities.

◈ DESCRIPTION

This study was designed to explore the instructional (school) situation with the aim of finding out how teachers teach English to young learners and how those learners are encouraged to acquire a foreign language. Data were collected from March to May 2003 from more than 45 public primary schools located not only in the city of Adana[1] but also in its surrounding towns. Multiple sources were used for data collection: a questionnaire and classroom observation to explore the subject from disparate perspectives, and an analysis of the MNE's documents, discussed in the preceding section.

Questionnaire

The survey questionnaire covered four main sections and was administered to 50 teachers (see the appendix). The first section of the questionnaire elicited personal information about the teachers and their experiences teaching young learners of English. Among these teachers, 27 were graduates of ELT departments, 2 were graduates of mathematics and biology departments, and 21 were graduates of the French and German departments. Although their teaching experience ranged from 2 to 16 years, all of them had been teaching in primary education during the previous 4 years. Only 7 of the non-ELT teachers had received local in-service training. All 50 of the teachers had been using MNE-approved books.

The second section of the questionnaire focused on teachers' classroom practice, and the first set of questions in this section dealt with the range of activities and the frequency with which teachers use the activities while teaching young learners of English. A large number of teachers generally gave students handouts as supplementary aids, while only a few used pictures. Many teachers did not have access to tape recorders, and none had access to computers. Few teachers used videotapes and overhead projectors. None of the teachers used poems or stories, but 5 used games and songs and 6 used postcards, rhymes from games and songs, and real objects to supplement lessons. Fifteen teachers sometimes used puzzles and flashcards, and 9 stated that they used dialogues, role-plays, and simulation activities, especially for Grade 6–8 students.

The next set of questions in the second section addressed the methodology teachers use while teaching reading, writing, grammar, and vocabulary. With regard to reading, the most frequently used technique, practiced by 32 teachers, was having students read the text aloud, one by one. Twenty-two teachers always read the text aloud while students listened, and 20 teachers said they generally "translated the reading text into L1." The technique of "students reading the text quietly followed by a discussion" was practiced by only 5 teachers, whereas "students preparing questions related to the text" was sometimes used by 28 teachers.

Clearly, there is no single correct method for teaching young learners of English to read. Yet the method that concentrates on meaning from the beginning is favored. As Scott and Ytreberg (2001) remind, "traditionally, reading aloud is often thought of

---

[1] With a population of approximately 1.5 million and a total area of 14,030 square kilometers, Adana is located in the southern part of Turkey, in the Çukurova region, which has fertile agricultural lands. It is the leading producer of cotton and citrus products and is renowned for its textile industry. Being one of the oldest settlements in Anatolia, the city houses many historical sites.

as reading round the class one by one, and although many children seem to enjoy it, this type of reading aloud is not to be recommended" (p. 57) because it is of little interest to the listeners and is an inefficient way to use lesson time. However, they suggest that reading aloud is a useful technique when the teacher uses it as a means of checking students' pronunciation.

As for the method of teaching writing, 42 teachers always had students write words more than once, and 25 sometimes used dictation and guided writing. Letter writing was already in the curriculum of upper grades, so it was often practiced. Only 6 teachers gave students project writing. Unfortunately, some teachers had students copy the reading text into a notebook as homework. Yet Halliwell (2000) maintains that "activities set up by the teacher should 'require both mental engagement and actual occupation'" on the part of the students and notes that "copying is not mentally engaging" (p. 22). When students are asked to copy the text into a notebook, they have to concentrate and physically do something to copy accurately, but this activity does not require students to understand or comprehend the text.

The majority of the teachers, 38 in all, always taught grammar giving a Turkish explanation, which 23 teachers sometimes followed by using actions, demonstrations, and examples. Although the MNE advocated teaching grammar in the context of games, only 6 teachers taught grammar in the context of games and stories. Scott and Ytreberg (2001) point out that the actual teaching should include only the barest minimum of grammar taught as grammar—and then for the older children only. They suggest the best time to introduce simple grammar is either when a student asks for an explanation or when a teacher thinks a student will benefit from learning some grammar.

This study found that teachers tended to present vocabulary by giving the Turkish meaning of a word, and that teachers might be justified in switching to the L1 to save time and forestall complication. Halliwell (2000), however, argues that "teaching in the target language must very decidedly *not* take the form of simply giving the target language equivalent of the mother tongue explanation" (p. 16). She states that systems other than words exist for carrying meaning, such as mime, demonstrations, word recognition, games, and so on. Another technique the surveyed teachers often used was giving examples to illustrate the meaning of the word. They sometimes used pictures for vocabulary instruction, too.

The third section of the questionnaire was devoted to the assessment procedures employed by the teachers and the frequency with which they assess students. All teachers gave an achievement test, as required by the MNE. Thirty-two always gave a quiz, and 3 gave project work. In the open-ended part of this section, responses indicated that teachers took into consideration students' in-classroom participation and daily homework during assessment. The most frequently used question type, fill-in-the-blank, was followed by translation, question-and-answer, multiple-choice, and true-false. In the open-ended section, responses showed that picture description and sentence transformation were also employed.

The final section of the questionnaire aimed to elicit teachers' opinions concerning the MNE curriculum and its relevance to young Turkish learners of English. The first positive aspect of the curriculum was the age at which children started learning English. Teachers stated that lowering the starting age had a positive influence on children because they took great delight in learning English. The young learners' capacity for learning English was high; young learners have good memories, which enable them to memorize and learn words rapidly and acquire pronunciation easily. Another positive aspect was that the books published after the educational reform in 1997 were colorful, full of pictures, written in simple and comprehensible language, and easy to implement, particularly for Grades 4–5.

The most unfavorable aspect of the curriculum, as stated by the teachers, was class size. An average of 40–50 students per class made it increasingly difficult for the teachers to complete the curriculum, which was already too dense, particularly for Grades 6–8. It has been suggested that the quantity of the input to which young learners of English are exposed needs to be reduced. The next issue was lack of teaching time. At present, the teaching hours allocated for each grade make it difficult to pay individual attention to students and conduct additional consolidation activities. Another point of difficulty was that many schools lacked equipment and materials (e.g., computers, tape recorders, VCRs, extra course books) for reinforcement activities.

Teachers offered two suggestions to improve the young learners' curriculum. First, they suggested that it be revised to make it more suitable to the age and level of learners in Grades 6–8 and that the curriculum of these grades be simplified to allow more time for practice. Second, because the classroom was the only place students were exposed to the English language, teachers suggested that school learning be combined with students' natural exposure to the language, such as contacting tourists or visitors to give young learners additional practice in English.

Observation

As a follow-up to initial responses on the questionnaire, 18 teachers volunteered to have class observations that would provide a more detailed picture of the English language instructional practices in public primary schools.

The teaching style of 10 of the teachers could be characterized as largely teacher centered, using the transmission model as the predominant method of teaching through the grammar-translation method. Ironically, these teachers were the graduates of ELT departments, yet they had not received any university training regarding teaching English to young learners, nor had they received any in-service training. Although teaching children differs from teaching adults (Harley, 1986; Krashen, Scarcella, & Long, 1982), these teachers had a tendency to impose their previous experience with older learners on their young learners of English. Implementing the same approach to teaching such dissimilar learning groups resulted in a lack of motivation in the young learners. Despite the MNE's objectives to be communicative and to teach grammar through games, these teachers remained unable to translate these curriculum objectives into their instructional practices.

As mentioned by Halliwell (2000), children's capacity for conscious learning of forms and grammatical patterns is relatively underdeveloped. In contrast, all children bring with them enormous instinct for indirect learning. Unfortunately, very few of these teachers attempted to build on this asset.

The remaining 8 teachers who were observed used the communicative approach. They used differentiated tasks and adopted different approaches to address the varied learning needs of students. These teachers were graduates of French and German departments and had previously received in-service training. One sample activity from an observed class follows:

In this activity, the teacher integrates total physical response into the game to teach imperatives to Grade 4 students. She acts out, and uses intonation to convey the meaning of what she says:

"Sit down."

"Stand up."

"Move aside."

After students become familiar with imperatives, the teacher encourages each student to participate and actively involves each student in the game by giving short sequences of instructions:

"Simon says sit down." (Students sit down.)

"Simon says stand up." (Students stand up.)

The teacher sets up a communicative situation by engaging the students in the game. Students act out sequences of instructions. If a student acts out incorrectly, the student loses the game. The final student to complete the game is the winner and is given a reward. In this activity, the teacher creates a rich, active, meaningful, and memorable source of input for young learners of English.

◈ DISTINGUISHING FEATURES

Based on the experience gained from this study, three pedagogical implications are addressed: first, for the MNE in terms of its language policy for young learners of English; second, for teacher education programs at universities; and, finally, for schools and practicing teachers of English.

Language Policy

The findings demonstrate that the current language policy objectives, syllabus specifications, and intensity of teaching English in primary education need revision. Because the main objective of teaching English to young learners is awareness raising, rather than gaining solid linguistic achievement, more feasible and appropriate goals need to be established, particularly for students in Grades 6–8. In addition, curriculum designers need to establish coherence and continuity between Grades 4–5 and 6–8.

Teacher Education and Teacher Development

Because teachers are the main resource for the learning process, teacher education departments need to take the teaching of young learners of English seriously. Considering the growth of English in the young learner population in Turkey, every university teacher education program focused on young learners should integrate the study of foreign language acquisition into its coursework.

In addition, the duration of trainees' teaching practice time in primary schools needs to be extended to give prospective trainees systematic school-based teaching experience with young learners of English before the trainees enter the professional community. Spending time in a classroom with such students would help teacher candidates make stronger connections between their university courses and the actual demands of teaching young learners of English, and would guide them in developing understanding to help all children become better learners. As emphasized by Huie and Yahya (2003), teacher candidates need to be made aware of the problems inherent in the extensive use of traditional instructional practices, such as copying and filling in the blanks, and they should be trained to use approaches that allow young learners of English to use language in creative and meaningful ways.

Finally, in-service teacher development opportunities need to be increased for teachers already engaged in teaching young learners of English. Professional development should be promoted, particularly for those who are experienced primary teachers in other subjects, but also for recruits entirely new to language instruction and those language teachers more accustomed to teaching and assessing English with older learners in secondary schools. As part of this initiative, teachers should become more aware of the differences between teaching young learners and teaching adults, and they should adopt methodology that will be more conducive to young learners' acquisition of English.

Classroom Practice

Much of what is suggested here for language policy and teacher education programs also applies to practicing teachers. Teachers should implement instructional strategies based on foundations in language acquisition theories to help young learners of English improve their L2 acquisition. Thus, a better understanding of how children acquire English as a foreign or second language would help teachers be more effective instructors, particularly in earlier grades. Teachers engaged in programs for young learners of English could be trained in action research, which would provide continuous monitoring of student progress and help shape instruction.

◈ PRACTICAL IDEAS

Based on the findings of this study, some practical guidance for educators can be extracted and applied to a variety of teaching contexts:

- Be tolerant and create an acquisition-friendly environment to facilitate young learners' acquisition of the L2.
- Be encouraging and guiding rather than demanding.
- Be creative—use games, songs, stories, and interesting activities.
- Provide adequate exposure to language using variety to meet students' different learning styles.
- Use concrete materials and familiar concepts, particularly for very young learners of English.
- Be student centered, using pair and group work.
- Don't teach the language like a set of rules or a formula (subject + verb + object); provide an element of indirect learning.
- As suggested by Halliwell (2000), increase student participation by choosing activities that involve both mental engagement and actual occupation.

- Relate new materials to students' real-life experiences to enable them to make associations between their L1 literacy knowledge and the new concepts to facilitate the acquisition process.

⟡ CONCLUSION

Teaching English in Turkish primary schools has become a challenge. The high demand for primary-level English teachers called for the establishment of new sources of teachers. Many teachers have found themselves teaching in primary schools, even though they have not been trained for this level. In-service training can be established to help them transition.

On the whole, the results obtained by means of questionnaires, classroom observations, and analysis of the MNE curriculum demonstrate that the syllabus of young learners of English is appropriate, particularly for Grades 4–5, and that the curriculum would make the teaching and learning more effective and result in better performance in communicative skills, provided that the number of hours devoted to each grade were increased.

Target syllabus requirements seem essentially realistic. However, there exists a gap between the MNE objectives and actual classroom instructional practices. Analysis of the syllabus and textbooks, and study findings obtained from questionnaires and observations, confirm the need to strengthen the communicative orientation of ELT as advocated by the MNE.

Although this study was carried out in only one major province in Turkey, I believe that the findings illustrate a nationwide trend. However, much remains to be investigated. Future research should be directed toward increasing the number of schools under investigation to ensure representative results.

⟡ CONTRIBUTOR

Yasemin Kırkgöz is currently a lecturer at the ELT department of the Faculty of Education at Çukurova University in Adana, Turkey. She has served as vice director and director of the Center for Foreign Languages. She completed her master's degree and doctorate at Aston University in Birmingham, England. Her research interests include teaching English to young learners, teacher education, and classroom research.

⟡ APPENDIX: SURVEY QUESTIONNAIRE

I. Personal Information

1. The university/department you graduated from: _____

2. How long have you been teaching English? _____

3. How long have you been teaching English in primary education? _____

4. Have you ever received any training to teach in primary education? _____

5. At the moment which grade(s) do you teach? _____

II. Teaching Methods

Please use the following scale in answering Questions 6–13

Always	Generally	Sometimes	Rarely	Never
(5)	(4)	(3)	(2)	(1)

6. Which supplementary aids do you use and how often?

   Pictures

   Tape recorder

   Computer

   Video

   Overhead projector

   Handout

   Other _____

7. Which of the following activities do you use and how often?

   Poem

   Game

   Story

   Song

   Puzzle

   Flash card

   Other _____

8. In reading classes, which of the following techniques do you use and how often?

   Teacher reads the text while students listen.

   Teacher has the students, one by one, read aloud the text.

   Teacher asks the students to read quietly, followed by a discussion of the questions.

   Teacher translates the text into Turkish.

   Teacher asks students to prepare questions related to text.

   Other _____

9. While teaching writing, which of the following techniques do you use and how often?

   Students writing the words a couple of times.

   Dictation

   Letter writing

   Guided writing

   Term project

   Other _____

10. While teaching grammar, which of the following techniques do you use and how often?

Teacher provides Turkish explanation.

Teacher illustrates using examples.

Teacher uses body language.

Teacher teaches in the context of stories.

11. While teaching vocabulary, which of the following techniques do you use and how often?

Teacher gives first language equivalent.

Teacher uses pictures.

Teacher illustrates with examples.

Teacher gives synonym/antonym.

Other _____

III. Assessment

12. How often do you use the following means of testing and assessment?
    Achievement test

    Quiz

    Project

    Students' in-class performances

    Other _____

13. In the exams, which type of questions do you use and how often?
    Multiple-choice

    True-false

    Matching

    Comprehension

    Translation

    Other _____

IV. Opinions of MNE's Curriculum

14. What are the three positive aspects of the MNE's curriculum?
    1.
    2.
    3.

15. What are the three negative aspects of the MNE's curriculum?
    1.
    2.
    3.

16. To what extent is the MNE's ELT curriculum appropriate to young learners' age and cognitive development? _____

17. What could be done to improve the present ELT curriculum? _____

18. Please explain any other comments you may have: _____

CHAPTER 7

Flavoring the Salt: Teaching English in Primary Schools in India

Jayashree Mohanraj

◈ INTRODUCTION

India has a long tradition of English language teaching, which dates back to Macaulay's Minutes in 1835.[1] Since then, the purpose of teaching English, the status accorded to English in schools and colleges, and the role English plays in the social and professional interactions have undergone several changes. These changes have a direct bearing on the levels at which learners are introduced to English and the methods and the materials used for teaching the language.

This chapter discusses the teaching of English in primary schools in India, focusing mainly on the curriculum and teaching materials used in these schools. The chapter particularly focuses on English instruction in Andhra Pradesh, a state in South India.

◈ CONTEXT

To understand the teaching of English at the primary level in India, it is essential to understand the history, compulsions, contexts, problems, and relevance of English in such a multicultural and multilingual country.

India has 4,653 language communities. The Constitution, VIII Schedule,[2] lists 18 official languages. English is taught in India as a second language in schools, and it is the medium of instruction in the universities and in higher and technical education.

The introduction of English to India in 1835 was a landmark in India's history of education. The Education Act of 1835 changed the course of relations between the states within the country and the country's relations with other countries. Although Macaulay's reason for Indians to learn English was to serve the purposes of the British government to some extent, ironically, knowledge of the English language brought power to the hands of Indian leaders during the freedom struggle. The Resolution on

---

[1] Hon. T. B. Macaulay was an advisor to the then governor general of India, Sir William Bentinck. In his famous minutes, Macaulay recommended that Indians be educated in English, the purpose for which was to make Indians think like the British and take jobs as clerks to help the British administration (i.e., the East India Company).

[2] The Indian constitution has a specific section of recommendations on recognizing languages as official languages. To date, 18 languages have been offered such recognition. English is one of them. Further, English is given the status of associate official language at the national level.

Educational Policy (1913) brought in an expansion of primary education, but English continued to be taught only in high school. Although the government intended to extend English language education only to those in higher education and the upper classes, the masses were attracted to schools that offered it because an English education ensured jobs. The situation is not very different in the first decade of the 21st century, an age of globalization and open markets. After gaining independence in 1947, the Indian people realized that knowledge of English led to empowerment in the modern world, and this realization helped to retain English language instruction in the academic institutions.

Within a few years of independence, efforts to improve English language teaching (ELT) in India began. Several commissions and conferences undertook a periodical review of the status of English. A look at various language commissions provides insight into the policy makers' thinking about the level at which English should be introduced. The Official Language Commission, under B. G. Kher's chairmanship, recommended 7 years of English instruction at the primary school level, beginning at age 5, culminating in the receipt of a pre-School Leaving Certificate (S.L.C.) at age 12 (Kher, 1957, p. 79). Almost 10 years later, the Report of the Education Commission of 1964–1966 expressed a view that commissioners were not in favor of teaching English as a second language at the primary level. However, Professor Gokak (1963), chairman of the Conference on the Teaching of English in Primary Schools, stated that there had been rapid changes in the thinking about the proper age and level for teaching English in schools. Although committee after committee recommended that the number of years of English instruction should not be fewer than 6, there has been variation from state to state regarding implementation of the recommendation. This variation is possible because the Indian constitution provides for the central as well as state governments to establish laws and frame policies on education.

The first feature of the English language instruction policy in India is the indecisiveness of the policy makers, which could be a result of the multicultural, multilingual, and multidimensional nature of Indian society. Whereas members of one school of thought look at teaching English as a means of empowering learners and equipping them with language to achieve success in the world, another group, more conservative in thought, is concerned about survival of regional languages and feels that the hegemony of English will be detrimental to maintenance of these languages. Yet a third and moderate group perceives the potential for a peaceful coexistence of the languages.

The second feature is the level at which learners need to be introduced to English. Several educational commissions appointed by the government reiterated that introduction to English should occur in Class VI or VII (in the age group of 11–12 years) after the child attains a reasonable competence in the language of home:

> While the formulation of the exact curriculum, etc., are matters for educational experts to consider, we would tentatively advance the view that it would probably suffice for the purposes that we have specified, if instruction in the English language commences in the secondary school at a stage about five year pre-S.L.C. (Kher, 1957, p. 79)

Several education commissions subsequently appointed by the government of India have echoed this opinion. But in recent years this thinking has undergone a change. Apart from the urgency felt because of globalization, Noam Chomsky's psycholinguistic theories of language learning, which state that a child 5–15 years of age has facility for learning several languages simultaneously, seem to have strengthened the view that introduction to English should start in the primary school. In addition, socioeconomic factors seem to have led policy makers to recommend the introduction of English at the primary level. English has increasingly been recognized as a tool for access, success, prosperity, prestige, and upward mobility. Even rural first generation learners aspire to learn English to secure for themselves a place in the successful and respected social class.

The National Curriculum Framework for School Education (National Council of Educational Research and Training, 2000) advocated that English should be taught in Class III (at 7–8 years of age). As a result, several states, including those in North India that not long ago campaigned for the removal of English from the curricula, have introduced English in Class III and, in some cases, as early as Class I (at 5–6 years of age).

Whether the change in policy was based on political or academic considerations is difficult to determine. One major factor that contributed to the paradigm shift could be globalization and the changed role of English in the society and in academia. Hence, once again attention has been drawn to English language instruction in the country. Fifty years of indecisiveness in education has made the situation very complex, and the complexity can only be understood by discussing the intricacies of the Indian education system.

The postindependence years have brought about many changes and improvements in education. An important aspect of educational development in the past few decades has been the continuous and sustained effort to develop a national system of education. The Education Commission, appointed in 1964, recommended a 10 + 2 + 3 pattern of education (referring to the number of years spent at each major level), which was accepted by parliament within the Resolution on National Policy on Education in 1968. Children start primary education at 5 years of age. Classes I–V are considered primary, Classes VI and VII are upper primary, and Classes VIII–X are secondary (for a total of 10 years). Classes XI and XII are higher secondary (for a total of 2 years). After Class XII, learners enter a professional course or pursue a 3-year degree course in a college. Universities offer postgraduate studies and research courses.

The data pertaining to the number of schools and the number of teachers at various levels reveal the enormity of the education programs in India. For example, per the official 1993 data, India had 822,486 schools: 570,455 primary, 162,805 upper primary, 65,564 secondary, and 23,662 higher secondary (Department of Education, Government of India, 1993a). At the same time, India had 4,197,555 teachers: 1,623,379 primary, 1,129,747 upper primary, 829,405 secondary, and 615,024 higher secondary (Department of Education, Government of India, 1993b).

Structure of Primary Education

Figure 1 summarizes the complex organizational structure of primary education in India. At the apex are the National Council of Educational Research and Training (NCERT) and the National Council for Teacher Education (NCTE). The NCERT assists the central and state governments with academic matters related to school education, providing academic and technical support. The NCTE regulates and

TABLE 1. NUMBERS OF TEACHERS AND SCHOOLS IN INDIA (1993)

Level	Schools	Teachers
Primary	570,455	1,623,379
Upper primary	162,805	1,129,747
Secondary	65,564	829,405
Higher secondary	23,662	615,024
Total	822,486	4,197,555

maintains norms and standards in teacher education. State government and private agencies (schools run by individuals or groups of individuals not associated with the government) control the schools at the state level. Some schools are overseen by local self-governing bodies and other agencies, such as social welfare departments, and some are governed by private agencies. Schools use a variety of models for language instruction, including English language only, bilingual education, Indian language only, and combined English and Indian language. Schools can be classified by their location—urban, semiurban, rural. There are also schools for tribal children and schools for social classes or castes.

Curriculum Development

Before independence, textbooks were mainly an individual and commercial initiative. However, within a few years of independence, efforts began to improve ELT in India. Around 1950, the Madras presidency sought help from the British Council on effective methods of English language instruction. In 1952, Dr. Jean Forrester developed the first structural syllabus for learners of English in India.

An important development in education during the next few decades was the professionalism surrounding curriculum development, syllabus design, and the preparation and evaluation of textbooks. The NCERT at the national level formulated guidelines for developing syllabi, an effort which helped achieve a broad commonality in the scheme of studies and the content of courses in this vast country. At the state level, each state develops syllabi and teaching materials with the help of state councils of educational research and training (SCERTs) and textbook boards. Further, the state

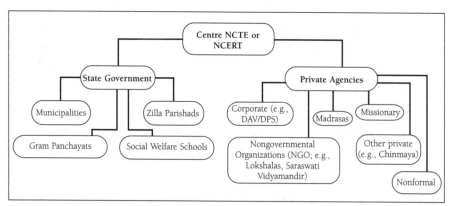

FIGURE 1. Organizational Structure of Primary Education in India

institutes of education (SIEs) provide technical support to research and develop activities related to formulation of curriculum and preparation of textbooks.

Curriculum development is a dynamic process that involves a constant search for qualitative improvement in response to the needs of society and the aspirations of learners. Education should be designed to meet the complex needs of individuals in a developing societal context. This means designing the content and process of education so that it develops the requisite knowledge, understandings, skills, and attitudes for learners to be in tune with the social, economic, and political ethos of the country. Another consideration should be the changes and developments taking place in the global context.

The National Curriculum Framework for School Education (National Council of Educational Research and Training, 2000) stated that because of the changed socioeconomic scenario, as well as the individual and national requirements generated by globalization and information technology, the introduction of English in Class III seems to have been necessary. It should not be introduced earlier than this because

- the learners' first language should be strong enough to be used as a resource for learning the second language

- the first 2 years of school, in the vast majority of cases, are to be devoted to instruction in the school language or regional language

Although schools run or aided by the government adhere to the national policy, schools run by private agencies have always had the freedom to teach English as early as Class I. The Kendriya Vidyalayas (central schools with a uniform curriculum), which are controlled by a central body that uses the NCERT curriculum, introduce English in Class I. By introducing English instruction at the primary level in the government schools, where most of the children from lower and middle classes study, some equity is established. However, critics disagree with this point of view for different reasons.

The IX Plan (1997–2002)[3] treated elementary education as a crucial investment in human resource development. The planning process has thus shifted from the state and national levels to the district level. Textbook design has also undergone change. In the later half of the 1990s, textbooks were revised in response to the pedagogic practices adopted under the District Primary Education Programme, a World Bank–sponsored program that has undertaken the Sarvasikhsha Abhiyan, the implementation of the world declaration of Education for All, by 2015.

Language Learning in Multicultural Contexts

Children living in the multilingual Indian society grow up with at least two languages (e.g., the language of the home and the language used in the immediate society or region), and they have no problem communicating in these languages with equal facility, without one language interfering with the other. Although acquisition of the

---

[3] Since independence, India has planned its development in terms of 5-year periods. Each plan period focuses on a specific area. The IX Plan focused on education at large and the universalization of primary education. India sought help from the World Bank to open in-service training centers, develop materials at district levels (small administrative zones), and implement projects such as the District Primary Education Programs on a massive scale.

first language is faster and more natural, it is nonetheless true that learning the second, third, and fourth languages happens more easily between 3 and 6 years of age or by the age of 15. Hence, it might be worthwhile to introduce both English and the regional language at an early age. The bilingual education system introduced in Kendriya Vidyalayas illustrates the language learning abilities of children in a multilingual society. For more than three decades these schools have simultaneously introduced children to two languages, English and Hindi, in Class I. In India, Hindi is the official language and English is the associate official language. Some subjects, such as science and mathematics, are taught in English, whereas social studies is taught in Hindi.

Introducing children to English at an early age should not pose a problem to their cognitive, emotional, or social development, but a problem does seem to lie elsewhere. The caution sounded by Gokak (1963) is worth recapitulation:

> There have been rapid changes in the thinking about the proper age level for the teaching of English in schools. Quite a few states have changed over to introducing English from Class III onwards. The State of Gujarat has changed to introduce English in Class VIII. The objection to these changes is not based on the thinking that they are impracticable. But rather, it would really be hazardous to change over to another arrangement without properly trained teachers, a well-defined syllabus and planned text materials. It is certainly not desirable to implement the change and then cast about for ways and means of making it effective. (p. 4)

Andhra Pradesh has been one of the first states to implement the new policy for English instruction by developing and using the curriculum and materials. This state's actions are worth examination in light of Gokak's statement.

◈ DESCRIPTION

India has 29 states and 5 union territories. Andhra Pradesh has a total of 55,901 lower and 9,804 upper primary schools. The total enrollment in 2001 was 6,060,394 children in the lower primary and 2,628,185 children in the upper primary schools. The state has three types of schools for English language education, each of which begins teaching the language differently:

- Class I and all subjects are taught in English.
- Class I along with Hindi and all other subjects are taught either in Hindi or English.
- Classes III and IV and all the other subjects are taught in the regional language (in Andhra Pradesh the languages are Telugu and Urdu).

Although formal teaching of English continues to begin in Class V in the state, in 1998–1999 Andhra Pradesh introduced English instruction informally in Classes III and IV in all government and government-aided schools. This conforms with the NCERT guidelines. As said earlier, although the NCERT is at the apex in matters of school education, such as textbook preparation, teacher training, school guidance, and monitoring in general, the state governments have freedom to make decisions in all matters within the broad NCERT framework. Thus, education is the joint responsibility of the state government as well as the central government.

The Department of School Education of Andhra Pradesh introduced a 6-year syllabus in 1990 for Classes V–X, the sole objective of which was to equip learners with a vocabulary of 1,000–1,200 words; mastery of 100 frequently used structures; and the ability to participate in day-to-day conversations in English, to read and understand simple English texts, and to write paragraphs correctly in English. It was felt that a controlled but informal exposure to the language in Classes III and IV would adequately prepare learners to receive the formal instruction in English in Class V. Two suggestions were made:

- The new book for Class III should be learner-friendly[4] because most of the pupils happen to be first-generation learners.

- By the end of 2001, the book must prepare the learners psychologically and provide them with a reasonably good foundation in the basics so that they might listen, speak, read, and write English in an acceptable way (Government of Andhra Pradesh, 2002, p. iii).

These suggestions are significant in light of the caution sounded by the University Grants Commission English Review Committee in 1965, namely, that taking English down to Class III or Class V means taking it down to the level at which education is expanding rapidly, where it is reaching the farthest and smallest villages, to classes in society that have not had even the remotest connection with education (*Report of the English Review Committee,* 1965).

Textbooks in Andhra Pradesh

The textbooks examined in this study are for those learners who do not speak English at home. These learners' societal environment is very different and local in texture. Most of the learners use Telugu or Urdu at home and with peers. The textbooks have been designed with the objective of familiarizing learners with English under friendly and nonthreatening conditions. Teachers at the primary level should supply children with stories, poems, jingles, songs, and pictures. Teachers should allow children to begin selecting for themselves and create an atmosphere of freedom and pleasure in which the children can use words. In fact, wherever there is scope, it is desirable that teachers take care not to separate reading, writing, and talking or to isolate English from the other arts. Thus, if learning can be made enjoyable, if the text is chosen with care, and if the classroom methodology is suitable, children will enjoy learning languages. It is in this light that the English language teaching program and the materials used should be examined.

The textbooks for Classes III and IV for the regional medium schools in Andhra Pradesh are called *My English Workbook.* An expert committee appointed by the state government prepared the textbooks. The committee consisted of education specialists, teacher educators, and teachers with rich experience in teaching at the primary level, which gave legitimacy to the materials. The books were piloted in representative schools before they were introduced in all government schools in the state, and the state's department of education conducted orientation programs for teachers at the primary school level. The orientation aimed to help teachers develop awareness

---

[4] A term adopted from the computer field is *user-friendly.* Materials produced are termed *learner-friendly* when they take into account learners' chronological and psychological age and their ability to understand and use the materials. This incorporates the classical concept of selection and gradation.

about communicating with learners, and helping them communicate with each other, in English. The orientation was also meant to familiarize teachers with the books and instruct them in how to use the books efficiently to achieve the objectives, which, according to *My English Workbook*, are to

- familiarize pupils with the spoken and written forms of English
- make learning English an enjoyable activity
- help learners understand the language spoken by the teacher and the classmates
- help learners speak English words and short sentences with the help of the teacher
- help learners read and understand simple words and sentences
- help learners trace and write words, phrases, and sentences
- help learners recite rhymes

The design of the books supports the realization of these objectives. The total number of hours for English instruction in Class III is 75 hours per year (150 periods, 30 minutes each). In Class IV, the time increases to 80 hours (160 periods). Both books have two main sections: activities and lessons. In Class III, activities are taught in the initial 20–30 periods, and the rest are devoted to lessons. In Class IV, 20–40 sessions are set aside for activities, with the remainder devoted to lessons.

The objectives of the textbook activities are to give learners practice in motor skills[5] and to familiarize them with the shape and size of the letters as they move toward the stage of reading readiness. At the end of the activities section of Class III, learners become familiar with the spoken and written forms of English. Activities such as coloring pictures and drawing lines to match pictures make learning English enjoyable. Children learn simple words and phrases and are provided with opportunities to interact with peers using simple sentences. Audiocassettes with simple rhymes help them hone their listening skills. The Class III book gives instructions to learners in their mother tongue and provides guidelines for the teachers in English. The Class IV book provides instructions to learners in both the mother tongue and English. This conforms to the directions of the NCTE Task Force, which states that during early stages of development schoolchildren must become acquainted with language in general, and with its uses in thinking and communicating, much of which must be accomplished through the dialect they already speak. As children gain experience in listening to and understanding informal English, especially through contact with teachers, school programs can gradually begin to teach standard informal English.

◈ DISTINGUISHING FEATURES

The conception for the Class III and IV *My English Workbook* emerged from the thinking that the English textbook for Class V was not elementary enough for

---

[5] The motor skills here refer to the type of muscle control required to form letters of the English alphabet. This is necessary because the strokes and curves of the Telugu/Urdu letters are different from that of English.

beginners with non-English backgrounds and it would be better to develop something new instead of modifying the existing Class V textbook. Further, *My English Workbook* is introduced in a noncurricular course, which helps it to be nonthreatening to learners as it helps them learn. Hence, a helpful approach is adopted in Class III and IV textbooks. To ensure this approach before introducing the books formally, a panel of reviewers was asked to comment on the book, and care was taken to orient teachers before the books were introduced in classes.

The design of the books obviously recognizes the importance of the learning process and the psychology of young children. A nonthreatening environment for learning is fostered through the use of bilingual instructions, slow pacing, the grading of language items, involvement of learners in activities that interest them, and use of culturally familiar names and situations. The Class III book introduces children to simple activities, and the Class IV book provides them with language games and interesting stories. Writing activities are limited to tracing and writing letters in Class III. Learners are then encouraged to write words and simple sentences.

My English Workbook also comes with a teacher's handbook. Teachers receive elaborate notes at the beginning of the book and teaching guidelines and steps at the beginning of each lesson. These important features provide adequate help to teachers who have not attended the orientation. The step-by-step guidelines, as shown in Figure 2, provide assistance in planning lessons. Another feature of the teacher's book is the notes of caution, which are boxed items that tell teachers what not to do. For example, they are asked not to allow children to use pens because, given the learners' age and developing psychomotor skills, writing activities are limited to tracing and writing words and simple sentences.

LESSON 4	
NOTE TO THE TEACHER	
LISTENING/SPEAKING	
1. Greeting	Your pupils will greet you. Respond appropriately.
2. Rhyme	Follow the instructions given in Lesson 1.
3. Story	Narrate the story with expression. Use miming and action when possible. Rehearse the story before class. Let your pupils close their books and listen. On the third or fourth day, let them look at the pictures of the story. You need not ask any questions about the story.
4. Revision	Ask the pupils to look at each picture and say the sentence with it. Then say the sentence a number of times and ask your students to repeat it after you.
5. New Sentences	Ask the pupils to look at each picture and say who or what it is.
6. Vocabulary	Ask the pupils to look at what the boys and girls are doing. Then say the words. Ask pupils to repeat after you.
7. Reading	Read the sentences aloud. Let the pupils listen to you. Then ask them to read each sentence.
8. Writing	Ask the pupils to trace and copy the sentences.

FIGURE 2. Sample Lesson Plan

◈ PRACTICAL IDEAS

My English Workbook is not revolutionary in terms of approach or materials, but it is certainly simple, down to earth, and practical. The objectives mentioned earlier are modest and achievable in most EFL settings, if the following steps can be taken:

- Ensure that course books do not make undue demands on teachers and learners.
- Consider reasons that might prevent teachers' from being resourceful in the classroom.
- Exploit children's language learning potential in multilingual settings.

In light of inadequate resources and some limited teacher experience, the design of the textbook and the audiocassettes are features that deserve special mention. Teacher resourcefulness in the English classroom may be rather modest for two reasons: teachers' own English proficiency might be limited, and most of them might not have had preservice training in teaching English. Hence, the elaborate help given in the teacher's book aids them in handling the textbook reasonably well and gives them an intensive orientation to teaching English effectively in the classroom.

◈ CONCLUSION

The idea of introducing learners to English at an early stage of primary education has caught on throughout all the states in India. Each state has produced its own set of textbooks for the English classroom. The flexible, practical approach of the textbooks introduced in Andhra Pradesh, as discussed in this chapter, takes into consideration the limited teacher experience at the primary level and the children's ability to learn in a multilingual setting. Although the objectives stated in the two textbooks seem to be achievable, such an approach to teaching a second or third language needs to be explored further.

Other states in India, as well as countries where English is taught and learned as a second and foreign language, could emulate the Andhra Pradesh experiment. The careful thinking that created the learner-friendly teaching program described in this chapter certainly attempts to meet the needs of the hour, and it initiates new thoughts about teaching English in a multilanguage setting.

◈ ACKNOWLDGMENT

I gratefully acknowledge the input provided by Mr. Ramabhadracharyulu, Special Officer, English Studies, Government of Andhra Pradesh.

◈ CONTRIBUTOR

Jayashree Mohanraj teaches at Central Institute of English and Foreign Languages in Hyderabad, India. She has taught in three states in India and has wide experience as a teacher educator. She knows eight Indian languages and is an established translator who has translated Oriya and Telugu works into English.

CHAPTER 8

Is Grade 3 Too Early to Teach EFL in Vietnam?

Ha Van Sinh

◈ INTRODUCTION

In 1995, English as a foreign language (EFL) was officially introduced in Grade 1 to 7-year-old children in Nha Trang, Vietnam. Then, just a year later, English instruction shifted to begin in Grade 3 to 9-year-old children. Hesitance was expressed about expanding the program to all primary schools in the province at the time. Did this hesitation result from concerns about the negative effects of early bilingualism imposed on children's linguistic and cognitive development? Or did the concerns center on the potential for ineffectual management of a large primary school EFL program? These questions were frequently raised and discussed in academic circles. Most local EFL professionals seemed to support the early start of primary school EFL instruction based on the assumption that children are able to learn languages more easily than adults. Nonetheless, empirical experience was not very helpful in handling the queries from the public.

I therefore decided to explore the issues by reviewing the relevant literature and examining the EFL instruction in a primary school in Nha Trang, its affect on children, and the perceptions of parents and other stakeholders. The investigation involved Nha Trang education authorities, primary school teachers of both English and Vietnamese, 80 Grade 4 pupils in two non-EFL primary schools, 91 pupils in an EFL primary school, and their parents. First, I examined the EFL pupils' study records in Vietnamese and English language classes to establish a correlation between their current stage of development in both languages. Second, I compared the non-EFL primary school pupils' study records with the developmental patterns of Vietnamese. Third, I sent questionnaires to the EFL pupils' parents, the students' teachers of English and Vietnamese, and the education authorities to elicit their perceptions and expectations about the issues. Finally, I examined the implementation of the EFL program in the school to see how EFL was being taught in the classroom.

◈ CONTEXT

Vietnam's economic and political changes over the past decade have brought about a more significant role for EFL in all spheres of life. English has become an effective means of attaining well-paying jobs and promotions and accessing higher education.

Parents are concerned that their children not only learn basic English but also achieve high levels of English language proficiency. Some language institutes, generally serving adults, now attract a large number of children who are 6–12 years old.

Although EFL has been officially taught in secondary schools since the 1950s, teaching EFL in primary schools was not introduced in Nha Trang, the capital of Khanh Hoa Province, until 1995, which was earlier than in other major cities in Vietnam. Education authorities in major cities, such as Ha Noi, Ho Chi Minh City, Hue, Da Nang, and Nha Trang, decided to implement a primary school curriculum with English as an optional subject. This curriculum was first implemented in Grade 1. Then, due to criticism that this addition created a heavy workload for Grade 1 students, the Ministry of Education and Training (MOET) and Khanh Hoa decided to delay implementation of the English curriculum until Grade 3, "when the first language has been relatively established" (T. Nguyen, personal interview, 1999).

In 1996, 17 of the 36 primary schools in Khanh Hoa began teaching English in Grade 3 using this latest program. The schools that have not implemented the program are mostly in the countryside, where schools are understaffed and parents cannot afford extra school fees for EFL. Where it is implemented, there are two 40-minute classes per week, and there is no official textbook. The teachers, most of whom graduated from the local teacher college, use the suggested textbooks of the provincial department of education and training.

◈ DESCRIPTION

This study involved 171 Grade 4 students, 91 parents, 2 teachers of Vietnamese, 1 teacher of English, 1 Nha Trang municipal education official, and 1 primary school assistant principal in Nha Trang, where English is being taught as an optional subject to students in third through fifth grades. One of Nha Trang's 17 EFL schools was selected because the principal of the school was a very open and supportive colleague. It was, therefore, convenient for me to collaborate with both teachers and students to collect data.

Ninety-one students in this study were from two of the eight Grade 4 classes in the primary school. The parents of these students provided information concerning their perceptions of early bilingualism and their support and assistance for their children's EFL learning. The other 80 Grade 4 students were from two non-EFL schools in the same locality, which were randomly selected from the list provided by the municipal education official. All three schools were under the supervision of the same municipal department of education and implemented a similar core curriculum (i.e., the national nine-subject primary school curriculum).

The two teachers of Vietnamese taught all of the content subjects. The teacher of English was one of two English language teachers in the EFL school, and she taught the two classes involved in the study. The assistant principal of the school and the municipal education official were responsible for implementing, and evaluating the implementation of, the EFL syllabus in this school and in the province's other primary schools that taught English.

This study was conducted in three phases. First, the study records (grades from ongoing assessments and final exams) of all of the students were collected to examine the results of Vietnamese instruction. Then, a questionnaire was given to parents, teachers, and the education authorities to collect data about their perceptions, support, and knowledge of the EFL program. Finally, an analysis of the school EFL syllabus and classroom observations was conducted to gauge the effectiveness of the EFL program.

In the first phase, I calculated the average of the EFL pupils' grades in Vietnamese in Grades 2, 3, and 4 to establish a base grade before and after incorporation of EFL into the curriculum. I also calculated an average of non-EFL pupils' grades in Vietnamese and compared it with that of the EFL pupils (see Table 1). The total number of pupils from the two EFL classes was 91. However, due to the missing study records of English in Grade 3, eight of the pupils were removed from the data analysis. Table 1 shows that there is a gradual decline in EFL pupils' grades in Vietnamese subjects from Grade 2 to Grade 4, whereas there is almost no change in the non-EFL pupils' grades.

In the second phase, I used the completed questionnaires to collect opinions on the effect of early bilingualism on pupils' first language. The results indicate that there is a strong belief in the positive effect of early bilingualism among education authorities, teachers, and parents (see Table 2).

TABLE 1. AVERAGE GRADES IN VIETNAMESE OF EFL AND NON-EFL STUDENTS

| | Vietnamese Subject Grades | | |
Pupils	Grade 2	Grade 3	Grade 4
EFL school (*n* = 83)	9.39	9.18	8.40
Non-EFL school A (*n* = 48)	7.60	8.08	7.67
Non-EFL school B (*n* = 32)	7.15	7.60	7.59

Note. In Vietnamese schools, the learner's study result is graded according to a decimal system, ranging from 1 to 10: 1–4 = unqualified, 5–6 = average, 7–8 = good, and 9–10 = excellent.

TABLE 2. OPINIONS ON THE EFFECT OF EARLY BILINGUALISM ON PUPILS' FIRST LANGUAGE

| | Feels English Has a Negative Impact on First Language | |
	Yes	No
Municipal Education Official *n* = 1		1 (100%)
Assistant Principal *n* = 1		1 (100%)
Teachers of Vietnamese *n* = 2		2 (100%)
Teacher of English *n* = 1		1 (100%)
EFL Pupils' Parents *n* = 91	7 (7.7%)	84 (92.3%)
Total *n* = 96	7 (7.3%)	89 (92.7%)

TABLE 3. PARENTAL SUPPORT AND ASSISTANCE

	Number of Responses (n = 91)	Percentage
Both parents support the incorporation of EFL in the curriculum.	66	79.5%
One parent supports and assists the child in learning English.	40	48.19%
Both parents support and assist the child in learning English.	32	38.56%
Parents object to the incorporation of EFL in the curriculum.	17	20.48%
Parents do not support or assist their child in learning English.	11	13.25%

The questionnaire elicited parents' perceptions about their support of their children's English language learning. The results show that the parents who completed the questionnaire greatly support and assist their children in learning English (see Table 3).

Parental perceptions of the benefits of early bilingualism and the current EFL syllabus are presented in Table 4. The data were tabulated from the questionnaires completed by EFL pupils' parents and indicate that the parents involved in the study agreed on the necessity and appropriateness of the current EFL program for primary children.

Based on data collected from the EFL pupils' study records and the questionnaires from the parents, I compared the average grades in English achieved by EFL pupils with and without parental support and assistance (see Table 5). The comparison reveals a strong correlation between parental support and assistance with children's achievement in learning English at school. The data collected in this phase of the study reveal a consensus among those surveyed on the positive effect of early bilingualism and the essential role that parents play in promoting pupils' motivation and results of their English learning.

In the third phase of the study, I summarized observation with field notes. The analysis focused on type of interaction, teacher talk, and the approaches and techniques that teachers used in conducting lessons. A summary of the field notes revealed pupils were involved in an insufficient number of class hours and had little access to English both outside and inside the classroom. In addition, they were not provided with many opportunities to interact with each other because of the teacher-fronted type of classroom interaction. Personal communication with the teachers also revealed that they were not trained to teach English to primary school children.

⊗ DISTINGUISHING FEATURES

The study provides evidence of a gradual decline in EFL pupils' grades in Vietnamese subjects from Grade 2 to Grade 4, and indicates a strong belief in the positive effect of an early start in EFL and its current curriculum among education authorities, teachers, and parents. The study also shows a strong correlation between parental support and assistance and children's achievement in English at school. However, the pupils were not exposed to a language-rich environment or involved in a sufficient number of class hours. Moreover, there was a lack of classroom interaction due to a lack of primary school teacher training. Two main themes emerged from the results of the study that truly distinguish the features of this program: positive attitudes toward early bilingual education, and insufficient EFL teacher training.

The perception that early bilingualism has little negative effect on children's linguistic and cognitive development (Baetens-Beardsmore, 1982; Clyne, Jenkins, Chen, Tsokalidou, & Wallner, 1995; Genesee, 1995; Piper, 1993) was shared by virtually all those involved in the study (92.7%). Table 2 indicates that the administration, the teachers, and 84 of the 91 parents thought that early bilingualism had no negative effect on children's first language, and only 7 parents said it had negative effects. However, the EFL pupils' study records show that their grades on ongoing assessments and final exams from the Vietnamese subjects declined during each year of English instruction (Grade 2: 9.39; Grade 3: 9.18; Grade 4: 8.40; see Table 1).The study records of 80 pupils from two non-EFL primary schools do not follow the same pattern of results as that of the EFL pupils. As can be seen in Table 1, the results show Vietnamese language grades in these schools was lowest in Grade 2 (7.60, 7.15), highest in Grade 3 (8.08, 7.60), and then a bit lower in Grade 4 (7.67, 7.59). Two teachers of Vietnamese expressed their hypothesis about these results: "Even when pupils do not have to learn EFL, the results in Vietnamese usually decline due to the increasingly challenging requirements of the subject" (personal communication).

More than 79% of the parents who completed the questionnaire supported the incorporation of EFL into the curriculum (see Table 3). Only 1 of the 91 parents said it was an additional burden for children (Table 4). This result correlates with the research on the benefits of mutual development of a first and second language (Collier & Thomas, 1999; Pica, 1994; Swain, 1981). Similarly, 54.94% of the parents agreed that simultaneously learning a first and second language assists children in their development of metalinguistic awareness, and 13.18% added that mutual development of a first and second language has a beneficial impact on first language development (see Table 4).

Of the parents surveyed, 57.14% claimed that the younger the children, the better they acquire a foreign language. Nevertheless, the EFL program for primary schools was first introduced in Grade 1 (7-year-old pupils) and then shifted to Grade 3 (9-year-old pupils) a year later. The education officials explained that in Grade 3 the pupils' first language system was well established, and the incorporation of the program into Grade 1 would overload pupils academically. This supports Scott and Ytreberg's (1993) theory stating that 8- to 10-year-old children's ability in abstraction, generalization, and systematization assists them in learning a foreign language. In addition, Baetens-Beardsmore (1982) and Dunn (1985) also support the theory that preadolescent children's language acquisition ability is superior to that of adults. Parents whose children started to learn a foreign language in Grade 1 affirmed that their children reached a high level of attainment after the first year of the program in the trial school (personal communications).

My experience of teaching EFL to children in a language center in 1989–1992 demonstrated that Grade 3 children acquired a foreign language much faster than children in Grades 1 and 2 when they were put in the same group. The faster acquisition of English exhibited by Grade 3 children may have resulted from advanced development of the first language system or from their advanced cognitive abilities in general, and consequently the children in Grades 1 and 2 could not keep

TABLE 4. PARENTS' PERCEPTION OF EARLY BILINGUALISM AND THE CURRENT EFL SYLLABUS

	Number of Responses (n = 91)	Percentage
Children are motivated and interested in EFL learning.	73	80.21%
The current EFL syllabus is appropriate and suitable for children's age.	68	74.72%
The current EFL syllabus is not a heavy workload for children.	61	67.03%
Early bilingualism is necessary because the younger the better to acquire a language.	52	57.14%
Early bilingualism is necessary because simultaneous learning of the first and second language assists in better development of metalinguistic awareness.	50	54.94%
The current EFL syllabus increases the workload for children.	9	9.98%
A possible negative influence on children's first language development may exist.	7	7.69%
Early bilingualism is unnecessary because it is an additional burden for children.	1	1.09%
Early bilingualism is necessary because mutual development of first and second language has beneficial impact on first language development.	12	13.18%
The EFL program is necessary preparation for the compulsory Year 6 EFL program.	2	2.19%
The EFL program is necessary preparation for children's further study in higher education levels.	1	1.09%
EFL helps improve children's pronunciation of the first language.	1	1.09%
The number of class hours in the current EFL syllabus is so small that children cannot master the required language and language skills.	1	1.09%

up with their Grade 3 peers. However, in both cases (the early start of EFL in Grade 1 and mixed classes of Grades 1, 2, and 3), there is no evidence to show that these children's foreign language acquisition was not affected by other internal or external factors (see Pienemann & Johnston, 1987). Hence, an attempt to decide whether it is better to start an EFL program in Grade 1 or Grade 3 requires further research in the Vietnamese context.

The EFL program for primary school children in Nha Trang received a great deal of parental support, but it required more social and pedagogical support. The questionnaires revealed that 79.5% of parents approved the incorporation of EFL into the primary school curriculum, and 86.75% assisted their children's learning. More than one third (38.56%) of the pupils received assistance with their EFL learning from both parents (see Table 3). Because young children learn English to be able to speak English with peers or adults, rather than to be able to find a good job

TABLE 5. COMPARISON OF PUPILS WITH AND WITHOUT PARENTAL SUPPORT AND ASSISTANCE

Number of Children n = 83	Average Grades		Number of Children Who Obtained Grade Lower Than 8	
	Grade 3	Grade 4	Grade 3	Grade 4
With parental support and assistance n = 72; 86.75%	(6506:72) 9.03	(6449:72) 8.95	8 11.11%	10 13.88%
Without parental support and assistance n = 11; 13.25%	(908:11) 8.25	(941:11) 8.55	5 45.45%	2 18.18%

or get promoted, a sound parent–child relationship, whereby parents transmit their enthusiasm, interest, and language input (when possible), seems to sustain the children's enthusiasm to learn a foreign language (Abe, 1996; Dunn, 1985; Tucker, 1999). This study shows that there may be a correlation between parent support and children's high scores in English class: 86.75% of the students (those who were supported and aided by one or both parents) had an average English grade of 9.03 (in Grade 3) and 8.95 (in Grade 4), compared with the average marks of 8.25 (in Grade 3) and 8.55 (in Grade 4) obtained by the 13.25% of students who did not receive parental support or assistance. Although several pupils who had no support or assistance from their parents obtained high grades, in general, the more support and assistance the children had, the higher their grades in EFL (see Table 5).

However, although they were being supported and assisted by adults, the EFL pupils did not have an English-language-rich environment outside the classroom. The pupils involved in this program had little access to English outside the classroom and limited exposure to spoken and written English inside the classroom. The common sources of English language contact were textbooks with a limited source of supplementary materials, such as songs and poems in English, and some English-language children's picture books or cartoons. Coupled with an insufficient number of class hours (two 40-minute class periods per week), the lack of a language-rich environment may slow the acquisition of a foreign language (Dunn, 1985; Houwer, 1999; Lotherington, 1996; Newman, 1999; Scott & Ytreberg, 1993; Vale, 1995). The current timetable in Khanh Hoa EFL primary schools allows for two 40-minute classes per week, which is equal to the minimum amount of class time suggested by Rosenbusch (1995). Some (e.g., Nicholas, 1983) have suggested using a timetable that allows for a sufficient amount of time to develop language at the initial stage. With such limited time, and with the lack of a language-rich environment, these two 40-minute classes per week may not be adequate.

Although 74.72% of the parents considered the current EFL syllabus appropriate and suitable for their children's age and said that their children were motivated and interested in learning EFL, the teacher of English involved in the study said that the textbook was only partially suitable: "We do not have enough time to cover all the syllabus, which has no review section to consolidate what they have learned, especially in Grade 5." When asked what changes she would make to modify the textbook, she said, "I would cut down the syllabus and add more review exercises. More guided writing tasks would be added to help pupils' master structures better.

Songs would also be included to motivate children. I would also like to have more listening lessons with language tapes or a language lab."

Research has shown that the success of an EFL program for children requires well-qualified staff and an appropriately designed syllabus (Rosenbusch, 1995). Data collected in the third phase of the study revealed that the current syllabus was unsatisfactory and the staff insufficiently qualified. The syllabus, which aimed to prepare pupils for secondary schooling, included only some textbooks, written either by native speakers of English or by Vietnamese English language specialists and supplemented by a limited number of songs, games, or readers. Moreover, there was no coordination or articulation across levels of instruction. After a 3-year course of EFL in primary school, pupils will have to continue learning EFL as beginners in Grade 6 because only a beginning EFL course is offered in secondary school. Being placed beside beginners and repeating the tasks and structures they have already studied surely will result in boredom and a lack of motivation (Singleton, 1989). Hence, if the purpose of the program is to prepare primary school pupils for their secondary schooling, as expressed by the municipal education official, the assistant principal, and the English teacher, the curriculum should be articulated between primary and secondary programs and well planned, as suggested by Marinova-Todd, Marshall, and Snow (2000).

The second theme highlighted in this study was the virtual lack of an EFL teaching component in Vietnam's teacher training colleges. The two teachers of English at the EFL primary school used to be teachers of Russian and were sent to be retrained to teach English to secondary school children. The teacher of English in the study admitted that she had not been trained to teach children. She said she had to observe some Vietnamese classes to find a suitable way of teaching English to her pupils. Obviously, she admitted the dissimilarity between teaching English to children and adults and the need to adapt her teaching. As mentioned earlier, the introduction of a foreign language into the school curriculum needs to take into consideration young children's specific educational development. Second language experts and teachers have markedly shown unanimity on age-specific approaches to teaching a foreign language to children (Abe, 1996; Cook, 1996; Dunn, 1985; Enright, 1991; Hudelson, 1996; Klein, 1993; Phillips, 1993; Scott & Ytreberg, 1993; Ur, 1996; Vale, 1995). These approaches reflect heterogeneity in teaching techniques as well as attitudes to suit children's particular cultural, cognitive, emotional, linguistic, and physical development.

In a class I observed, the English teacher checked to see if pupils knew how to tell the time in their first language before starting the time lesson in English because concepts and activities should fit not only the mental age of the pupils but also their first language knowledge base and physical development (Vale, 1995). Apart from this, the classroom atmosphere did not promote much involvement in the lesson, and the formal setting required pupils to perform in controlled practice and written work. Although the teacher tried to incorporate structure, function, and grammar into the lesson, as suggested by the author of the textbook (Pham, 1998), she dominated the class with mostly teacher-initiated interaction and focused on accuracy with controlled practice.

The textbook uses a topic-based approach with pictures primarily for reading and listening activities. Writing tasks are incorporated to reinforce the grammatical structures presented in each unit. Each lesson ends with a game and a summary table of the structures or grammar points. Speaking activities aimed at providing more interaction among learners are not included. Young learners' development requires a holistic and activity-based approach to teaching and a language-rich environment, both of which help to reduce learners' anxiety in the classroom (Abe, 1996; Dunn, 1985). However, this textbook does not seem to match this need; hence, some modification of the textbook and its supplementary material is required.

Because the data were collected from a limited population and do not reflect the whole situation of the province, more research must be carried out before refinements to the foreign language policy can be made. The decline in the Vietnamese grades of the 83 EFL pupils, for example, necessitates further investigation, as do the results of the other EFL classes and the study records of non-EFL pupils in this school in the previous years. Such an investigation will help clarify whether the same decline occurs for non-EFL pupils in this school and whether it is caused by the increasingly challenging requirements of the Vietnamese subject or the added subject of English.

◈ PRACTICAL IDEAS

The limited data do suggest that teaching EFL to primary school children in Nha Trang has gained a great deal of approval from parents and teachers, who perceive that the early introduction of EFL into the primary school curriculum brings about cognitive, cultural, and linguistic benefits for children. Hence, the program will be able to expand at the same time that social and pedagogical support is increased to ensure success. This support should improve the current deficiencies in the following areas: qualified teachers of EFL for primary schools, appropriate teaching methodologies and instructional materials, coordination across levels of instruction, and appropriately designed syllabi. This section presents some practical ideas that could be implemented in Vietnam.

Define a Model Curriculum for an Uninterrupted Sequence of EFL Instruction Across Primary and Secondary Levels

As suggested by Rosenbusch (1995), there should be a steering committee to clarify the rationale of the program, consider its advantages and limitations, and then define a model curriculum for an uninterrupted sequence of EFL instruction across primary and secondary levels. In a country where the education ministry takes full responsibility for the planning and design of curricula, provision of instructional materials and supervision should occur at all levels, and research should be conducted on a national scale to affirm the optimal grade for starting EFL learning in primary schools. The steering committee should involve in the research teachers and teacher trainers who have a good understanding of early bilingualism and sound experience in teaching EFL in the early grades.

Integrate the Teaching of EFL to Primary School Children Into the EFL Programs at Teacher Training Colleges

This integration would aim to provide well-qualified staff for primary schools in Vietnam. There is no better place for teachers to receive relevant knowledge and teaching practice than in local teacher training colleges, whose programs are closely connected with real classes in primary and secondary schools. The training program should be designed to provide teacher learners with knowledge about early bilingualism and approaches that reflect heterogeneity in teaching techniques and attitudes to suit children's particular cultural, cognitive, emotional, linguistic, and physical development.

Encourage Local Education Authorities to Take a More Active Role in Teacher Training Programs

Local education authorities should coordinate with the local teachers' college to retrain primary school EFL teachers who have insufficient English language skills and qualifications to teach the foreign language to children. As mentioned earlier, a teacher in this study said that she had been trained to teach secondary school students and thus had to observe how primary school children learned and were taught Vietnamese. She then applied the methodologies of teaching Vietnamese to teaching English to her primary school pupils. Many teachers of Russian who became redundant (a large number were once trained to teach Russian to secondary school students as the first-priority foreign language) were retrained to teach English to secondary students. However, after they were retrained, the need for EFL secondary school teachers declined and they were offered teaching jobs in primary schools. The local education authorities, therefore, should work with the local teachers' college to design and implement an in-service training course for these EFL primary school teachers.

Ensure That Primary School Syllabi Allow Sufficient Time for Language Development

Differences between teaching English to young learners and older students imply the need for a specifically designed syllabus for primary schools. This syllabus must allow for a sufficient amount of time to develop language at the initial stage. With two 40-minute classes per week and the lack of a language-rich environment, pupils in the current EFL program do not have enough opportunities for practicing, revising, or staying motivated to learn English. A syllabus with at least three 40-minute classes per week, in which pupils meet every second day, may be necessary. Furthermore, young learners may better be served by an initial-stage syllabus, as suggested by Dunn (1985), which aims to equip them with the basic level of communication in simple language to enable them to talk and write at a basic level about themselves, their immediate surroundings, and their interests. This syllabus should be implemented in Grades 3–5 in Vietnam; upon completion of Grade 5, children would be ready to recycle language at a linguistically and cognitively more advanced level in Grades 6–12.

Take a Holistic, Topic-Based Approach to Syllabus Design

A syllabus designed with a holistic, topic-based, and activity-based approach creates informal cooperative learning situations without abstract or overabundant grammar instruction in the second language. In addition, the language classroom needs to have pictures, posters, and maps to expose children to English on a daily basis. However, this will be achieved only when the Vietnamese school receives sufficient funding from the local government and parents.

Encourage Community and Home Support for the Primary EFL Program

Continuous home and community support as well as coordination between teachers and parents are needed to sustain children's enthusiasm and to provide financial support to implement the program. Whereas education authorities take responsibility for curriculum design and teacher training, parents should be willing to provide some financial support to the primary school where their children are involved in an EFL program.

◈ CONCLUSION

This investigation has provided a direction for policy makers and educators in making decisions about language policy and integrating primary school EFL training into teacher training programs in Vietnam. An EFL program for Vietnamese primary school children is worth promoting and investing in to bring about a generation ready for a world of mutual understanding and technological advancement. However, the early introduction of a foreign language requires continuous development of children's first language as well as support for the second language. Grade 3, therefore, is not too early to teach EFL, on the condition that it is fully supported and sustained by the government, language specialists, teachers, and parents, and includes a curriculum aimed at developing both first and second languages of students.

The perceptions of the benefits of early bilingualism among the surveyed parents, teachers, and education authorities are supported and shared by many second language experts and educators throughout the world (e.g., Baker, 1996; Clyne et al., 1995; Galambos & Goldin-Meadow, 1990). The study shows that parental support is an important factor in a successful EFL program for children. The pupils who were supported and aided by one or both parents gained higher grades than those who had no parental support and assistance. The limitations on incorporating an EFL program into the primary school's curriculum, however, include the lack of instructional materials, adequate teaching and learning facilities, and teachers with English language skills and EFL instruction qualifications; insufficient exposure to classroom instruction for young learners; and a meager English language environment. The continuity of the program across primary and secondary levels also needs to be considered.

The hesitation about expanding the program to all primary schools results from the current understaffing and difficulty in funding. The later start of EFL programs (i.e., Grade 3 instead of Grade 1) was due to the education authorities' belief that Grade 3 pupils' first language is well developed and they are more ready to learn a foreign language. In addition, my experience in teaching EFL in the early grades also indicates that Grade 3 students are quicker learners than students in Grades 1 and 2. This can be explained by the children's mutual development of their first and second languages, whereby second language development is promoted by the positive transfer of language concepts and literary skills from the high level of the first language system developed during the early primary school years (Collier & Thomas, 1999).

Until now there has been no documented research into the negative effects of early bilingualism on children's general linguistic and mental development (Baetens-

Beardsmore, 1982; Clyne et al., 1995). Many studies (e.g., Baker, 1993; Clyne et al., 1995; Cummins, 1979; Galambos & Goldin-Meadow, 1990; Genesee, 1995; Rosenblum & Pinker, 1983) have examined the benefits of early bilingualism. EFL programs for primary school children are therefore worth investing in, albeit with detailed planning—curriculum design and social and pedagogical support from the community, including education authorities, teacher trainers, and parents. However, the educational department must make the necessary investment in teacher training and support for an EFL program to succeed.

At the moment, EFL courses for very young learners in major cities such as Hanoi and Ho Chi Minh City are mushrooming, and the children enrolled in them are exposed to a more English-language-rich environment with modern facilities and qualified teachers. The courses are also strongly supported by parents. However, these courses are for only a very small population of privileged children from these two cities. Attempts to teach English to primary school children on a national scale are facing a serious lack of both social and pedagogical support and thus require comprehensive reform efforts.

◈ CONTRIBUTOR

Ha Van Sinh is a senior lecturer of English at Nha Trang Teacher College in Vietnam. He has a master's degree in teaching English to speakers of other languages from the University of South Australia, Adelaide, and a doctorate in teacher education from La Trobe University, Melbourne. His interests are foreign language teacher education and second language acquisition.

CHAPTER 9

A Local Approach to Global English: A Bulgarian EFL Model Based on International Children's Culture

Lilia Savova

◈ INTRODUCTION

Bulgaria has a long tradition of teaching foreign languages in elementary school. I can still remember how my paternal grandmother would quote legendary authors from antiquity in Latin! She followed with a painfully detailed account of how her elementary school teacher had managed to accomplish that extraordinary feat. Even in her late 70s, when she could hardly remember the events of the day, she could proudly recite the fateful lines of Caesar's demise. Modern languages have long since taken the lead in the Bulgarian elementary school curriculum, first French and German, and now English.

This case study focuses on teaching English as a foreign language (EFL) in Bulgarian public elementary schools. It begins with an explanation of the general educational context in which EFL learning occurs. It then describes the main components of the elementary EFL curriculum (e.g., unit objectives, content topics/themes, communicative functions, language material). It also discusses a three-part model comprising a literacy-focused approach, a theme-oriented method, and children's culture-based techniques. Finally, it summarizes the applications and adaptations of this approach-method-technique model in varying educational contexts nationally and internationally.

◈ CONTEXT

Teaching English to elementary school children in Bulgaria occurs in three types of instructional settings: as part of the public school core curricula, at individual private schools, and in one-on-one private tutorials. EFL was added to the public elementary school curricula in the early 1980s as an elective to meet an ever-growing demand for early childhood foreign language education. At that time, public schools were the only form of organized schooling in the country. After the fall of communism in the early 1990s, private schools emerged to offer alternative modes of education at all levels—elementary, middle, high school, and college and university levels. On the other hand, private tutorials for children have existed as a home schooling alternative for many years. The development of foreign language curricula—and EFL curricula in particular—in Bulgaria is driven by powerful economic and cultural traditions that arise from the fact that Bulgaria is a small European country whose global integration relies heavily on the foreign language proficiency and multicultural awareness of its citizens.

Elementary EFL in Bulgaria is part of the national core curriculum that includes an introduction to humanities, science, art, and physical education. The content and goals of elementary EFL in Grades 1–4 of the public school system reflect the social, psychological, physical, and intellectual development of 6- to 9-year-old children. Literacy in EFL occurs parallel to native Bulgarian literacy and to knowledge growth in other subject areas. The primary goal of EFL literacy at these early levels is oral proficiency. Written proficiency in English is developed based on well-established listening and speaking skills in English and on Bulgarian literacy skills, both oral and written. EFL instruction is also integrated with all other elementary school subjects. Furthermore, it is closely aligned with the Bulgarian middle school national educational goals. Even though parents and EFL program developers strongly believe that young children should learn English to prepare for their future career realization, they understand that instrumental and integrative motivation alone (Richards, Platt, & Platt, 1992, p. 238) are not enough. Instead, young children in Bulgaria are predominantly intrinsically motivated to learn English. EFL program and materials developers offer elementary school children opportunities to do what they can do best (e.g., play games, sing songs, engage in other fun activities linked to learning a new language).

◈ DESCRIPTION

As part of the foreign language core curriculum, EFL is taught in Grades 1–4. The appendix provides a sample EFL curriculum for these grades. It defines unit objectives and content through the discussion of topics and themes, communicative functions, and language material to be introduced in each unit (Savova & Alexandrova, 1986, p. 47).

◈ DISTINGUISHING FEATURES

Three main features distinguish the EFL curriculum in the Bulgarian elementary public schools:

- a literacy-focused approach based on the children, their individuality, and their overall linguistic, academic, psychological, physical, and intellectual development

- a theme-oriented method featuring the children's surroundings (e.g., family, school, society, nature)

- children's culture-based communicative techniques or activities and behaviors that are typical for children of the same age (e.g., games, sports, humor, fun)

Figure 1 illustrates how the EFL curriculum is built on these three principles.

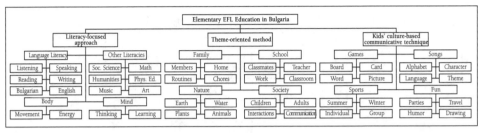

FIGURE 1. Distinguishing Features of the Elementary EFL Curriculum in Bulgaria

Literacy-Focused Approach

In Bulgarian public elementary schools, reading and writing in English are introduced to 7- and 8-year-old children in second grade—a time of dramatic changes in their physical, psychological, and intellectual development. At that time, they have already had a year of reading and writing in Bulgarian and a year of oral English. As they build their literacy in English based on their oral and written fluency in Bulgarian and on their knowledge and skills in other disciplines, children can benefit from appropriate educational strategies and techniques.

A central issue in children's overall development is literacy. In first grade, they learn the Bulgarian alphabet and use that knowledge to read simple words, phrases, and short texts. It is important to note that, unlike English, Bulgarian is a phonetically based language with a one-to-one sound–symbol correspondence; each letter from the Cyrillic alphabet has only one pronunciation. For example, the Cyrillic letter *A, a* is always pronounced as /ʌ/ as in *cut*. The same letter in English can be pronounced /eɪ/ as in *baby*, /æ/ as in *cat*, /ɑ:/ as in *arm*, /ɔ:/ as in *all*, and /ə/ as in *alive*. Moreover, in English, two different pronunciations of the same letter may exist in the same word, as in *away*. This example demonstrates how the two alphabets share a common symbol but differ in pronunciation. That means that children who can write the Bulgarian letter *A, a* will have no problem writing it in English. However, they will have to learn its different pronunciations in English. Some of these have similar counterparts in Bulgarian. For example, the pronunciation of *baby, answer, all,* and *alive* will be understandable because of the existence of similar phonemes in Bulgarian. However, the pronunciation of /æ/ in *cat,* for which there's no corresponding Bulgarian phoneme, will be a major problem. Similar problems exist with all vowels and many consonant phonemes. Thus, letter practice activities are designed in accordance with the specific orthographic and phonetic difficulty each English letter presents and do not necessarily follow the order in which letters appear in the English alphabet.

To develop accurate orthographic and pronunciation habits, the elementary EFL curriculum uses an eclectic activity-based, theme-oriented approach with strong structural and functional components (i.e., practice is both meaningful and purposeful at all stages). For example, simple letter recognition activities are presented as letter puzzles. The activity in Figure 2 instructs students to circle the correct letter and leads to the creation of a picture, which serves as immediate feedback and

Instruction: Color the boxes with the letter "o." What do you see?

a	q	b	a	c	p	b	c	q	c
g	p	c	d	o	b	g	a	d	b
b	c	d	o	b	o	a	d	a	q
p	g	o	o	o	o	o	b	c	a
a	q	o	b	c	d	o	a	b	b
q	c	o	c	b	g	o	q	d	q
b	a	o	q	a	q	o	c	b	c
q	q	o	o	o	o	o	d	q	d
c	a	b	q	g	q	b	a	a	c
p	b	p	d	q	a	c	q	b	d

FIGURE 2. Letter Recognition Puzzle

instant reward. Thus, the completion of an "o" recognition puzzle is ultimately about creating a house.

Similarly, a later lesson about a New Year's party shows characters dressed as different professionals and animals. For Bulgarian students, these situations are authentic because they reflect a common practice to celebrate the New Year's holiday at mask parties. The students are guided to talk, read, and write in the roles of these characters. They practice the names of familiar professions and animals as they ask and answer yes/no questions in situations created in a mask-induced mystery activity (Savova & Alexandrova, 1991, p. 43). Initially, children write only to record what they have already heard, said, and read. Gradually, they use the alphabet code, which consists of pictorial representations of letters, to create coded messages, which are usually titles of children's books, such as *The Little Red Hen*, or utterances in response to accompanying pictures. At a more advanced stage, children write to describe objects and people, to talk about their friends' likes and dislikes, to record conversations, and to write letters about various events.

Literacy in English develops through the use of knowledge, skills, strategies, techniques, and activities that are developed in other subjects in the elementary school curriculum. From math, the English class adapts some logical word problems as well as arithmetic problems that require counting, addition, subtraction, and multiplication. From the humanities and social sciences, it draws information about different people and places, their cultures and customs, their present and past. Most important, EFL uses materials and activities from music, art, and physical education; throughout elementary school, children sing specially composed songs about the book characters:

Nick's sleeping in his room [3 times]
And he can't see you
But he'll be up soon

Fred's playing loud music [3 times]
And he can't hear you
But it'll be over soon

Tony's reading in his room [3 times]
And he can't meet you
But he'll be here soon

Jane's doing homework [3 times]
And she can't chat with you
But she'll be done soon

Everybody's doing something [3 times]
And they can't be with you
But they'll join you soon

Other songs are about animals, food, holidays, colors, and various children's activities. Learners are often asked to draw and color pictures and then use those in information gap activities, and in memory and matching games. Children's art is one of the recurring topics throughout the elementary EFL curriculum. The EFL course in the second grade opens with a children's art exhibition, a rare children's international event, which provides the context for the introduction of the book characters. Physical education, too, offers valuable activity-based learning for the EFL classroom. Children are often engaged in movement to demonstrate actions as part of EFL classroom projects or as part of song activities similar to this one:

Children, touch your desks
Children, jump high
Children, sit down and smile
Children, take your pens and write

Children, move your chairs
Children, run fast
Children, sit down and write
Children, open your books and read

Overall, literacy development in English in the Bulgarian elementary public school system incorporates effective classroom practices from across the elementary school curriculum and is consistent with young children's physical and mental development.

Theme-Oriented Method

The second distinguishing feature of the Bulgarian EFL elementary curriculum derives from the representation of the child's inner world in relation to the world outside. The latter includes both closer and more distant surroundings, such as family and school on the one hand and society and nature on the other. These themes serve as foci for content organization.

Family and school are frequent sources of real-life reference and context. The Bulgarian EFL elementary curriculum acknowledges the importance of these two environments for the child's passage into the world at large. The EFL book based on the curriculum introduces family members, roles, and relations through family albums, parties, and holidays. Along with these festive occasions, the EFL book characters are also involved in more mundane daily tasks such as chores and routines. These themes are a major contextual frame for a large part of the EFL content. Texts and activities reflect young children's limited life experience and their preoccupation with the here and now, with the familiar and the known. In second grade here is an example of how a family, whose son is visiting Bulgaria as a participant in an international children's art exhibition, might be introduced in a dialogue:

Anna: Hello, Nick. Who's this?
Nick: This is my mother. And that is my sister, Kate. She's a little girl. She's five.
Anna: And who's this?
Nick: This is my father. And that's grandpa.
Anna: And who's this?
Nick: This is my grandma. She's very nice. And this little thing here is my dog, Sally.
Anna: And this is you, Nick.
Nick: No. This is my brother, Bob. He's eight, and I'm eight too.

Through family and school activities, young children are introduced to the more complex worlds of nature and society. Some class activities use situations occurring in the park, in the yard, at the farm, in the mountains, and on the beach. Different locations allow introduction of basic notions such as formal and informal, and child–adult interactions. Thus, the elementary EFL class introduces young children to their surroundings and more specifically to that part of the outside world that is most familiar to them.

Children's Culture-Based Communicative Techniques

The third distinctive feature of the elementary EFL curriculum in the Bulgarian public schools, children's culture-based communicative techniques, provides a medium for both learning and teaching. Set in themes from children's surroundings, learning is immersed in children's culture (e.g., games, songs, sport, fun activities that children of the same age share). The latter are basic components of the content and structure of the elementary school EFL curriculum. They make up most of its communicative activities. Games include board, card, and word games, as well as drawing and outside games. For example, one board game, a "snakes and ladders" type, limits communication to practice within the model: "What's this? It's a tree." Other board games focus on specific structures: "Does Anna's shop sell candy? Yes, it does./No, it doesn't." "How many bars of chocolate are in your pocket?" "Can you pick flowers in this park? Yes, you can./No, you can't." Similarly, card games focus on the practice of basic English structures such as these: "Is there a book in the picture? Yes, there is./No, there isn't." "Whose watch is this? Is it yours? Yes, it is./No, it isn't." "What's Tony doing? Is he swimming?" Games are generally used at the level of free expression because they provide authentic communication contexts within specific game rules. That's why all review sections include games. Game elements and elements of surprise and competition are included in most class activities.

Specially written songs also offer opportunities to learn correct structures and pronunciations in English through the repetition of texts, tunes, dances, and movements. Sport and other enjoyable activities complete the children's list of favorite projects. By using English to play games, sing songs, talk about parties and travels, tell jokes, laugh, and draw, children are immersed in a comfortable environment of creative learning experiences.

The Bulgarian Model

The literacy-focused, theme-oriented, culture-based model of the Bulgarian elementary school EFL curriculum could be interpreted as an application of Anthony's (1963) approach-method-technique model. Both models are three-member hierarchical constructs, as shown in Figure 3. First, both "Literacy-Focused Approach" and "Approach" refer to a set of correlative assumptions about the axiomatic nature of language learning. Whereas the latter is all encompassing and refers to any language learning context, the former is subject specific and addresses a particular type of language learning situation, which is that of EFL elementary school children. Second, both "Theme-Oriented Method" and "Method" refer to an overall procedural plan for the presentation of language content, all of which is based on the selected approach. The psycholinguistic literacy-focused approach could yield different methods. The theme-oriented method selected in the second category comprises elements of structural, functional, and situational methods with an emphasis on the thematic lexicalization of grammar. And third, both "Children's Culture-Based Communicative Techniques" and "Technique" refer to what actually takes place in the classroom. More specifically, this category refers to children's favorite activities. On the whole, each model reflects the hierarchical integration of its three components.

◈ PRACTICAL IDEAS

The literacy-focused, theme-oriented, children's culture-based model discussed in this study is an example of a local approach to global English language instruction. Even though it is designed to meet the requirements of the national core curriculum for Bulgarian elementary schools, it has wider applications that derive from the

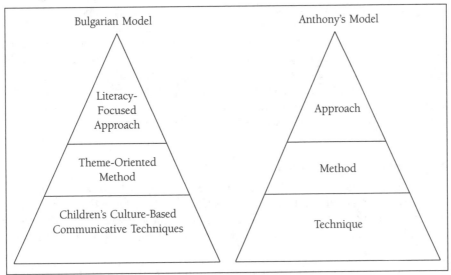

FIGURE 3. Two Hierarchical Models: The Bulgarian and Anthony's (1963)

universal appeal of its age-determined distinctive features. Its literacy-focused approach represents well-established traditions in child education. Its theme-based method is in harmony with child education curricula. And its children's culture-oriented communicative activities reflect common practices in children's home and organized schooling activities. In this section, I suggest ways that this model could be used in other child education settings. I also explain how its distinctive features could be applied to meet specific classroom objectives.

Literacy-Focused Approach: Applications

Literacy development may be organized according to several local factors, such as the exact age when children start learning EFL, the nature of the corresponding mother tongue in comparison to English, and the general program goals of elementary education in the school. Age, for example, is a very decisive factor at the elementary education stage of children's development. At 4 or 5 years of age, children may have to spend a longer time acquiring oral English. Here are some applications to consider:

Have Children Listen to and Repeat Short Language Samples in English That Are Modeled by the Teacher

The samples could be common words and phrases, minidialogues, or short stories used in everyday interactions and classroom settings. The younger the children, the more natural it will be for them to accept the foreign language as a means of communication in the classroom and the easier it will be for them to acquire foreign pronunciations. Frequent recycling of oral language is essential because children's memory span is very short.

Begin Reading and Writing Monosyllabic Words With the Introduction of the English Alphabet

First, children can learn how to pronounce easy words, such as *pen, boy, girl,* and *book,* in a variety of tasks: listen and say, draw and say, look and say, point and say, do and say, and remember and say. Then they can begin oral reading by imitating their teacher, who points to the text and reads aloud. Thus, they are encouraged to read globally (i.e., to remember each word, not so much as a string of letters but as a whole word). Later, they can try to read independently, beginning with choral reading and moving on to individual oral reading. Their first writing may be the completion of the words they learned orally. After they practice writing a letter, they may use it to fill in a gap. For example, they may have to write *n* in *pe_* to complete the word *pen.*

Consider the Children's First Language Relative to EFL

Even though elementary school children are still learning the basics of their first language, the nature of that language affects how they perceive and acquire English in their native countries. EFL professionals can consider the native language's phonological system relative to English. In doing so, they may answer questions such as the following:

- How many and what are the vowels and consonants in the first and second language?

- Which of the second language vowels and consonants have adequate sound equivalents in the first language, and which do not?

- Of the existing first language sound equivalents, which ones are only slightly similar to their second language counterparts, and what other phonemes might they be confused with?

- Which second language phonemes have no first language equivalents and what makes them difficult to pronounce?

The answers to these questions may then be used in the selection and arrangement of the EFL content. For example, if some Asian students find it difficult to pronounce *r* in initial position, it might be a good idea to call one of their EFL book characters *Ron*.

Compare the Basic First and Second Language Structures and Analyze Their Morphological and Syntactic Features

Look for similarities and differences in the most widely used basic structures. EFL program developers may respond to these questions:

- How is the English verb different from its first language counterpart?

- How is tense expressed in the first and second languages?

- Is tense in the first language a grammatical or lexical category?

- Are there any morphological tense markers in the first language and, if so, are they similar to those in English?

- How are present actions expressed in the first and second languages?

- What English structures would be best selected as the communication minimum for specific child learners?

Answers to these and other similar questions could be helpful in deciding what structures are introduced first, second, and last.

Consider Selecting Appropriate Situations After Identifying Core Phonetic and Grammar Components, Contexts, and Their Related Semantic Fields

These situations could be used as contexts to introduce basic English structures. For example, a birthday party might be a good opportunity to talk about food, presents, cards, games, good and bad manners, and guests. Children's limited life and language experience reduces the list of appropriate themes to a minimum; however, the few familiar and safe topics, such as the family, may be used for different purposes several times during the course. On one occasion, a child's family could be introduced to talk about family members; on another occasion, the topic might be vacations or hobbies. In all cases, themes should be culturally appropriate.

Use School Program Goals as Curriculum Goals

Elementary schools that are music, art, science, mathematics, or foreign language magnets can place a different emphasis on learning English. Thus, it may be appropriate to think of a more extensive integration of EFL and art education in an art magnet, where products from art classes may be used as realia or visuals in the EFL class. Teachers may choose to integrate the following activities into other subjects:

- Use songs from music class with English texts in the EFL class. Some of the techniques used in music education can be adopted in the EFL class. Music tunes can be used to demonstrate English intonation.

- Use simple experiments from science class to describe actions and give advice and directions. Scientific knowledge may be used as a conversation topic in EFL content.

- Use simple problems from math class to talk about quantity, ordinal and cardinal numbers, addresses, telephone numbers, and age.

- Incorporate movement, games, and exercises learned in physical education class into EFL songs and games. These activities can be a rich source of kinesthetic components to EFL tasks and activities.

Overall, the literacy-focused elementary EFL approach discussed in this study may be customized in accordance with learner age and first language as well as with program goal specifics. It may also affect the selection of a corresponding language teaching method.

Theme-Oriented Method: Applications

The theme-oriented method developed for Bulgarian elementary schools may be applied in other educational settings. Each application will depend on the particular approach selected in that setting, as well as on the cultural appropriateness of the themes selected.

Consider School-Specific Needs

As mentioned earlier, approach selection can be determined by learner age and first language considerations as well as by specific program goals. Although learner age in elementary school may be similar around the world, native tongues and program goals vary. The latter can have a major impact on the choice of criteria for selecting EFL content and materials, especially when the native language is significantly different from English. As program goals tend to vary from one type of elementary school to another, even within one country or region, main curriculum foci may be largely determined by prevailing school-specific needs rather than by national or international standards.

Consider Local Cultural Practices

Theme selection in the elementary EFL classroom depends on the corresponding cultural conventions. The family, school, nature, and society themes listed in Figure 1 might be entirely or partially appropriate in some cultures and totally inappropriate in others. In such matters, a heightened cultural awareness and sensitivity is the teacher's best guide in each EFL classroom.

Children's Culture-Based Communicative Techniques: Applications

Just as the instructional approach and method described here can be adapted to specific educational settings, the supporting communicative techniques may also be used with or without modification. Many songs, games, sports, and other enjoyable activities may be used as is, simply because they constitute independent communicative events defined by their own conventions and rules. On the other hand, creative adaptations of these activities in terms of content and difficulty may enhance EFL learning significantly. The following ideas involve technique adaptation.

Consider the Relevance of English-Based Games in the Particular Country or Area

Game models can be changed to include relevant language content (e.g., "Who's this?" could be replaced by "What's this?"). The content of the game can also be changed. For example, objects could replace people in the original version (e.g., "It's a girl" could be changed to "It's a book"). Game models, content, and rules may be adapted for students of different EFL proficiency levels.

Situate Songs Through a Variety of Before and After Tasks

Before the actual singing of the song, a series of tasks targeting language and content issues may be designed. Songs may also be first presented as poems. Postsinging activities may include transforming songs into games, stories, and dialogues, both oral and written. Some songs may even be rewritten with name or word substitutions; others may be used as models for the composition of new songs.

Select and Adapt Sports Activities According to Regional Factors

American football may be a great topic in some countries, and virtually unknown in others. Winter sports may be part of everyday life in Scandinavian countries, but in tropical climates they make no sense.

Select Enjoyable Activities

Children's parties, playground games, and drawing activities are probably universal class activity favorites that could easily be adapted to local traditions and customs. For example, it may be common in some places to have the whole family go to the children's playground; in other places, however, it may be only mothers who accompany children.

◈ CONCLUSION

This chapter discusses elementary EFL education in the Bulgarian public schools in connection with Anthony's (1963) approach-method-technique model, which may well be one of the most influential English as a second language models developed so far (Richards & Rodgers, 2001). The Bulgarian version constitutes one of many possible interpretations and applications. It is a literacy-focused, theme-oriented, children's culture-based model, which I used to analyze the EFL elementary school core curriculum and the Grade 1–4 materials designed for that curriculum. In that analysis, I emphasize the hierarchy of its three distinguishing features. The first, its literacy-focused approach, is axiomatic and takes into account important psychological, physiological, and academic factors contributing to a child's overall development. The second, based on that approach, is a theme-oriented method that calls for language content and organization that use familiar topics. And the third, children's culture-based communicative activities, implement both of the first two features.

◈ CONTRIBUTOR

Lilia Savova is professor of English in the English Department of Indiana University of Pennsylvania, where she teaches graduate courses in the MA TESOL, PhD TESOL, and composition programs. She specializes in methodology, linguistics, assessment, technology and literacy, and instructional design.

◈ APPENDIX: EFL CURRICULUM, GRADES 1–4

Unit Number	Discussion Topics and Themes	Communicative Functions	Language Structure Samples
1	Hello friends International children's pictures exhibition	Introducing people Naming people and qualities	*Who's this?* *It's Anna.* *What's this?* *It's a white dove.*
2	Participants in the picture exhibition visit the EFL class	Introducing people Asking questions Giving positive and negative answers	*What's your name?* *I'm Molly.* *My name's Molly.* *I'm not Anna.*
3	The family The family album	Introducing and describing people Naming people's qualities and age	*This is Jane.* *She's five.* Numbers 1–10 *My, your, his, her, its, our, their*
4	Art Jane's pictures	Asking questions Giving positive and negative responses Beginning and maintaining a conversation Agreeing and disagreeing	*Is it a girl?* *Yes, it is.* *No, it isn't.*
5	The child's room Furniture, toys, school supplies	Reviewing and summarizing the communicative functions from Units 1–4	Review and summary of the language structures from Units 1–4
6	Sports and games At the sports ground	Talking about possession Asking questions Giving positive and negative responses Maintaining and ending a conversation Expressing opinions	*Whose car is this?* *It's Fred's.* *Mine, yours, his, hers, its, ours, theirs*

Unit Number	Discussion Topics and Themes	Communicative Functions	Language Structure Samples
7	The farmhouse Farm animals	Comparing qualities Indicating close and distant objects Expressing opinions Describing objects	*This is a brown cow, and that's a black horse.* *What color is the pig?* *It's pink.*
8	Work Jobs and professions	Asking about one's job Providing information about one's job Expressing supposition and doubt Asking for help	*What am I?* *You're a farmer.* *Are you a farmer?* *Yes, I am.* *No, I'm not.*
9	Culture, tradition, holidays	Celebrating the new year Expressing one's feelings Expressing surprise, happiness Asking questions Giving positive and negative responses	*What is Jane?* *Is she a lion?* *No, she isn't.* *She's a tiger.*
10	Hobbies and fun Solving puzzles	Reviewing and summarizing the communicative functions from Units 5–9	Review and summary of the language structures from Units 5–9
11	Sports Winter sports	Expressing requests, orders Giving instructions Expressing support	*Molly, sit!*
12	Shopping Buying clothes and shoes	Expressing approval Asking for and giving information	*What are these?* *They're yellow dresses.* *No, they're not.* *They're yellow blouses.*
13	Health and sickness Doctors and patients	Beginning, maintaining, and ending a conversation Describing things	*Are they nurses?* *We're nurses.* *You're doctors.*
14	Nature and wildlife	Asking about locations Describing locations	*Where do bears live?* *They live in the forest.* Adverbs of place
15	Children and the world around them Society, nature, wildlife	Reviewing and summarizing the communicative functions from Units 10–14	Review and summary of the language structures from Units 10–14

Unit Number	Discussion Topics and Themes	Communicative Functions	Language Structure Samples
16	The family Parents and children	Expressing preferences Expressing positive and negative opinions Expressing wishes	*Do you like dancing?* *Yes, I do.* *No, I don't.* *I like reading.*
17	Shopping Buying food	Describing actions Expressing agreement or disagreement	*Does he sell milk?* *Yes, he does.* *No, he doesn't.* *What does he sell?*
18	The child's home	Being polite Describing places	*There's a table in the kitchen.* *There are some chairs in the kitchen.* Prepositions of place The indefinite article
19	The family Family roles, responsibilities, and chores	Expressing indefinite quantity Asking for specific information Providing specific information	*Is there any bread on the table?* *Yes, there's some.* *No, there isn't any.* *Are there any biscuits?*
20	Fun and games	Reviewing and summarizing the communicative functions from Units 15–19	Review and summary of the language structures from Units 15–19
21	The daily calendar Time and schedules	Asking for and giving information about the time of actions Offering clarifications about time Expressing likes and dislikes Making suggestions	*What's the time?* *It's 8 o'clock.* *Tony goes running at 8 o'clock on Mondays.* Adverbs of time
22	The family Breakfast at home	Naming definite quantities Asking for things politely Making suggestions Asking for and giving information about food Expressing a warning	*How many slices of bread are there?* *How much sugar?* *How many spoonfuls?* *A cup of milk, please.* *I'd like some jam, please.* Prepositions

Unit Number	Discussion Topics and Themes	Communicative Functions	Language Structure Samples
23	Tourism and traveling Vacation at the beach	Describing present actions Beginning, maintaining, and ending a conversation Expressing how you feel Asking people to do things	*What's Molly doing?* *She's eating ice cream.* *I'm reading.* *We're playing ball.* *Nick, come out.* *Aren't you tired?*
24	Art Visual art Helping others	Describing present actions Describing people Asking for and giving information about present actions	*Is Molly swimming?* *Yes, she is.* *No, she isn't.* *What am I doing?* *Am I jumping?* *What are you doing?*
25	Fun and games	Reviewing and summarizing the communicative functions from Units 20–24	Review and summary of the language structures from Units 20–24
26	Nature Weather and climate The four seasons	Describing the seasons Talking about the weather Expressing intentions Describing habitual actions	*It's cold in the mountains.* *It often snows there.* *It's always sunny at the beach.* *I'm going home.*
27	Tourism and traveling	Asking for and giving information about the time Describing present and habitual actions Expressing suggestions	*What's the time?* *It's five to ten.* *It's half past six.* *It's quarter to eleven.* *Let's go.*
28	Tourism and traveling Souvenirs from Bulgaria	Describing quality and possession Expressing likes and dislikes Expressing joy and gratitude	*What have you got?* *I've got mittens.* *Have I got a present?* *Yes, you have.* *No, you haven't.* *I haven't got a blouse.* Possessive pronouns
29	Tourism and traveling Mountain hiking	Expressing ability and inability Encouraging people (not) to do things	*Can Tommy climb up the tree?* *Yes, he can.* *No, he can't.* *Who can climb that tree?* *You can do it, but I can't.*

Unit Number	Discussion Topics and Themes	Communicative Functions	Language Structure Samples
30	Country life The farmhouse and farm animals	Reviewing and summarizing the communicative functions from Units 25–29	Review and summary of the language structures from Units 25–29
31	Culture, traditions, holidays Choosing birthday presents	Asking for and giving information about events Expressing intentions Expressing approval	*When's your birthday?* *It's in September.* *I'm giving Anna a skiing hat.* *What a lovely hat!*
32	Culture, traditions, holidays At a birthday party	Congratulating people Expressing feelings Expressing agreement and disagreement Expressing possession Asking for and giving permission	*Has Nick got a sandwich?* *Yes, he has.* *No, he hasn't.* *This cake is mine and that's hers.* *You can't have cake now.*
33	National history History of Sofia: Sofia then and now	Describing past places, events, and actions Asking for and giving information about past places and events Comparing quantities, qualities, and features	*Was there a stadium there?* *Yes, there was.* *No, there wasn't.* *Were there any schools?* *Yes, there were.* Adverbs of time
34	Nature and wildlife in antiquity	Describing past actions Asking for and giving information about the appearance and the abilities of extinct creatures	*When did this animal live?* *It lived 100 million years ago.* *Did it have four legs?* *Yes, it did.* *No, it didn't.* *Could it fly?* *No, it couldn't.*
35	Fun and games Children and the peace movement	Reviewing and summarizing the communicative functions from Units 30–34	Review and summary of the language structures from Units 30–34

PART 3

Teacher Development for Primary EFL

CHAPTER 10

Developing Teachers in the Developing World of Sri Lanka

David Hayes

◈ INTRODUCTION

Much international experience shows that investment in in-service teacher training/development[1] (INSET) can have a positive impact on the quality of schooling (Pennycuick, 1993). There is not, however, a simple one-to-one correspondence between any INSET course and improved practice in the classroom. There are sufficient examples of in-service courses having limited or no impact on the teachers involved, particularly in the long term (see, e.g., Ibrahim, 1991; Lamb, 1996; Moon & Boullón, 1997), to give considerable pause for thought. Ibrahim (1991), for example, studied the in-service training program for the introduction of a new primary school curriculum in Malaysia, which consisted of a cascade system ending in a diluted version of trainers' courses. According to Ibrahim, "the evidence suggests that the courses had a surface effect but not the impact that could bring deep assimilation of all the KBSR [new primary school curriculum] features" (p. 125). As this experience indicates, there is always the prospect with short, one-off teacher training courses of surface adoption.[2] Teachers may adopt external features of a new curriculum (e.g., in terms of discourse, how they describe their teaching objectives or the classroom activities they claim to use in lesson plans or discussions with supervisors or head teachers), while in practice they continue to use the tried and trusted methods with which they have long been familiar. A similar disjunction between rhetoric and practice has been found in Western contexts, too. Alexander (1984), for example, in the course of his investigations into progressive primary education in the United Kingdom, commented that "the progressive rhetoric is apparently espoused across most of the range of actual primary practice . . . despite a wide variety of practices, some of which . . . are totally inconsistent with the rhetoric" (p. 14). In discussing any in-service teacher development program, then, as this case study does, one must be extremely careful when making claims of success, lest one fall into the trap of equating rhetoric with classroom practice.

---

[1] *In-service training* is the most commonly used term in Sri Lanka, the context of this case study, although the training activity discussed in this study is best described as part of a process of teacher development.

[2] I do not intend to imply any blame here. There are many good reasons that teachers choose not to implement innovations introduced to them in in-service courses. However, for many teachers working in government systems, there is often little overt choice as to which classroom methods they should be using.

With that caveat, I hope to show in this chapter that it is indeed possible for an in-service program to bring about change in classroom behaviors in line with curriculum innovation mandated by central educational authorities (i.e., in a situation where teachers have no choice as to whether or not they should adopt the innovation). The country under study is Sri Lanka, where English is taught formally as a subject at the primary level, beginning in Grade 3 (although there is some informal teaching that starts in Grade 1). I am particularly concerned with government schools that implement a standard curriculum nationwide. I begin by discussing the context in which the program has operated, referring to language policies and the status of English in the wider society as well as to economic considerations. No article on education in Sri Lanka would be complete without taking into account the ethnic conflict that has bedeviled the country for decades, and this case study is not an exception. I then move on to describe in some detail the teacher (and, inevitably, trainer) development program for primary English teachers against the backdrop of national curriculum reform, which aims to transform classroom pedagogy for all subjects from a fundamentally transmissive model to one that is activity based and child centered. I describe key features of the training/ development program so that lessons can be applied in other, similar contexts. I also provide practical advice for project planners and project implementers from the experience of the program.

◈ CONTEXT

The government of Sri Lanka is currently making considerable efforts to promote the use of English in the country and aims to offer, as a minimum, English as a subject to children in all grades in all government schools throughout the island, with the prospect of some schools being allowed to teach other subjects in the English medium (National Education Commission, 2002). This is partly a result of language policies but perhaps more directly attributable to economic imperatives. The recent report by the National Education Commission on English policy in education notes that

> English has been taught as a compulsory second language from Grade 3 for around half a century but has failed to ensure proficiency in spoken or written English among the student population and continues therefore to be an agent of social differentiation. Moreover studies have indicated that with the high incidence of unemployment from the end of the 1960s, proficiency in English has emerged as a critical factor in graduate unemployment, particularly in the context of a shrinking public sector and expanding private sector since the 1970s. (p. 1)

Language policies have been contentious in Sri Lanka for some time and have played a role in the longstanding and well-documented conflict between the majority Sinhalese and minority Tamil communities. (The civil war has been in abeyance since early 2002, although a fragile peace process was suspended in November 2003 because of political problems between the president and the prime minister.) Tension between the two communities, which existed for much of the 20th century, was exacerbated by the 1956 Act of Parliament, which made Sinhala the sole official language and thus devalued Tamil as well as English, the language of the former colonial power. The status of both Tamil and English has changed since then, with Tamil now given official status as a national language and English deemed the "link language" between the communities. Whether official pronouncements are reflected in everyday reality is another matter. For all practical purposes, members of the Tamil community tend to learn and use Sinhala in dealings with their Sinhalese country-men, whereas Sinhalese rarely learn Tamil. It would be true to say that English is most widely used among members of the socioeconomic elite, a group for whom English has long functioned as a strong second language (and for some a first language), irrespective of official language policies. For them, use of English is a marker of high status within a highly stratified society, a badge of distinction, as the National Education Commission (2002) notes. The converse is also true (i.e., that lack of fluency in English is correlated with low status).

Attitudes toward English among school-age children vary enormously. In an exercise on first-word responses, Lo Bianco (1999) asked Sinhala-medium and Tamil-medium children in Grades 6 and 9 to say, in their mother tongues, the first things that came to mind in response to the words *English*, *Tamil*, and *Sinhala*, written in their own languages. Translated responses[3] to *English* included the following:

> "They destroyed our discipline, culture and everything."
>
> "Sinhalese morals and culture were damaged by English people."
>
> "International language."
>
> "Very capable people."
>
> "I need a high knowledge of English." (Sinhala-medium children; Lo Bianco, 1999, p. 56)
>
> "English is everywhere."
>
> "Easier to speak than Sinhala."
>
> "When I go for interview I will be helped with English."
>
> "International language." (Tamil-medium children; Lo Bianco, 1999, p. 58)

What is notable here are the lack of comments from Tamil-medium children about the negative influence of English on local culture, and an emphasis on seeing English in instrumental terms, the latter response being also evident from Sinhala-medium children. While I can only speculate as to what primary-age children in Grades 1–5 might feel toward the language, these reactions give a clear indication of the complex sociocultural pressures that exist in Sri Lankan society with regard to English and the range of possible reactions that children can evince by later stages of schooling.

These pressures are inevitably connected to the wider socioeconomic world, and as previously intimated, Sri Lanka, like so many other countries, is subject to economic imperatives and the forces of globalization. These forces have a powerful impact on perceptions of English as the language of modern technology and economic advancement (Block & Cameron, 2002). Recognizing, but leaving aside, the question of whether mastery of English for most Sri Lankan children currently in school will indeed lead to an economically prosperous future or whether such a

---

[3] Translations from the original Sinhala and Tamil were made by Sri Lankan colleagues of mine and are recorded here exactly as in Lo Bianco (1999).

future will remain chimerical, demand for English is strong and political backing immensely powerful. As Kandiah (2000) notes,

> not a day passes without several affirmations of the importance of English by various important figures [in Sri Lanka]. Pronouncements about the language and the need to teach and learn it emanate from the most significant official figures and institutions, and are then given real substance in the forms of plans, strategies and so on, the implementation of which is seriously pursued. (p. 14)

The teaching and learning of English, therefore, is far from value-neutral; it is not just another subject in the school curriculum. Moreover, formal teaching of English begins in Grade 3, and it is also there that it begins to play its part in contributing to the overall objectives of lessening social differentiation and contributing to the achievement of social harmony between communities. These objectives are encapsulated in the first two of the nine national goals for education (National Education Commission, 1992):

1. the achievement of national cohesion, national integration, and national unity

2. the establishment of a pervasive pattern of social justice and the active elimination of inequalities

Set against this complex context, a comprehensive program of education reform has been underway since 1997 (National Education Commission, 1997), and within this reform in the primary school curriculum English is taught as a foreign language. It might be argued that redressing patterns of social inequality and contributing to social harmony between communities are rarefied goals for teaching English at the primary level. However, education as a whole has its part to play in establishing the preconditions for social harmony and greater equity among future generations (Department for International Development and World Bank, 2000). It is therefore essential to recognize that these goals form an important element in the backdrop of primary education in Sri Lanka and help to shape all activities aimed at improving schooling for children, including the teacher training/development program for English, which is the subject of this case study.

◈ DESCRIPTION

The teacher training/development program for English language teachers was a component of a British-funded project, the Sri Lanka Primary English Language Project (PELP), which ran from 1996 to 2003.[4] The overall training program had as its major aim improvement of the quality of teaching basic English in primary schools in Sri Lanka by establishing a training cadre with the sustainable capacity to implement improved, locally based training for English language teachers. It was

---

[4] I was project manager/lead consultant for PELP. Although nominally an English language project, PELP's mandate eventually went beyond training, curriculum, and textbook development for English to encompass mentoring school in-service advisors and writing supplementary readers in Tamil and Sinhala as well as English.

operationalized through a network of 30 regional English support centers (RESCs), in-service centers that predated the project and that remain the education ministry's[5] normal vehicle for in-service training for teachers of English. The RESCs continue to operate nationwide, even in conflict areas such as Jaffna and Vavuniya in the north of the island and Batticaloa in the east.[6] As an indicator of the demanding schedule of the system, in a typical year the centers conduct about 1,000 one-day courses attended by approximately 6,000 teachers. However, a teacher's mere attendance is no guarantee that content will be implemented, so I now turn to a more detailed description of PELP's teacher training program before considering its most distinguishing features.

Trainers

Because PELP operated a cascade system of training, it seems appropriate to begin the discussion with the trainers—the four full-time staff each RESC was allowed by the ministry. RESC staff members are government English teachers who have applied for posts in their local centers. They have been selected after an interview by the staff of the ministry and the National Institute of Education (NIE), which jointly run the RESC network. In Sri Lanka, until very recently specialist English teachers were trained to teach the entire range of ages from 7 to 18. As is common in so many education systems, teaching at the secondary/high school level is considered to be more prestigious; primary school teaching is undervalued and the complex professional skills needed to teach young children underrecognized. The perceived importance of secondary teaching resulted in a cadre of trainers with experience predominantly at the postprimary level. PELP then had the challenge of helping these trainers improve their knowledge and skills in three areas: first, the management of their in-service resource centers; second, the writing and delivery of in-service courses; and third, but perhaps most important, primary English teaching.

How has this been accomplished? A number of opportunities for development have been available to RESC staff during the life of the project, including

- workshops conducted by project staff focusing on areas such as resource center management, trainer skills, and primary English language teaching (ELT) methodology
- workshops conducted by visiting international consultants in areas such as mentoring, materials writing, and multicultural education
- intensive 10-week courses for selected trainers at universities in the United Kingdom
- frequent monitoring and support visits to RESCs conducted by highly qualified British volunteers (themselves primary school teachers)
- opportunities for RESC staff to work collaboratively and visit each other's centers for mutual professional input, guidance, and support

---

[5] The full official name is the Ministry of Human Resource Development, Education & Cultural Affairs, but "ministry" is convenient shorthand.

[6] These are the three major towns in an area that the Liberation Tigers of Tamil Eelam fought for as their homeland.

- an annual RESC conference where trainers offer sessions for their peers, based on their own successful primary teaching and training practice, and attend sessions with outside speakers

A pervasive focus throughout these development opportunities, sometimes explicit and sometimes implicit, has been strengthening RESC staff's capacity to teach at the primary level. As part of the follow-up to workshops, all staff have been required to make available in their centers special programs for children from local primary schools, involving, for example, such activities as songs and games, storytelling, and displays in English. These are staples of primary classrooms in many Western countries, but innovations for most primary English classrooms in Sri Lanka.

Teachers and Courses

With growing expertise in their primary-level ELT skills, RESC trainers were better able to provide relevant, practical training for teachers from primary schools in their catchment areas. These teachers, like the RESC trainers, had also been trained to teach English across all age ranges and generally found themselves ill equipped to deal with classroom realities at the primary level. The emphasis of their initial teacher training was largely theoretical, and when they were posted to schools they tended to fall back on the methods their own teachers had used, methods that were long outmoded in terms of present-day curriculum requirements. To redress this situation, project staff and RESC trainers decided in an early meeting on a series of 12 topics for in-service courses, which their experience indicated would provide a basic foundation in English as a foreign language (EFL) instruction in the primary classroom (see the later section titled "Training Materials"). Unlike the initial teacher training, the emphasis of these in-service courses was to be solidly practical. It could thus be said that the project's training courses aimed to improve upon perceived deficiencies in initial teacher training by providing teachers with the practical classroom skills and techniques to which they had so far not been exposed. The need for courses of this kind is perhaps best encapsulated in the words of one trainer, who said of his own experience of initial teacher training, "I think our training college teachers were not good models because we get knowledge from the books and we got theories explained in the classroom but we didn't see the models so we couldn't translate the knowledge into application skills."[7]

Each RESC decides on the exact program of courses to meet the constraints of its own specific regional situations. Teachers may apply to attend the courses when they have been advertised, with only two provisos: that they have their school principal's consent because courses take place during school time, and that they agree to attend all of the courses offered because the courses form an integrated whole. Neither the project nor the ministry set any targets in terms of numbers of teachers to be trained. However, as mentioned previously, statistics collected annually showed that every year approximately 6,000 teachers attended about 1,000 one-day courses. This is a considerable achievement given that teachers are not paid for attending the courses and are not reimbursed for travel expenses. It also speaks volumes about the quality

---

[7] This comment is taken from an in-depth interview that I conducted in late 2002 as part of ongoing doctoral research.

of the training offered by the RESCs. Teachers would not continue to come to courses if they did not feel they were gaining something of direct relevance to their everyday teaching lives.

Training Materials

The 12 topics for in-service courses were as follows: children learning languages; lesson planning; listening skills; spoken English; basic reading; basic writing; songs, rhymes, and games; class management; classroom language; vocabulary presentation; course book supplement use; and assessment. Again, there may be nothing surprising in the choice of topics, but their focus on the implementation of techniques and methods as well as the opportunity for real-life practice was a considerable innovation for in-service teacher training in Sri Lanka, where previous practice centered on strategies that were at best rational-empirical and often simply power coercive (Kennedy, 1987). Although I have said that the courses were very practical, practice was, of course, informed by theory, and all materials made explicit the links between theory and practice at appropriate junctures.

The materials were written in modular format by teams from the RESCs. Draft materials were used on a trial basis in RESCs and revised based on peer feedback as well as feedback from teachers who attended the first courses. All materials referred to course books in use in schools and promoted the activity-based, child-centered pedagogy required by the national curriculum. Input from non–Sri Lankan project staff came in the form of advice on training material formats, methodological choices in primary ELT, and final editing of the modules. There were, however, no project prescriptions regarding exact content of the training modules; this remained the preserve of the RESC staff members, based on their experience in Sri Lankan schools and their knowledge of the new national curriculum.

Support for Broader Educational Reform

PELP is not conducted in isolation from but in harmony with broader educational reform objectives. The in-service program has had a positive impact on one of the common problems associated with much in-service work: that training does not respond to immediate needs and, therefore, is negatively evaluated by teachers who see it as one more burden added to their busy schedules. However, the program does not simply act as an implementation agency for ministry pronouncements; it attempts to take into account the microrealities of teachers' working lives and to show how curriculum reforms can improve teaching and learning conditions for teachers as well as children in schools. In so doing, there is an attempt to adapt the educational reforms to classroom realities rather than, as is so common, ignore them (Torres, 1996).

◈ DISTINGUISHING FEATURES

A number of features, taken as a whole, make this in-service program distinctive. All of these features contribute to its success in terms of direct implementation of classroom behaviors advocated in the courses. As O'Sullivan (2001) notes, in-service programs are rarely evaluated in terms of classroom impact, but since its inception PELP has monitored the impact of its activities at the classroom level. Evaluation reports indicate year after year that teachers who have attended RESC courses exhibit classroom behaviors that are more child centered and activity based than those of teachers who have not attended the courses (Coleman, 2002). Not only that, but children taught by RESC-trained teachers consistently outperform children taught by teachers who are not RESC trained (Coleman, 2002).

The Immediate Practical Relevance of Training

I previously mentioned recipients' perceptions of initial teacher training in Sri Lanka as predominantly theoretical. I also indicated that project materials were strongly practical in focus. Evidence indicates that teachers in developing countries (like most teachers worldwide) place the most value on training that has immediate relevance to their classrooms (Hayes, 1997a, 2004), and this has certainly been the experience in Sri Lanka. One teacher who attended PELP courses commented, "They [RESC trainers] taught us many activities, which we can use in the classroom and they made us aware what teaching in a primary classroom is all about. So we understood something and we gained something from the program. This is my impression of the program. I think it is a success."[8]

Opportunities for Reflection on and Analysis of New and Existing Practice

It has long been clear that, irrespective of official pronouncements, it is teachers, not ministry officials, who decide which methodology will be used in their classrooms and thus determine the success or failure of educational reforms (Fullan, 1991). Nevertheless, education systems continue trying to bring about rapid change in teaching and learning behaviors through regular curriculum reforms, often without reference to existing classroom realities (Torres, 1996). Based on this notion, it is important for in-service programs such as PELP to work with existing classroom realities. If teachers are asked simply to replicate techniques and activities from an in-service course, it is likely that they will try things once and then discard them if not immediately successful. For teachers to appreciate fully the characteristics of a new curriculum and methodology, it is crucial that they be given opportunities to reflect on both new techniques and their current practice. If the new techniques can be demonstrated to improve practice, or are seen as a progression of existing practice, then there is a much greater chance of implementation being consistently pursued after the course. The RESC training modules encourage this reflection and analysis first by relating theory to practice. For example, in the listening skills module, before examining listening activities for the primary classroom, there are tasks whose objectives include gaining insights into the complex nature of listening and helping teachers understand what good listeners do. It can then be seen how activities promote the use of skills and strategies that are required for effective listening. The modules (e.g., in basic writing) also ask teachers at various times to demonstrate their own methods of teaching so that their practice can be related to model lessons presented by the trainers. In this way, new and existing practice can be analyzed and

---

[8] This comment was given in an interview conducted by one of the project coordinators at the National Institute of Education with teachers who had undergone the in-service training.

discussed and the effectiveness of various methods of teaching can be stimulated. Similarly in the assessment module, an early task objective is to have the opportunity to reflect on present assessment procedures prior to examining other appropriate ways of assessing teaching and learning for primary-age children. With tasks such as these, it is hoped that teachers can make sense of new techniques and incorporate them into their teaching-learning schema for daily use.

The Cyclical Nature of Training

This process of incorporation following reflection and analysis is assisted by the cyclical nature of the training program. All RESCs follow a day-release model of training with, generally, one training day per week over a 3-month period. Such a model enables teachers to experiment with the new classroom methods and activities that they have learned in their training. The model also gives teachers the opportunity in succeeding weeks to ask for clarification of or additional assistance with the previous week's topic area if they encountered any difficulties or issues they could not resolve. Thus, teachers receive support in the implementation process over an extended period, ameliorating the danger of lack of follow-up being associated with limited implementation (O'Sullivan, 2001).

Easy-to-Use Materials for Novice Trainers

Recognizing at the outset of the project that RESC trainers had no experience of task-based, experiential training, the project coordinators decided to develop in-service materials for teachers in a modular format, which provided considerable support to trainers as they began to come to terms with what was for most a radical departure in training styles. These materials were written in an easily accessible style with a little jargon, which was confined to key teaching terminology. The program began with general and module introductions with guidance on the necessary preparation. The format consisted of trainer's notes on the left-hand page and associated teachers' tasks on the right-hand page. This enabled trainers to relate clearly their instructions for tasks with the teachers' materials. The instructions were precise and gave suggested answers for teachers' tasks where relevant. All tasks had written objectives so that trainers and teachers alike could see the purpose of the activities in which they were engaged. However, none of these features precluded the scope for personalization and adaptation (see the next section), which was positively encouraged on courses for RESC trainers.

Opportunities for Reinterpretation of
Training Experience by Both Teachers and Trainers

Although all RESCs use a common bank of materials for their in-service courses and, as shown earlier, these materials have been developed in a format that provides a great deal of support for the novice trainer, this does not mean that the materials are prescriptive; indeed, far from it. There is no requirement that the modules always be used as they are. PELP recognizes that different local exigencies will result in common materials being modified to meet local needs. Also, as trainers develop confidence, they inevitably see the potential to reinterpret according to their own experience. As one trainer reported, we have worked and we have done what we want, not what others do. They [the training materials] give a task and the answers we give are according to our own experiences. It can suit our needs here. We take the teachers needs actually.

Similarly, as I noted earlier, teachers are the ones who ultimately decide which methodology to use in their classrooms. So, recognizing again that personalization of training experiences is a necessary and indeed welcome feature of any in-service training program, project evaluation involves evidence of common activity-based, child-centered teaching-learning behaviors in classrooms, but the precise, local application of these features varies from school to school and from teacher to teacher.

Collaborative Patterns of Professional Learning

In the training there has also been a strong concern to promote a collaborative pattern of professional learning between trainers and teachers, which is "embedded in the life and work" (Hargreaves, 2000, p. 165) of the centers and the schools that they serve, this being seen as the most effective model for professional development. The collaboration is evident in RESCs as staff work together to prepare courses, training materials, and programs for children. It is also noticeable between trainers and the teachers they work with when trainers are asked to do follow-up work with schools and when they work together on teacher initiatives—for example, initial reading programs.[9] From a wider perspective—both geographical and in terms of the network—collaboration is also evident between centers as trainers from different regions offer each other expertise in their specializations. Practical examples of this include trainers from the west coast assisting those from the northeast in evaluation and trainers from the central province working with others in the west on teaching aids and displays. And there is collaboration between teachers who have attended courses, which in themselves promote cooperative task-based learning, and who continue their relationship beyond the courses. It is hoped that a culture of self-initiated, self-sustaining continuing professional development will take root and prosper well beyond the lifetime of the project.

Ownership of Training Programs and Processes by Sri Lankan "Insiders"

From this study, I hope readers have gained a strong sense that there is very limited direction by foreign project staff and a far greater sense of Sri Lankan ownership of the training programs. Without such ownership by Sri Lankans, sustainability is unlikely, and the whole future of the in-service training programs postproject is under threat. The role of foreign "outsiders" has been one of guidance and support as the project has sought to instill an ethos of participatory development in all of its activities. That this has been successful can be seen in the comments given by one RESC staff member during an interview with one of the project coordinators:

> Personally if I tell about me, it's from the foreigners that I learnt how they get things done, how they go round and get the people to work. They have done

---

[9] Both Tamil and Sinhala use their own scripts, so learning to read and write in English requires additional skills on the part of the teacher.

that to us. They have really done that to us in a shrewd way. Ultimately we have done all the work. They have only guided us. And by that we have really been satisfied.

Working Within Established Structures

In development programs, criticism is sometimes directed toward projects that replicate existing structures rather than work within them. This approach leads to a situation in which, when foreign funding is withdrawn and reliance is placed on more restricted local resources, local staff members are unable to sustain the levels of activity generated by the well-funded project. Sustainability of activity is clearly a key issue and one that PELP has managed by ensuring that training programs are conducted through institutions (the RESCs) that predated the project and are the ministry's usual vehicle for in-service training for English language teachers. PELP has simply worked to strengthen the RESCs and their staff's capacity to plan and deliver effective in-service activities for teachers. This effort has largely been achieved through the staff development activities already discussed, although the project also helped to improve the RESCs' resource base with book and equipment purchases. Considerable time was also spent in meetings with ministry officials, developing contacts and winning increased support for the RESC network. A concrete indication of success in this area can be seen in the ministry's decision to quadruple the recurrent funding for RESCs during the project's lifetime. Officials at the highest levels speak highly of the contribution of the centers' in-service education, and a World Bank teacher education project in the ministry has praised the RESCs as models for development of in-service centers for other subjects.

Supporting National Educational Reform Programs

Another criticism of some foreign-funded development programs is that they do not work in harmony with national educational objectives. This has particularly been suggested of ELT programs, many of which have in the past attempted to introduce communicative language teaching approaches without analyzing whether such approaches are culturally appropriate within the host educational systems (for a discussion of relevant issues, see, e.g., Coleman, 1996; Holliday, 1994). It is common sense that innovations that are culturally at odds with the remainder of the education system are likely to experience failure once project support ends, a process that Holliday (1992), in an apt medical analogy, characterizes as tissue rejection. It should be clear from the preceding discussion that PELP has never been in this position. Educational reform in Sri Lanka has been initiated by the government's National Education Commission (1997) through its *Reforms in General Education,* and it is the curriculum specifications developed from this (see, e.g., Primary Education Planning Project, 2000) that PELP and RESC staff have had to follow when considering the content of training materials. In so doing, in-service training for primary ELT is guaranteed to work in harmony with all other reform processes, which, in turn, ensures as a bare minimum surface acceptance of the training content by administrators and teachers (deeper change at the classroom level is promoted by the training approaches discussed earlier).

Being Concerned With Evaluating Impact at the Classroom Level

O'Sullivan (2001) states that evaluation of INSET has long been problematic and has usually been concerned with course evaluation rather than evaluation of impact at the classroom level. In contrast, PELP has consistently focused on the impact on teachers and the children they teach. In annual impact assessment exercises, RESC staff members gather data from classroom observation and assessments of children's competence and confidence using standardized instruments developed with outside consultancy support. The large amount of data gathered is sent to a UK university for independent processing. The annual analyses have shown consistently, as noted before, that teachers who attend RESC courses exhibit classroom behaviors that are more child centered and activity based than those of teachers who do not attend these courses, and that children taught by RESC-trained teachers consistently outperform children taught by teachers who are not RESC trained. In addition, the more courses a teacher attends, the greater the chance that these patterns will occur (Coleman, 2002). These results confirm the value of the in-service courses delivered by the RESCs and their general approaches to training.

◈ PRACTICAL IDEAS

There is such a wealth of experience in PELP that deciding on a focus for practical ideas emanating from the project is far from easy. A number of products, including the *Primary English Teacher Training Modules,*[10] might offer useful models for readers working in similar contexts to adapt to their own circumstances. However, readers are most likely to be familiar with the pedagogical content of these materials, so instead I offer practical advice to those planning for or working on educational development projects. I confine my discussion to two or three instances of general advice for each group, the instances being linked across the groups. This advice might be valuable to readers working on in-service programs in any context (and for any subject); the major difference between Sri Lanka and many other contexts as far as in-service teacher development is concerned is probably one of levels of available financial and material resources, rather than fundamental differences in basic educational philosophy.

Project Planners

Acknowledge That Educational Change Is a Long-Term Process

When introducing an innovation into an educational system, a whole host of factors need to be taken into account, as Markee (1997) notes:

> Curricular innovation is a complex, multidimensional phenomenon. . . . It is a socially situated activity that is affected by ethical and systemic constraints, the personal characteristics of potential adopters, the attributes of innovations, and the strategies that are used to manage change in a particular context. (pp. 39–41)

---

[10] The *Primary English Teacher Training Modules* are published in-house by the project and are not available commercially. However, further information about them may be obtained from the director of the Department of English, National Institute of Education, Maharagama, Sri Lanka.

Development projects, perhaps influenced by the need to demonstrate that donor agency money is being well spent, may expect too much too soon and thus fail to achieve deep-seated change. PELP was fortunate to run for more than 6 years, providing time to address systemic constraints, to develop contextually appropriate innovations in training and relevant strategies to manage change, and to begin to have an impact on the characteristics of adopters. I therefore advise that any development project concerned with curricular innovation should last a minimum of 5 years.

Accept That Projects Need Realistic Objectives

Flowing from the previous point is a recognition that well-planned projects require realistic objectives for the available time and resources (both human and material). PELP's purpose was "to improve the quality of teaching in basic English skills in Sri Lankan primary schools" (Department for International Development, 2002, p. 1), but there were no specific targets set for this improvement, such as *an improvement of a minimum of 10% in children's scores on standardized tests for all four language skills.* Instead, the improvement was to be measured by a

> change in attitudes and skills of teachers of English in primary schools manifested in: participation in teacher development activities; local sharing of good classroom practice; application of new ideas in the classroom based on RESC courses and new materials; and receptivity towards the new curriculum for Grades 3 to 5 and ability to use new materials with confidence and skill. (Department for International Development, 2002, p. 9)

Of course, these indicators needed to be measured, and I have already discussed to a certain extent how that was done. The point I want to make here is simply that setting unobtainable targets for improvement in performance risks a project being labeled a failure when so many other worthwhile objectives are probably being achieved. I advise practitioners to avoid setting quantifiable performance targets when dealing with what is essentially human resource development. Instead, focus more on long-term attitude change and changes in classroom practice, measured as part of a supportive observation process.

Host Country Teachers, Trainers, and Ministry Officials Are Partners in Development

Educational staff members in the host country must be seen as partners in, not objects of, development. Project design should ensure that major decision making is in the hands of steering committees that include expatriate project staff but are headed by senior government officials. The host country's system and schoolchildren are affected by project activities, not the donor agency, so mechanisms are required to generate a sense of ownership from the outset. Steering committees need to meet regularly, and projects should report progress on a monthly basis to the host ministry as well as to their own funding organizations. Unless issues of confidentiality are involved—and these should be rare—the same report should be delivered to all stakeholders.

Project Implementers

Acknowledge That Change in Teacher Behavior Is a Long-Term Process

As Markee (1997) points out, curricular change centrally concerns people. Trying to bring about change in people's behavior involves a fundamental reorientation in individuals' thinking, their deepest schema regarding effective teaching and learning behaviors. This reorientation may involve a challenge to long-held beliefs, so strategies for change must allow scope for (re)examination of existing practice alongside innovations. These strategies are most likely to be normative-re-educative in nature (Kennedy, 1987), working at the deepest level of beliefs underlying behavior. If, as Fullan (1991) says, "educational change depends on what teachers do and think—it's as simple and complex as that" (p. 117), those of us who play a part in implementing educational development projects need to recognize not just that teachers are at the heart of reform processes, but also that changes in classroom behavior will take considerable time to take root. Project planners and implementers would be well advised not to expect too much too soon.

Allow Scope for Reinterpretation of Training Experiences

Related to the first point, project implementers must recognize that rigid adherence to prescribed ways of working, whether in the classroom or the training room, is not just impractical; it also denies practitioners the agency that lies at the heart of their professional sense of self. For both of these reasons, it must never be expected. Rather, I advise acknowledging that teachers and trainers reinterpret what they receive in courses in the light of their own prior experience, and that they adapt the unfamiliar to fit with existing schemas of the known, not implement innovations wholesale. Havelock and Huberman (cited in Bishop, 1986) offer some pertinent comments:

> It is important to understand that innovations are not adopted by people on the basis of the intrinsic value of the innovation, but rather on the basis of the adopter's perception of the changes they personally will be required to make. Those designing, administering and advising projects do not generally have to make very many changes themselves. Their task remains the same. It is others who will have to modify their behaviors and very often to modify them rapidly in fairly significant ways, and with little previous or even gradual preparation. (p. 5)

Practitioners should be wary of thinking that they know what is best for other teachers. Practitioners should also be understanding when expected changes do not materialize in classrooms. After all, if strategies that promote reflection on existing and new practice are not adopted, it could be that the teachers have decided that their existing practice is preferable to a proposed innovation. Reexamining and deciding to continue with existing practice is just as valid an option as modifying practice—even though I doubt many ministry officials would agree.

Value Host Country Expertise

Staff members of a development project are often deemed experts by their host country counterparts, and there may be expectations that these experts have all the solutions to education problems in the host country. This is far from the case.

Outsiders do have a range of expertise that will, of course, be valuable when adapted to the local context, but the adaptation can only be done by those with in-depth knowledge of that context—insiders rather than outsiders. Insiders also have their own areas of professional expertise beyond contextual knowledge, and an effective project allows for genuinely collegial modes of working. Insiders and outsiders should be engaged in learning from each other. This mutual enrichment has the potential to contribute so powerfully to the innovation process and, in so doing, to enhance its chances of success.

◈ CONCLUSION

Systemic education reform is a complex process. It is difficult in a relatively brief chapter such as this to do justice to the part played by PELP in supporting effective in-service teacher training/development through the RESCs, but I hope I have given some flavor of the project, its activities, its ways of working, and its achievements. Writing one year after the official end of the project, I note that the future lies wholly in the hands of Sri Lankan teachers, trainers, and ministry officials. These are safe hands. Although as with any system there will be areas of difficulty and tension, the broad momentum of in-service training in the RESC network continues. On a trip to Sri Lanka in March 2004, I visited a RESC on short notice and was delighted to see a busy center full of schoolchildren who had been brought by their teacher for a special program, and trainers who were planning a full program of courses. Long may they continue to flourish.

◈ CONTRIBUTOR

David Hayes is a freelance consultant for the Asian Development Bank, British Council, RAND Corporation, and World Bank. His doctoral study at the University of Birmingham, in England, focuses on the lives and careers of nonnative-speaking teachers of English in Sri Lanka and Thailand. He has managed innovation in educational projects in Sri Lanka, Thailand, Vietnam, Cyprus, Malaysia, and Nigeria, and he is committed to work that enhances educational opportunities for disadvantaged people in developing countries. His most recent book-length publication is the edited volume *Trainer Development: Principles and Practice From Language Teacher Training*.

CHAPTER 11

The Pyramid Scheme: Implementing Activity-Based Communicative Language Teaching and Supervision With Primary Teacher Educators in Egypt

Mary Lou McCloskey, Linda New Levine, Barbara Thornton, and Zeinab El Naggar

◈ INTRODUCTION

Primary English language education in Egypt was quickly implemented in autumn 1994. Previously, English had been taught beginning in the sixth year. As of 1994, it began in the fourth year of primary school. Few primary teachers had received any training for their new roles as English language educators, so, as has happened in such situations elsewhere in the world, teachers of other subjects were drafted to fill in. These teachers had varying amounts of competence in English and little or no education in English language methodology.

In Egypt, subject area teachers in schools are closely supervised by representatives from the Ministry of Education (MoE). English language supervisors with experience in secondary schools were assigned to help these new primary English teachers. However, the supervisors also had little knowledge or understanding of an appropriate methodology of teaching English to young learners. Furthermore, although their title had been changed from "inspector" to "supervisor" in 1986 by Ministerial Decree no. 64, many of them had limited awareness of their advisory role as supervisors, viewing themselves instead in an evaluative role as inspectors.

We have been working since 1998 on a primary English language teacher education project at the Integrated Language Teaching Program II (IELP-II) in Cairo. One of us has been a member of the Egyptian advisory board to IELP-II, a project participant, a consultant, and an editor of the publication *Spotlight on Primary English Education Resources* (SPEER; El Naggar, Fadel, Hanaa, McCloskey, & Thornton, 2002). The rest of us have served as consultants in the various training and writing stages of the project. One of us served as editor of SPEER, and two of us served as developmental editors. All of us coauthored chapters of the final book, along with Egyptian educators.

This project was funded by the United States Agency for International Development (USAID) and managed by two nonprofit agencies in Washington, DC:

Academy for Educational Development (AED) and America-Mideast Educational and Training Services, Inc. (AMIDEAST). A major goal of the project was to assist teacher educators from the faculties of education (FoE; equivalent to university schools of education or departments of education in other systems) and the MoE in improving primary English language education in Egypt. Our primary role in the project was to assist these teacher educators in developing

- their knowledge of communicative-based methodologies for young learners

- their skills in transferring this knowledge to teachers and student teachers in the classroom

- their attitudes toward both the use of communicative methodologies for primary education and their own roles in supporting and guiding teachers

An additional goal for the project was to facilitate collaboration among faculty and ministry teacher educators. Previously, there had been few opportunities for these two groups to work with one another in Egypt. Frequently, members of each group placed responsibility on the other for problems in Egyptian education. Our goal was to have members of these two groups, the MoE and the FoE, work together and come to appreciate and take advantage of one another's expertise.

Although IELP-II involved working directly with the ministry and faculties in improving the English language skills of primary teachers, the participants' intensive work in an English language environment also furthered this effort, especially for supervisors who had less background in English. We witnessed and nourished this increased participation and fluency as the series progressed; thus English language development at these higher levels became an unintended consequence of our work as well.

A pyramid scheme is usually thought of as a scam operation in which many people at the bottom pay money to people at the top in the hopes of making more money, although it is usually only those at the top who gain. We like to think of this project as a reverse pyramid scheme because the learning and experience of those at the top helped them spread knowledge and expertise throughout the entire pyramid.

❧ CONTEXT

In Egypt, English is the main foreign language taught in schools, and there are three basic types of schools. In the public or government school, English is taught only as a school subject and is offered in three 40-minute classes per week in primary (equivalent to elementary, Grades 1–5), five 45-minute classes per week in preparatory (equivalent to junior high, Grades 6–8), and six 50-minute classes per week in secondary (equivalent to senior high, Grades 9–11).

Experimental language schools were established by the MoE in 1978, after realizing that English had become a language for international communication and parents were interested in providing their children with quality education that they considered lacking in public schools. These schools were modeled after private language schools in the use of English as a medium of instruction. However, unlike private language schools, the experimental language schools suffer from overcrowded classrooms and unqualified teachers. These schools are semiprivate, with tuition fees that most middle-class Egyptian parents can afford.

In private language schools, English is taught both as a school subject and as a medium of instruction from kindergarten through the end of third-year secondary. These schools usually attract qualified teachers with good English language ability and have adequate resources, interested parents, and a motivated student body. There are also a few immersion language schools in other languages, including French and German, although most use English.

Our project was primarily focused on the needs of Egyptian teacher educators from the MoE and FoE who were training primary teachers in the Egyptian government schools. We also worked with other groups, however, and all teacher educators now have the opportunity to use the products of the project.

Like many other developing countries, Egypt faces a continuous increase in the student population, coupled with an acute shortage of teachers in all fields, particularly English. To overcome this problem, graduates of majors other than English are recruited to teach English with little or no training in either the language or methodology. With the introduction of English at the upper elementary (fourth grade) level in 1994–1995, the situation was further aggravated. MoE statistics reveal that of 11,270 teachers engaged in primary education at the beginning of this period, only 823 (7%) were specialists (i.e., had teaching degrees in English; Ministry of Education, Egypt, 1995). In September 2003, the age at which English was introduced was lowered even further to Primary 1, meaning that issues of teacher preparation were even more acute. However, the problems had begun 10 years before. In 1993, the Conference on the Development of Primary Education Curricula was held in Cairo. Recommendation 10 reads, "introducing the teaching of English or other foreign languages starting from grade 4 of the primary school . . . should be started at the full-day schools, provided that qualified language teachers are available" (Z. El Naggar, personal communication, April 2002).

The MoE formed a committee of Egyptian English language teaching (ELT) experts to draw up the necessary curriculum document that would guide the selection or writing of a new primary EFL textbook. There was an understanding that the English curriculum would be piloted at certain full-day schools before the full introduction of the program. However, a ministerial decree issued in June 1994 stipulated that English was to be taught to all fourth graders in the country (except for 200 schools that would teach French).

Hence, that academic year brought chaos as all schools rushed to fulfill this requirement. There were no qualified English language primary teachers available, so primary teachers of other subjects (some not even university graduates) were asked to teach English in their schools. English language supervisors at other levels were assigned supervisory roles at the primary level, regardless of their lack of training in English education or experience teaching English to young learners.

Over the next few years, some training was carried out, but in a fragmented and uncoordinated way. Meanwhile, teachers who spoke little English and who had no knowledge of the methodology of teaching English to young learners were still being appointed. Furthermore, they were being managed by overstretched supervisors who had little knowledge of young learners' needs and were therefore not in a position to offer support and guidance.

Meanwhile, FoE were becoming aware of the scale of the problem. When English was introduced at the primary stage, faculties were already preparing teachers to teach at the preparatory and secondary levels. No programs to prepare primary school teachers were available. Some departments of primary education in English were hurriedly set up, but they varied in organization of the courses, intensity, quality, and curricula offered. For example, at Ain Shams University, student teachers followed a 4-year program in primary education, specializing in English from the start. Twenty miles away, at Helwan University, student teachers also followed a 4-year program that qualified them to teach social sciences and English. In Mansoura, 90 miles away, the program was also 4 years long, but student teachers spent the first 2 years studying such subjects as curriculum design, methodology, and psychology, all in Arabic, without following any courses in English. It was not until the third year that teachers in training at Mansoura University began their English-related studies.

The situation was further exacerbated by the fact that lecturers in many of the FoE had little knowledge of the methodology of teaching English to young learners and would frequently use other lectures they had given on general issues of methodology in their courses for primary preservice teachers. It can therefore be understood that although primary teachers were being qualified, the qualification they received was far from uniform. This led to a general feeling of dissatisfaction at all levels within the MoE.

In 1997, the U.S. government funded IELP-II, which would be managed by AED and AMIDEAST. Leaders of this project, in consultation with key Egyptian educators, quickly identified primary education as an area of great need. They realized that for many teachers in Egypt, supervisors are the main, if not only, source of professional development, and it would be unrealistic to target teachers without targeting supervisors. FoE had little expertise in primary English language education, and their knowledge and skills needed to be upgraded as well. Two working groups of Egyptian ELT specialists were formed: one concerned with methodology, the other with supervision. They presented an overview of the current situation to the IELP-II program and established the initial objectives of the primary education program.

◈ DESCRIPTION

Stage 1. Primary English Language Institutes

We led three institutes (summer 1998, winter 1999, and autumn 1999) to develop the knowledge and skills of a selected group of teacher educators from FoE who taught and supervised university students studying primary education.

The Summer Institute (1998)

Approximately 50 junior and senior staff from FoE and 50 primary teacher supervisors from the MoE attended the 1998 Summer Institute. The participants represented various areas of upper and lower Egypt and differed widely in their content knowledge and their ability to understand and speak English. The summer institute ran for 5 consecutive days each, in two locations. The institutes engaged participants in 7 instructional hours each in two topics: activity-based communicative methodology for primary students (ABC methodology) and supervisory skills for primary educators. The objectives were determined by the joint committee of FoE and MoE methodologists and supervisors, and included the following:

Activity-Based Communicative Methodology
- Identify and use effective communicative language teaching techniques for young language learners.
- Discuss ways of dealing with aspects of classroom management in Egyptian primary classes, such as overcrowded classrooms, unmotivated learners, discipline problems.
- Identify and produce simple teaching aids that would attract pupils' attention and increase their interest in learning.
- Identify and describe specific strategies and styles that children use in learning a new language.
- Identify testing techniques to be used with young children.
- Present a one-page action plan about topics raised during the workshop or new issues that need resolving through action research.

Supervision and Evaluation of Primary Language Teachers
- Identify the features of nonjudgmental supervision.
- Discuss ways for supervisors to balance their evaluation and development roles.
- Select from a range of observation tools according to the purposes of the observation and the needs of the teacher.
- Demonstrate an understanding of the three-phase model of supervision (preconference, observation, and postconference) and how this could be used in an Egyptian context.

An added goal was that supervisors from ministries and faculties be brought into closer working relationships. An additional objective, therefore, was that MoE supervisors and FoE members work toward consensus regarding elements of good teaching practice.

The reality of the training situation led to rapid on-site revision and adaptation of the planned program. As consultants, we had developed the training modules without access to specific information about the knowledge and skills of the participants. Two of us had not been to Egypt before and had limited knowledge of the school system. Almost immediately, workshop objectives were modified at the two training sites to accommodate the participants' needs. For example, at one site, those of us conducting the ABC methodology workshops found that the six objectives identified by the FoE working group could not be addressed equally because of the participants' level of language proficiency and background knowledge of the content. So we focused instead on two objectives: identifying and using communicative language techniques for young learners and identifying and producing simple teaching aids for young learners.

During the first week of training, language issues became so acute that those of us who were native-English-speaking consultants occasionally requested the help of Egyptian colleagues to translate information into Arabic for some participants. An additional issue involved the British and U.S. accents of the consultants. Many of the participants had never spoken to native speakers of English and were confused by the differing pronunciations. As a result, we determined that as we worked toward the content goals of the institute we would focus on development of participants' English language skills as well.

The supervisory workshop objectives were similarly modified. For example, we provided optional readings and varied activities to accommodate differences in language and content knowledge.

A major goal of the IELP-II program and thus of the institute was the notion of sustainability. Sustainability required that all content learned in the institutes could be put to use in the Egyptian context, that the Egyptian participants could sustain the skills they developed, and that they could maintain whatever changes or improvements were made beyond the intervention. As part of this effort, we introduced the concept of action plans on the first day of the summer institute and worked with participants throughout the institute to develop specific action plans relative to the course content and the needs of their own situations.

Each participant developed an action plan during the workshop to implement an aspect of what he or she had learned. We encouraged participants to work with partners and, in particular, promoted MoE participants pairing up with FoE colleagues. The action plan concept was a new one for most of them, and they struggled with it, reluctant to commit to a long-term project with nebulous outcomes. We devoted more than 6 hours of the workshop to the development of action plans, also not totally confident that the effort would be worth the time. Action plans were to include the following sections: Project Topic, Project Goal, Project Plan to Achieve Goal, Resources Needed, Trial and Evaluation, and Outcome/ Conclusions.

By the end of each week's workshop, participants submitted copies of their plans to us, and we told them we would contact them within the next 4 months to check on the progress of the plans. Participants were expected to summarize their action plans at the 1999 Winter Institute in January–February.

Participant involvement and satisfaction were high at both training sites of the 1998 Summer Institute. Participants willingly engaged in the training activities, which were based on the objectives of the course. Activities included cooperative learning; learning English through songs, chants, and action routines for young learners; group discussions; creation of teaching aids; and evening social events and informal tea breaks. Attendance during the 5 days was more than 90% at both sites. Participants expressed eagerness to return for the winter institute.

The Winter Institute (1999)

The 1999 Winter Institute again combined FoE and MoE educators at two different sites for 5 days of training. Although the intention was for the participants of the summer institute to attend this winter follow-up, personal and professional obligations made this difficult for some, and a number of new participants took the place of absent trainees. Nevertheless, attendance at both sites was good, with a high proportion of returning faculty and supervisors among the 50 participants at each site.

The winter institute again provided participants with opportunities to develop knowledge and skills in relation to ABC methodology and supervision of primary educators. The 1998 Summer Institute had focused on oral language development; the 1999 Winter Institute moved toward methodology for developing reading and writing in primary English. Objectives for the second institute's ABC methodology workshop included

- teaching to specific styles and strategies of young learners

- creating a learning aid to assist learners with reading development

- describing the steps of a shared reading activity

- describing the steps in a language experience approach activity

- planning a reading lesson following the into-through-beyond model (i.e., teaching strategies and activities before, during, and following the reading selection)

Participants in the supervision workshop sessions differed widely in level of expertise and experience. As presenters, we addressed these differences by developing core issues in depth, then briefly visiting advanced topics within the sessions and providing optional readings and materials for those who wished to pursue the issues further. Core topics of these sessions included teacher observation, oral and written feedback to teachers, and varied approaches to teacher assessment.

During the workshops, many supervisors agreed that a developmental approach to supervision was helpful. Yet in role-play situations, most reverted to their traditional fault-finding roles as inspectors. Thus, more emphasis than planned was placed on actually practicing developmental supervision skills, not just talking about them. The action planning process also helped participants focus on more constructive approaches to supervision in a real context.

Participants had developed action plans at the 1998 Summer Institute, and some had carried out their plans before the 1999 Winter Institute. We asked those who had carried out their plans to present them during the first 2 days of the institute. A number of plans had been implemented well, and presentations indicated a thorough understanding of the content of the summer institute. However, it was apparent that a significant percentage of participants still had a weak understanding of exactly what was involved in action planning. As a result, we spent time going through the stages of the action planning process in more detail. We also expected returnee participants to write and present a revised or second action plan, improving or extending what they had previously sought to implement. New participants wrote a first plan. All plans were to be presented at the 1999 Autumn Institute. A popular feature of the winter institute was "office hours." After the training day, those of us who were presenters were available in a workshop space during evening hours so that participants could discuss their action plans. Many took advantage of, and appreciated, this mentoring opportunity. Many extended the range of the mentoring by discussing education plans, thesis proposals, and other academic works.

The Autumn Institute (1999)

The 1999 Autumn Institute was held as a follow-up to the 1998 Summer Institute and 1999 Winter Institute. This time, an Egyptian consultant was added to the international team. The institute was held in two 2-day sessions in Cairo, with 63 attendees (40 from MoE and 23 from FoE) at the two sites. The goals were to revisit what was learned during the previous institutes, develop presentation skills and share the results of participants' action plans, and develop ideas and plan for the next stage of the project—materials development.

Participants arrived at the autumn institute at staggered intervals due to travel delays. So we set up a game to review the material covered during the first two institutes: The Great SIWI (Summer Institute/Winter Institute) Remembered Game. The game was popular, and participants took home a game board (which could be adapted for teaching any language put onto game cards) as another item in the methodological "bag of tricks" from the institutes. Participants also summarized the knowledge, skills, and attitudes that they learned during the first two institutes; participated in demonstrations on how to present an action plan (a very bad example was included with humorous results); and prepared visual aids to present their action plans. Office hours were again held in the evening to provide participants with support in their preparations.

On the second day of the institute, all participants presented their action plans, a number of which had been developed in ministry-faculty groups or pairs. Participants, those of us serving as consultants, IELP-II staff, and other visitors completed evaluation instruments to provide the participants and IELP-II with feedback on the action plan presentations. The high percentage of completion of the action plans at this workshop and the quality of the projects showed great growth and depth of learning through the institute process. Some of the most important accomplishments of the institutes resulted from the development of action plans:

- One participant wrote a training manual based on ABC methodology for primary learners.

- One began research for her master's degree on cooperative learning.

- Two wrote a joint paper detailing the positive outcomes of implementing their action plan.

- Two evaluated their project using the three-level model of supervision.

- A number of participants began communicating with each other and with us by e-mail.

Figure 1 shows participant Abdel Gayed explaining his action plan.

After the presentations, participants spent time brainstorming and offering suggestions for the next phase of the project—materials development. Participants asked for a useful and usable set of resource materials for primary teacher educators in Egypt that would last beyond the lifetime of the IELP-II project. They suggested a number of topics for inclusion in methodology and supervision, and many completed forms to state their interest in being part of the materials writing team.

Participants at all three institutes especially loved singing, and we found it to be an excellent community builder as well as a rich tool for language development and teacher education. We incorporated many songs appropriate for English language learning into the institutes and often wrote new lyrics to familiar tunes to make teaching points or to celebrate our learning community. We included song sheets in the handout packets for all three institutes and, at the request of participants, sent out an audiotape we made with a volunteer IELP-II staff member, in which we sang the songs and told the stories shared at the winter institute. At the autumn institute, at the request of participants, we offered additional songs for English language

FIGURE 1. Abdel Gayed and His Action Plan

teaching. Then the participants wrote new lyrics to summarize what they had learned and to celebrate the end of the institute.

Evidence from the action plans and from the autumn institute evaluation instruments indicated that the goals for the institute series were being achieved. Ministry and faculty were collaborating on action plans, carefully listening to and learning from one another's presentations, and even choosing to sit together. Participants were putting the institute content to use; they had tried new checklists and assessment tools; had implemented new ABC methodologies with their teachers and student teachers; had brought in photos, artifacts, and assessment tools to show what they had done; and were learning to give one another supportive feedback on change implementation.

Participants were also disseminating the knowledge they had gained in a wider arena. Some action plans became the basis for master's theses, some were presented at EgypTesol conferences in 1999 and 2000, several were presented at the international TESOL convention in 2000 and 2001, and still others were presented at IELP-II's Returnee Conferences in spring 2000 and 2001. Another accomplishment was the positive feeling about the institutes. Evaluations from participants at all institutes revealed high marks on both the content and the process. Participants at the autumn institute were delighted to greet old friends from previous institutes on the first day—clear evidence that a network among MoE and FoE was in operation.

Stage 2. Materials Development Institutes

The response to the training received during the first three seasonal institutes far exceeded expectations. There was a consensus among participants that the new knowledge and skills acquired should be disseminated as widely as possible. They requested better instructional materials for teachers and teacher educators— materials geared specifically toward the Egyptian context that also provided an overview of best practices in teaching young learners. It was envisaged that these materials could be used in initial teacher preparation programs and could also form the basis of in-service training.

Both the IELP-II staff and we agreed that the Egyptian participants were the experts in what did and did not work in their own context and thus would be the most appropriate writers of any materials produced for this project. With input from themselves and us, IELP-II participants decided to help develop a resource book to

- inform professionals on primary English education
- provide opportunities for professional development
- keep professionals abreast of new developments in the field
- support supervisors and teacher educators in educating pre- and in-service teachers

In the interest of sustainability, we asked participants to volunteer their time to help develop the materials. Although they received a per diem to attend the materials development institutes, participants received no remuneration for the writing they did on their own time. We hoped that this volunteer experience might lead them to volunteer in the future to work on other educational projects in Egypt, even after the completion of IELP-II.

The participants had widely varying writing abilities. Some were high-level university professors who had previously published academic papers (though not necessarily resource books for teachers); others were junior faculty who had never published. The MoE supervisors had a wealth of practical experience of what did and did not work in an Egyptian primary classroom, but almost no experience writing in English. The university professors frequently had good written English, but most had no firsthand experience teaching young children.

At this point, four Egyptian leaders (three senior faculty members from universities and one retired counselor of English from the MoE) were invited to join the consultants from the United States and the United Kingdom to form the editorial board for the publication project. They named it Spotlight on Primary English Education Resources (SPEER) and began to share leadership roles in planning for the product and developing and leading the materials development institutes.

In winter 2000, the one-week Materials Development Institute I (MDI-I) was conducted. The materials development institutes were designed to help the volunteer writers develop skills and conduct research for writing and revising chapters on supervision and methodology topics, which they had studied and practiced in the primary English language institutes. Our aim was that, by the end of the institute, writers should be able to

- work effectively together
- determine criteria of an effective product

- understand procedures and ground rules for the materials development process, including
  — understanding roles and responsibilities of all those involved
  — agreeing on topics and features to be included
  — locating Internet resources for the project
  — accessing information on assigned topics
  — researching and writing texts
  — referencing sources
  — working with peers to give one another feedback
  — using, revising, and editing checklists

At MDI-I, participants developed and worked with editors and consultants to finalize a core list of 27 chapters. Writers were assigned to various topics according to their interests and experience. Because of the differing abilities and experiences of participants from the two core groups, ministry participants were often paired with faculty members, and the two served as reviewers of one another's writing.

The materials development institutes dealt with topics such as planning and outlining chapters, researching topics, and writing clearly and concisely. A particular challenge arose with regard to documenting sources. Copyright policies and proper documentation of sources are not always fully understood by all academics in Egypt. After a morning spent talking about plagiarism, one participant asked if it was acceptable to copy and submit a chapter from a book as long as he did not substitute his name for that of the author!

Another difficulty involved participants' access to the resources required to research their topics once they returned home. Books in Egypt are prohibitively expensive, and libraries are not always well stocked. As much as possible, we lent our own copies of books and tried to arrange for key extracts to be photocopied.

We had recommended that participants receive technological training before the MDI-I so that they could create electronic manuscripts, which would ease the editing and publication of the text. Timing made this impossible, but IELP-II agreed to reimburse participants for training in their own cities or for having the documents typed and put on a disk. We began to receive drafts of chapters both electronically and in hard copy, but it was clear that some of the writers were struggling to find up-to-date resources on which to base their chapters and did not feel comfortable drafting materials at this level.

As a result, the Materials Development Institute II (MDI-II) was held later in 2000. The aim of this institute was very practical: to push all chapters along toward a finished version. We invited a small number of additional writers from universities to help writers who were having particular difficulty drafting their chapters.

MDI-II was held at a facility that had a computer lab. The writers spent half of their time developing computer skills and the other half perfecting the skills of drafting and redrafting. During the computer sessions, all participants were taught how to use e-mail and the Internet to find resources for their chapters. For many, this was a particular highlight of the institute. One participant e-mailed an academic from the United States to ask her permission to use part of her work. He was delighted to receive a reply within the space of a few hours giving permission and offering encouragement. This was his first experience using e-mail!

A significant proportion of noncomputer time was spent working on individual chapters in pairs and small groups, and some writers managed to achieve two or more redrafts of their work during this time.

One challenge did occur, however, with some new members of the group from the universities. Although they were invaluable in that they possessed high-level writing abilities, their presence altered the dynamics of the institute because they tended to be extremely conscious of their own status as faculty members and on some occasions looked down on the writing ability of participants from the ministry.

A summative evaluation at the end of MDI-II nonetheless confirmed our view that the materials development process had been overwhelmingly positive for the vast majority of participants. The success occurred not only at the personal level, with many individuals reporting an increase in skills as well as self-confidence, but also at a wider institutional level, with a new cadre of educators who, having been through the materials development process, would be capable of contributing to other similar projects in the future.

Stage 3. Development of SPEER

We began to receive drafts of chapters shortly after MDI-II, although some senior faculty members had difficulty sticking to the deadline because of other work pressures. A mark of the success of the computer training was that the chapters actually arrived in electronic form, either on disk or by e-mail. However, they did vary in quality, and it was at this stage that the editorial board's work began in earnest.

Our first task was to review the chapters we had received and try to assess their usefulness and editing needs. We found that

- there was overlap among some chapters

- more than one chapter did not focus on the assigned topic

- some writers had included extracts from published sources without giving due credit

- a number of writers had not followed the guidelines we had set regarding required components (e.g., including a rationale and an understanding check)

The editorial board and the consultants worked to revise the chapters into publishable and useful form, while keeping the writers' voices intact.

Stage 4. Piloting and Field Testing

We were aware throughout the writing process that many aid-funded projects had similarly produced materials that failed to be used after the end of the project (Bishop, 1986). Therefore, we felt it was crucial to validate the usefulness of the SPEER materials in the Egyptian context—to know that the techniques advocated were actually usable by the average teacher in the average Egyptian school. We determined the need for piloting (FoE and MoE supervisors putting the SPEER supervisory practices into action) and field testing (pre- and in-service teachers putting the methodology practices into action in the classroom). To prepare individuals for these roles, we decided to hold a field testers' and piloters' workshop in winter 2001.

The planning and delivery of the workshop and the field testing and piloting that followed were key parts of this effort toward sustainability, toward ensuring that the SPEER techniques were practical in Egypt and would actually be used by Egyptian teachers in more than one classroom.

Piloters' and Field Testers' Workshop (2001)

In January 2001, 10 MoE supervisors and 9 FoE members attended the piloters' and field testers' workshop. These participants were not materials writers for SPEER, although some had attended one or more of the institutes. Each faculty member brought two student teachers to the workshop; each ministry supervisor brought two teachers, one a novice and the other more experienced. Care was thus taken in the sampling to ensure a balance of respondents in terms of geographical distribution and teaching experience as well as specialist/nonspecialist and ministry/faculty designations.

During the workshop, all participants received training in the basic concepts of child development and supervision and in the procedures for piloting and field testing. Then smaller groups received training in some of the supervisory and methodological techniques included in SPEER so that each participant became familiar with four types of techniques. From those four, participants selected specific topics of focus for their piloting or field testing, and they returned to their settings to try out the new ideas.

Data collection on piloting and field testing. Data on the piloting and field testing were collected in the following ways:

- Teachers filled out questionnaires on a technique they had tried, making sure to include details about how easy the technique had been to implement, whether they had to adapt it, and the reaction of the children in their class.

- Supervisors filled out questionnaires on supervisory techniques they had tried.

- Supervisors also completed questionnaires on field-tested lessons they had observed.

- Teachers and supervisors wrote short paragraphs (vignettes) on their own personal experience of implementing a technique (see Figure 2 for an example).

- Some participants received follow-up telephone interviews to probe further into the responses they gave. During these interviews, many of the field testers described the reactions of the other teachers in the schools and asked for additional copies of the materials.

Furthermore, both to have authentic artifacts to include in the SPEER guide and to ensure that the techniques had actually been implemented, we asked field testers and

---

Creating and Using Low-Tech Teaching Aids for Teaching English
pocket charts, word family strips, making books, word-cards and sentence cards
Sherine Wanis Wahba, Field Tester

Thank you for giving me a chance to know more about teaching English in primary school. I used almost all the low-tech aids which we had learned before [pocket charts, word family strip, making books, word-cards and sentence cards] in my classrooms. These aids helped me most of the time in teaching songs, shared reading new words, structures, and language functions.

Using a pocket chart was the most useful aid because it helped me many times in teaching songs, shared reading, new words and structures. It also was a good aid for pupils; they found it fun. I can say it's a wonderful thing for student to see the whole lesson in front of their eyes instead of showing cards one by one then put them on the table. That helped my pupils to fully understand the lesson.

I used the word family strip technique with 4th graders and also I used it after new words in order to make a connection between words.

When I used it with 5th graders, I found some difficulties because there were more than ten words ending with the same letters. But I tried to divide them into groups in order to make it easier.

Making Books: It was a good one, but I found difficulty in putting it in a suitable place where the whole class could see it (my class had fifty students). I was happy because my pupils saw it as fun and liked it.

Also **word cards** and **sentence cards** were helpful when I used them with pocket charts especially in teaching songs and shared reading.

In all lessons when I used these learning aids, students were pleased and they were racing to use these aids in class, even they asked me "How can we make one!" I am so satisfied with the results of student's understanding and I'll use them as much as I could.

FIGURE 2. Field Test Report

piloters to provide artifacts to illustrate what they had done. We were pleased and delighted to receive more than 170 artifacts in response, including more than 50 photographs of children practicing communicative techniques, many samples of actual student work, and copies of materials that teachers had developed or used.

This stage of the project was invaluable in a number of ways. It enabled us as consultants to fine-tune the content of the book, it widened the ownership base of the book, and it gave validity to the contents—that these techniques were both useful and usable in Egypt.

Dissemination. In 2002, the SPEER guide (El Naggar et al., 2002) was published by IELP-II through the Academy for Educational Development. It has since been widely disseminated in Egypt and beyond. The guide is also available online (see Ministry of Education, Egypt, 2003a), and permission is given to reproduce materials for educational purposes. A total of 4,800 copies of the book have been produced in four printings, and it is in great demand. Since publication, chapters of the text have been used in faculties throughout Egypt as course readings, and workshops have been held in various parts of the country to introduce its contents to primary teachers.

From 2000 to 2003, participants from the FoE and MoE carried out the STEPS project to develop standards for newly qualified teachers in Egypt (McCloskey et al., 2003). This project was a collaboration between IELP-II and the Center for the Development of English Language Teaching, a national education center based at Ain Shams University in Cairo. Many participants in this project had participated in the training leading up to SPEER, written chapters in the SPEER book, or both, and the SPEER work did much to inform the standards project.

In 2003, a new Primary 1 textbook was developed in anticipation of the introduction of English language instruction at the Primary 1 (6-year-old) level (Ministry of Education, Egypt, 2003b). The SPEER program laid the foundation not only for curriculum developers who worked on the program materials, but also for the training of the teacher trainers who prepared Year 1 English teachers to use the materials. The SPEER book itself was used extensively in these sessions, and 10 of the 28 chapters were copied for distribution as part of the training of the 8,000 newly hired primary English teachers.

Many editors and participants who worked on the SPEER project have presented on the project at conferences throughout the world, including the EgypTesol conference, the annual Cairo Conference for Returnee Participants held by IELP-II each spring (e.g., Thornton, Burch, & McCloskey, 1999), the TESOL convention in the United States (El Naggar, Fadel, Hanna, McCloskey, & Thornton, 2001; McCloskey, 2003), a regional TESOL conference in Jordan and other conferences in the region (Thornton, 2001), TESOL Arabia (El Naggar, 2004; McCloskey, 2004), and many others. Presentations at these events have led to wider use of SPEER in many countries other than Egypt.

◈ DISTINGUISHING FEATURES

A number of distinctive features contributed to the success of the IELP-II project.

Local Ownership

Many projects of this nature claim local ownership. SPEER is not only Egyptian owned, but it also was Egyptian conceived, planned, and executed. Egyptians were key decision makers at all stages in the process, and as consultants, we did our planning according to Egyptian goals, yet reacting to others' needs as they emerged.

Cultural Relevance

Communicative methodologies are popular in Western classrooms, but some argue that they do not easily transport to large classes in countrywide educational systems (Holliday, 1996). The constant eye on usefulness of the techniques was a key element throughout this project to ensure that the techniques were adapted for the Egyptian system and could be used in Egyptian classrooms.

Innovative Methodologies

The adapted methodologies are still very much activity based and communicative in nature. Egyptian educators report witnessing changes in the attitudes of teachers who had previously been very satisfied with frontal teaching. Teachers who said pair work was difficult in Egyptian classrooms are now comfortably using various cooperative learning structures. Teachers who said they could not teach because their classes were poorly resourced have made their own pocket charts (in one case out of old fertilizer bags) and other low-tech aids (Zohry, 2002).

Integration of Technology

Participants were exposed to the power of new technologies. They experienced how a single computer can be successfully used to present new information, to collect data from participants, and to search for information. They all received some exposure to the Internet and understood the usefulness of this tool for finding out about new techniques and the state of the art in communicative methodologies.

Experiential and Active Learning

Throughout the training, those of us working as consultants in each activity modeled the methodologies we were promoting, and participants were active in the learning process. They had opportunities to learn through a variety of different modalities and through actually participating in activities, which could then be implemented in Egyptian classrooms. The focus on active learning for this activity was critical partly because many of the participants struggled to understand the native English speech and accents of two of us consultants. Participation in group work and activities provided context for understanding the language, while also limiting the amount of aural-oral input in English. Cooperative work allowed for negotiation of meaning among participants in small groups. Thus participants at widely different language and knowledge levels were able to be included in the process.

Long-Term Timeline

We were fortunate to be able to develop the SPEER guide over a period of nearly 2 years. This gave us ample time for planning, writing, and field testing. The longer time period created opportunities for more participation by Egyptian colleagues, more collaboration among colleagues, and more reflection from all those involved in the project.

Long-Term Usability

The SPEER guide is a resource that will be useful over the long term in Egypt. Educators at schools and universities far from metropolitan Cairo can access the Web-based information at no cost. The SPEER guide has an Egyptian home and a mechanism to permit it to be added to, revised, and fine-tuned as it is used by a wider audience.

Changing and Evolving Content and Process

The institute series started off as a way to train a limited number of people in methodology and supervision. Although these teacher educators were able to disseminate their ideas to others, it was only through a wider materials project that countrywide dissemination could take place. The project changed and evolved as needs arose.

Qualitative and Quantitative Evaluation

As consultants and staff from the Monitoring and Evaluation Department of IELP-II, we took project evaluation very seriously. We evaluated every stage of the project—indeed, every activity—by a variety of means, including objective tests of information learned, application of rubrics (evaluation schemes) to participants' products (e.g., action plans, writings), and administration of questionnaires and other innovative assessment tools. Due to ongoing evaluation, we spent many long evenings revising plans to meet the needs of the group the next day. We carefully considered evaluation outcomes of a major activity in planning further steps. At the end of a long training session, we sometimes used imaginative and metaphorical means to elicit participant comments (and keep them going). Figure 3 shows a participant's "Nile River Evaluation," which compares aspects of the workshop to geological features of Egypt.

Nile River Evaluation

Instructions (given orally):

1. Draw the river. Draw a *falucca* [Egyptian sailboat] on the river. Write important things you learned at the Winter Institute on the sail.

2. Draw a bridge over the river. On the bridge, write the names of people who helped and supported you.

3. Draw some mountains across the river. On the mountains, write your goals for what you want to do with what you learned at the Winter Institute.

4. Draw a little house on the banks of the river. On the house, write suggestions you have for future institutes.

5. Draw a crocodile in the river. Write on the crocodile some of the challenges or difficulties of the institute.

6. Draw a palm tree. Label the tree with the best thing in the institute for you.

FIGURE 3. Nile River Evaluation

From *Spotlight on Primary English Education Resources*
Chapter 4: Songs and Chants

Who Is Salma?

The following is a chant for primary grade learners that will help them learn initial medial and ending sounds as well as first person and third person present verb forms.

Procedures:

First demonstrate the chant to all the students.

Then choose one student to be the "Star." Use that student's name in place of "Salma."

Put the chant on a chart, a pocket chart (a chart made of heavy card or cloth with pockets for word cards), the board or the overhead.

Using a pointer or ruler, follow under the words as you say them.

On the second time through, tell "Salma" that she can say her part along with you. Tell the class that they can say their part along with you.

Repeat several times over a week, with different students playing Salma's part. Gradually let Salma and students take over their roles. When students are ready, give them the teacher role as well.

Review the chant every now and then during the year—the children will love it!

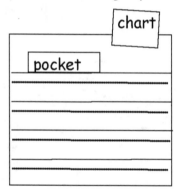

Who Is Salma?

(with thanks to Carolyn Graham)

Teacher:	Who has a name that starts with S?	*Teacher:*	Who has a name with an L in the middle?
Salma:	I do.	*Salma:*	I do.
Class:	She does.	*Class:*	She does.
Teacher:	What's her name?	*Teacher:*	What's her name?
Class:	Salma.	*Class:*	Salma.
Teacher:	Who has a name that ends with A?	*Teacher:*	Who is Salma?
		Salma:	I am.
Salma:	I do.	*Class:*	She is.
Class:	She does.	*Teacher:*	What's her name?
Teacher:	What's her name?	*Class:*	Salma
Class:	Salma.		

FIGURE 4. Who Is Salma?

Transfer of Responsibility

The Egyptian editorial board has had increasing responsibility for the project. A recent plan for two of us consultants to visit Egypt was canceled because the board felt it could easily carry out the tasks identified without our assistance. The Egyptian editorial board was responsible for managing the entire field-testing procedure, including collection and analysis of data and incorporation of findings into the SPEER guide. As such, they are well placed to manage other similar projects in the future.

◈ PRACTICAL IDEAS

The emphasis within SPEER was on practical techniques that can easily be applied in the Egyptian classroom, but many individual components of the project are practical and replicable in other sites. These include developing and applying knowledge about young children's language learning, identifying target country needs and adapting the program to them, providing training that is responsive to the culture of the participants, and developing a learning community of participants. Many of the materials from the SPEER book have also been used successfully in other countries. The short excerpt from the book (available online; see Ministry of Education, Egypt, 2003a) in Figure 4 illustrates how the techniques might apply to other primary teacher education pre- or in-service programs.

◈ CONCLUSION

SPEER offered opportunities for change that incorporated multiple resources, a long-term time frame, and rich and varied expertise. This combination, coupled with the fact that the project's origins lay in widespread dissatisfaction with the status quo, helped ensure its smooth adoption in the Egyptian context. These advantages may not hold true in other contexts; nevertheless, we feel that this project can provide a model for collaboration between faculties, ministries, and aid agencies. Many individual components of the project are practical and replicable: applying knowledge about young children's language learning, adapting the program to the target country's needs, providing culturally responsive training, and developing collaboration between and empowerment of the individuals involved. All of these factors led to a rich and renewable legacy as well as a possible model for implementing change in other settings.

◈ ACKNOWLEDGMENTS

We would like to thank Ghada Howaidy and Robert Burch for reviewing an earlier version of this chapter.

◈ CONTRIBUTORS

Mary Lou McCloskey, past president of TESOL, is an international consultant and author of professional texts, standards, and program materials in the field of English for speakers of other languages. She has worked with teachers, teacher educators, and departments and ministries of education on five continents and in 31 of the United States.

Linda New Levine is a consultant, staff development facilitator, and curriculum writer for teachers of second-language-learning children and programs teaching EFL in primary and secondary classrooms. She has taught ESL/EFL methods at Teachers College, Columbia University, and has conducted workshops with teachers and supervisors in Africa, Asia, and the Americas.

Barbara Thornton is an educational consultant, currently based in Brazil, who has worked with teachers in more than 20 countries on five continents. She has published widely in the field of teacher education and primary language teaching.

Zeinab El Naggar is a professor of English language teaching methodology at Ain Shams Faculty of Education in Cairo, Egypt. Through the Ministry of Higher Education Expert Committee for Faculties Education Reform, she has coordinated the work of faculties of education throughout Egypt to set standards for newly qualified teachers of English.

CHAPTER 12

The French Communicative Connection: Catching Up

Marlene Dolitsky

◈ INTRODUCTION

A recent European survey showed that France's youth have the lowest scores in foreign language competence compared with six other members of the European community: Sweden, Finland, Norway, The Netherlands, Denmark, and Spain (Laronche, 2004). This questionable claim to fame may be due in part to the traditional, negative attitude toward foreign languages in France, probably inherited from the time that French was the lingua franca of Europe (Charbonnel, 2002). Although between 1960 and 1973 there were a number of initiatives to teach foreign language in primary school, "a decree from the Education Nationale [French National Education Ministry] dated May 11, 1973, put an end to these undertakings" (Charbonnel, p. 1). Between 1973 and 1989, the general population in France thought that if children learned a foreign language too early, it would negatively affect their abilities in French. Principals, teachers, and school inspectors advised parents not to raise their children bilingually. The national education curriculum had no place for foreign language learning until sixth grade, the first year of middle school.

In 1989, the Education Nationale launched an experimental program to test the validity of beginning foreign language classes in primary school, aiming mainly at fifth grade. Schools took part in this program on a voluntary basis. The report of this study (Inspection Générale de l'Education National, 1993) concluded that the effect of foreign language learning in primary school was almost insignificant when the pupils arrived in middle school. At best, the early learners recognized and produced phonemes of English better than the later learners. Middle school English language teachers generally commented that there was only a slight and temporary advantage for early learners over those who began studying a foreign language in sixth grade.[1] After 3 months of foreign language study in sixth grade, the new pupils had caught up with the early learners. These observations, however, are controversial given the setup of the sixth-grade classes that contained early learners as well as beginners— what competence the early learners had acquired was ignored, and they were taught nothing new until the others had caught up (Chupin, 2005).

---

[1] This transition program refers to the necessary modifications in the foreign language curriculum that are brought about as foreign languages are progressively introduced first in fifth grade, then fourth, then third, down to kindergarten.

In spite of the controversial results, and the "lack of empirical support for the 'younger = better' hypothesis" (Nunan, 1999, p. 3)—which supports the view that the younger the child when foreign language study begins, the more easily the child will learn the foreign language—the ever-growing demand from parents for an early start in English has served as a catalyst for the decision to extend foreign language teaching to the primary schools. Since 2002, it has become officially mandatory for primary schools in France to teach a foreign language in third, fourth, and fifth grades. The government's objective has been to lower, year by year, the obligatory grade at which children are to begin foreign language learning, until all children begin a foreign language in kindergarten. This means that all third, fourth, and fifth graders would have been studying a foreign language in 2003. This objective proved to be overly optimistic: In 2003 only 95.6% of fourth- and fifth-grade students in public schools nationwide studied foreign languages (Legendre, 2003). And with the focus primarily on fourth and fifth grades, fewer third graders (55%) and kindergarteners (6%) received foreign language instruction. However, these percentages are increasing slowly as school districts develop the foreign language competence of their teachers. Rather than bringing specialized language teachers into the primary schools, the Education Nationale has decided that "foreign languages are to be taught only by generalist classroom teachers who will be trained to teach this subject" (de Gaudemar, 2001, p. 2). The shortage of primary school teachers who are sufficiently fluent in English and have been trained in foreign language pedagogy represents the greatest obstacle to meeting this staffing challenge. For this initiative to succeed, the main thrust must come from focused training of primary school teachers both in English language and English as a foreign language (EFL) teaching techniques.

It is the teachers' colleges (Institut Universitaire de Formation des Maîtres, IUFM) that end up with the responsibility to train the new teachers entering the profession and the experienced teachers who need additional skills to carry out their new, supplementary teaching duties. Until now, teachers who were not inclined to teach a foreign language could refuse on the grounds that they did not have the competence; in many cases, school districts brought in specially certified instructors to do the job. But at the time of this writing, the education ministry is putting pressure on teachers to fulfill the language teaching requirement themselves.

◈ CONTEXT

France's Education Nationale is geographically divided into 25 Académies (translated here as "school districts"). Each district has its own teachers' college (IUFM), which may include more than one teaching center. The teachers' colleges are linked to the universities in the same geographical location, but these universities do not belong to the school districts. The teachers' colleges have a symbiotic relationship with the school districts. The colleges work very closely with the schools in their districts; the teachers in training do all of their practice teaching in schools in the same district as their teachers' college. Generally, newly graduated primary teachers are assigned to schools in the same district where they studied. Whereas all of the teachers' colleges must train new teachers to fulfill the same national curriculum set up by the Education Nationale, they are free to set up their own programs, and these may vary among the different districts according to district priorities. The Paris school district has made development of foreign language programs a priority since 1999 (Plan de Formation Académique), evidenced by requirements that training programs be set up by the Paris teachers' college.

The training program in English for students at the Paris teachers' college includes courses both in language, to improve teachers' fluency, and in EFL methods. Teachers in training learn to create materials for English language classes and to plan a logical progression for learning in line with the Education Nationale's English curriculum. In addition, they may choose English for their specialization in practice teaching.

This training is extremely practical and pragmatic and uses as its pedagogical base the teacher learners' own work as teachers. It is a partial answer to the problems posed, on the one hand, by the Paris district's need to prepare teachers to teach a foreign language in their primary classes in short order, and, on the other hand, by the low level of language competence of many of these teachers in training. The program is based on the understanding that it is not necessary to wait for ideal conditions to get primary school language programs started; rather, teachers with even a basic level of ability in English and a willingness to work hard and prepare well can give children a good start in foreign language learning. True or false, this working hypothesis seems to me to be a necessity to get a new program off the ground because, when countries first initiate programs in primary school English, teachers often lack competence in foreign language fluency.

With the strengthening of the European community, communication among its member nations becomes more important. Competence in foreign languages has come to be perceived in France as a key element in functioning as a full-fledged European citizen.

The decision to begin teaching foreign languages earlier than sixth grade is based on the belief that "foreign language learning helps to structure children's knowledge of the world around them" (Duhamel, 1995, p. 1649) and that early language learning will lead to greater language competence later on. For this reason "pedagogical methods should emphasize active discovery"; the specific aims are to "arouse their interest and respond to children's desire and pleasure to communicate" (p. 1650). Because "scientific research of the last fifteen years shows that . . . sensitivity to phonetic contrasts decreases with age until individuals distinguish only the phonemes of the language of their environment" (p. 1649), the methods adopted by the Education Nationale for primary school up to fifth grade have emphasized the oral language functions (i.e., listening and speaking). The aim is to build good English phonetic abilities and to avoid possible interference with learning to read in French. Thus, the children do very little reading and writing, and only after learning the oral forms. This method differentiates the primary school curriculum from the middle school curriculum, in which reading and writing have always been an important part of foreign language instruction. Primary school language teaching is characterized by a "constant association between saying and doing, by accomplishing tasks and carrying out activities" (Duhamel, 1995, p. 1650), which has led to the use of a multisensory approach to language teaching and learning, whereby teaching activities are created to appeal to pupils' "different modes of sensory perception (auditive, visual, kinesthetic, even olfactive, gustative)" (Toulemonde, 1998, p. 1487).

However, even after 10 years of various ministerial decrees that foreign languages are obligatory in primary school, teaching English at this level remains controversial even as greater effort is being put into training teachers to carry out the work. The most recent study on the progress of language competence in France (*Evaluation des Compétences,* 2004) found that the French youth's ability to speak a foreign language is declining rather than increasing. A report chaired by Claude Thélot suggests that English should be taught as a language of international communication (*Pour la Réussite,* 2004, p. 23) and that it should be obligatory in primary school. This has awakened a hornet's nest of protest, beginning with upper-level English language teachers who are set against teaching "airport English" (Malingre, 2004, p. 11). English teachers do not want to give up the historical goals of foreign language learning (i.e., grammar and literature). They think that focusing solely on communicative needs, with much less emphasis on literature and culture, lowers their teaching standards, compared with other foreign languages that are taught and whose primary orientation is culture. The teaching of languages other than English is defended in the name of cultural diversity, to the point that Claude Hagège, professor at the renowned Collège de France, recommends that English be forbidden in primary schools. The conclusion of some is that foreign language learning in primary school has been treated more or less as a hobby ("Last but Not Least," 2004) because schools lack the necessary human resources and financial support.

Meanwhile, as the debate rages, firm in the knowledge that it is impossible to turn back and that France is condemned to succeed (Goutallier, 1993), the school districts are striving to make foreign languages (mainly English) an integral part of the primary school curriculum. In their role to train teachers in accordance with the decrees of the Education Nationale, the teachers' colleges redoubled their efforts to produce quality teachers (e.g., for the school year 2004–2005). The Paris teachers' college doubled the courses it offers to train students to teach English and developed a remediation program to improve the competence of in-service teachers.

In determining competence, France turned to the *Common European Framework* (Council of Europe, 2001a) to define the minimum language level that teachers should have reached to teach English. The *Common European Framework* "provides a common basis for the elaboration of language syllabuses, curriculum guidelines, examinations, textbooks, etc. across Europe" (p. 1). One of its intended uses is to help European countries plan for "language certification" and set "assessment criteria" (p. 6). France has accepted the following standards for oral comprehension and oral expression:

- Level B2 in oral comprehension, whereby teachers are able to "understand extended speech and lectures . . . follow complex lines of argument provided the topic is reasonably familiar . . . most TV news and current affairs programmes . . . the majority of films in standard dialect"

- Level B1 in oral expression, whereby they should be able to "connect phrases in a simple way in order to describe experiences and events . . . dreams, hopes and ambitions . . . give reasons and explanations for opinions and plans . . . narrate a story or relate the plot of a book or film and describe . . . reactions (pp. 26–27)

◈ DESCRIPTION

Teachers must be certified to teach English in primary school. The certification process is aimed at "verifying the abilities to teach a foreign language in primary school" (de Gaudemar, 2001, p. 1486) and takes place in the form of a one-on-one oral exam with a two-member commission. The candidate must listen to a (taped) text and answer questions about it, carry on a conversation with the commission, and be able to correctly answer questions about the national curriculum regarding foreign languages in primary school. In this way, the commission can assess whether the candidate has reached the levels in oral competence as described earlier. New teachers graduating from the teachers' colleges who have followed specific courses on teaching a foreign language in primary school (Toulemonde, 1999a) with those on teaching English in primary school, and who are considered apt to do so by the professors, do not need to take the certification exam. In this case, the teachers' college provides the school district with the names of these teachers, and they can teach English in their first teaching assignment as a generalist primary school teacher.

However, due to a shortage of primary school teachers qualified to teach English, and under pressure from the school district, the teacher trainers at the Paris teachers' college unofficially adjusted downward the absolute minimum level of language competence for certification of generalist primary school teachers. The teacher trainers decided that to teach English, teachers must at least possess all of the grammatical and phonetic forms that the pupils will ideally learn, as defined by the national curriculum (de Gaudemar, 2002). Thus, teacher learners are certified if their English competence corresponds to the ideal expectations for fifth graders at the end of their primary school English studies. This decision was made because, in the course of teachers' class work in English, there is no absolute need for them to speak or understand English at a level much higher than what they will teach to students. Having no choice but to begin English language instruction in primary school before all teachers are fully competent in English, those who are implementing it are counting on the teachers to "grow more professionally through their own learning and teaching of English" (Murphey, 2003, p. 1).

Because the new generalist primary school teachers are being asked to teach a subject (English) that they have not yet totally mastered, practice teaching sessions are being carefully conducted. The trainers hope the success that teacher learners achieve through the sound pedagogical methods they are learning will encourage them to improve their own English. Moreover, with an eye constantly on the future, the next generation of teachers should have greater foreign language competence because they will have been taught English earlier and better than the pioneers who are initiating primary school English.

◈ DISTINGUISHING FEATURES

Primary School Language Teaching in France's National Education System

France's Education Nationale has a highly centralized education structure. People have often wryly pointed out that at the time of the United Soviet Socialist Republic (USSR), France's Education Nationale was the world's second largest employer after the USSR's Red Army. It may now be first. Some have also jokingly said that if a child moves from Paris to Marseilles over a weekend, the child will begin school on Monday exactly where he or she left off on Friday. It should come as no surprise then that such a centralized organization sets the goals and learning objectives of a new subject, such as a foreign language, in the primary schools. Besides setting the curriculum, the Education Nationale has also designed the framework within which English is to be taught and implemented, placing importance on a cross-curricular approach linking foreign language instruction with the study of other school subjects.

The recommended methodology for teaching primary school English (de Gaudemar, 2002) is dramatically different from the grammatical-translation approach of the middle and high school foreign language programs. Lessons are to be enjoyable and based on situations and activities in which pupils use English in meaningful ways. The curriculum is based on a list of communicative competencies that pupils are to attain by the end of primary school. In the decree signed by de Gaudemar (2002), competencies are categorized into four types of communication:

1. speaking about oneself, whereby the pupil should be able to introduce himself or herself; give one's age, birthday, and address; describe family members and friends; and tell how he or she feels (e.g., hungry, thirsty, happy, sad, tired)

2. speaking about the environment, whereby the pupil should be able to designate a person or an object, give the date and time, talk about the weather, speak about food, describe someone or something (size, color, intensity), say where things are, and express simple chronological order

3. participating in classroom activities, whereby the pupil should be able to state whether he or she knows/understands or not and whether he or she likes something or not, express opinions, agree or disagree, get someone's attention, and refuse or accept something

4. using social and phatic functions of language, which include basic greetings and exclamations, the simple polite forms of *please, thank you, you're welcome*, excusing oneself, inviting, congratulating, and wishing others a happy birthday

In addition to teaching the children English, teachers should also guide pupils to understand that different languages do not map onto each other but follow different types of logic in how sentences and meaning are created. The language lesson is considered a royal road to multicultural understanding, and French pupils learn about children their own age in English-speaking countries (e.g., about family life, school activities, holidays, pets). They also receive basic instruction in history, art, and general civilization. Teachers are also encouraged to have children from immigrant families talk about their home language.

In all, the pupils are expected to leave primary school with an A1 level of language, as defined in the *Common European Framework* (2001):

> Can understand and use familiar everyday expressions and very basic phrases aimed at the satisfaction of needs of a concrete type. Can introduce him/herself and others and can ask and answer questions about personal details such as where he/she lives, people he/she knows and things he/she has. Can

interact in a simple way provided the other person talks slowly and clearly and is prepared to help. (p. 26)

Underlying this functional-communicative curriculum are the grammatical and phonetic forms needed to carry out language functions, for example, to correctly "speak of one's tastes—say what one likes: I like chocolate—say what one doesn't like: I don't like chocolate" (de Gaudemar, 2002, p. 15). This implies that the speaker can use the auxiliaries "do/does" and form questions and negatives with them, as well as conjugate the third person singular of "like" in the affirmative form. This communicative-grammatical approach has the advantage of offering teachers freedom regarding presentations, books, exercises, and activities. On the other hand, it creates challenges for teachers who learned English through a traditional, grammar-translation approach—they have few models in memory to implement a communicative approach to language learning in the classroom. As a consequence, training programs must help teachers develop an instructional style that is different from their own foreign language education.

The Paris Teachers' College and Foreign Languages

Since it was first entrusted in 1993 to implement language courses for future primary school teachers with a view to starting pupils earlier in foreign language learning, the Paris teachers' college has changed its program a number of times. It has done so in accordance with the increasing emphasis that the Education Nationale and the Paris school district placed on foreign language learning at the primary level (de Gaudemar, 2001; Lang, 2001; Toulemonde, 1999a, 1999b, 1999c). The change is evident both on the entrance exam, where candidates' foreign language abilities have greater impact on acceptance into the college, and on the increased hours devoted to foreign languages in the general training curriculum. In 1999, the teachers' colleges in France also became responsible for in-service teacher training, and by 2001, improving pupils' foreign language ability was one of the three main objectives of the Education Nationale.

Acceptance into the teachers' colleges is highly selective. Applicants must at least have the equivalent of a bachelor's degree (license), but a master's degree is more preferable. They can then apply to enter the first year at the teachers' college. A lucky few (approximately 300 per year in Paris) spend a year at the college preparing for the primary school licensing exam, although this does not guarantee that they will pass the exam. Those who are not chosen to prepare at the teachers' college can study for the exam through correspondence courses. The exam itself is spread over approximately one month. Candidates begin with written exams in French and mathematics, which are considered the most important subjects. Those whose grades are sufficiently high are allowed to pass to the next part of the exam, which includes pedagogy, two electives, and, since June 2006, an obligatory foreign language test (Duwoye & Le Bihan-Graf, 2005). Depending on the Paris school district's needs, between 250 and 450 candidates become teacher learners.

The Education Nationale requires that the colleges train all future teachers to be able to teach a foreign language to their classes, and a new foreign language curriculum extending from primary school through high school graduation to the training of all teachers was announced in May 2006 (Debbasch, 2006). In response, the Paris teachers' college will offer 28 hours of combined language and pedagogy courses to every teacher learner. At the end of the course, subgroups of two to four teacher learners will each create a lesson adapted to primary school pupils and present it to their classmates. Teacher learners can also choose to take 20 course hours specifically devoted to improving their proficiency in English.

Obviously, teacher learners with low proficiency will be unable to sufficiently improve their language ability with so few course hours. These learners will be advised in setting up a self-study program in the college's multimedia language lab so that they can achieve the proficiency required to carry out the tasks of language teaching.

Any trainee can choose to take a 5-week practice language instruction course. For practice teaching, a professor in the English department at the teachers' college partners with a master teacher in the Paris school district, taking a small group of student teachers to the master teacher's class. During the first week, the teacher learners observe the master teacher's English course. After the lesson, the teacher learners can ask the teacher questions and discuss the theory behind the various activities. Then the teacher learners decide, with help from the master teacher and the professor, which teacher learner will teach the next class, and then they determine the goals. The professor works with the student teachers to create lessons, help them choose materials, plan the progression, clearly determine the language to be taught to and elicited from the pupils, plan the student teachers' language, and structure the transitions from one exercise to another. The class of student teachers (usually singly or in pairs) is expected to teach one lesson per week for 5 weeks. Both the master teacher and the professor observe the lessons and comment on them during a follow-up meeting. The functions of the master teacher and the professor are to enhance student teachers' awareness of their achievements, to build student teachers' analytic ability so they can evaluate class work for continued progress of their students, and to continuously improve their own courses throughout the school year and over the years.

During the week, the trainee who teaches the lesson prepares a lesson plan and sends it to the professor, who checks the plan and makes any needed suggestions for improvement. On English Day, the student teacher teaches the English lesson to the pupils. The lesson is followed by a discussion with the master teacher, the professor, and the other teacher learners in the group, all of whom have observed the practice teacher's lesson. After analyzing the lesson and the needs of the pupils, another teacher learner takes over to teach the next week's lesson.

◈ PRACTICAL IDEAS

Help Teacher Learners Develop Their Own Lessons

Many manuals and methods, along with their accompanying instructional media, exist to support teaching English in primary school. The trainers' work can easily be limited to instructing teacher learners in how to use these materials. However, in a time of tightening budgets, this new subject in school is often the last to be allocated funds for books and materials. Another factor to consider is whether schools should, even if they have the funds, invest in expensive methods that require a course book and activity book for every pupil. Methods aimed at fifth-grade beginning English language learners will not be the same as methods aimed at younger beginners because of the different interests of the two age groups. For example, older children find pictures and stories aimed at younger children babyish and reject the use of such materials in class. As the education system achieves its goal of starting English in earlier grades, these costly and narrowly focused methods will become obsolete because those aimed at the interests of older children will not be adapted for use with younger children.

Focus Teacher Learners' Attention on Setting Clear Objectives

Teachers must always set objectives for the class they will be teaching. It is extremely important to distinguish between objectives and means: "listen to a song" is not an objective but the means to an objective (e.g., teaching the parts of the body with the song "Head, Shoulders, Knees, and Toes"). Objectives should focus on what pupils will to be able to say or do through language (e.g., greet each other correctly, use the auxiliary *do* when asking and answering questions about preferences, correctly distinguish /h/ and non-/h/ at the beginning of words). Planning a lesson means setting objectives and determining the best way to instruct pupils as they achieve those objectives. The Strategy of Objectives sheet (see Figure 1) is distributed by the trainer to help teacher learners determine the objectives of any given lesson. It is based on the neurolinguistic programming (NLP) technique of creating well-formed outcomes (Densky & Reese, 1993) and is divided into four parts: The first part defines the objective, the second determines prerequisites to attain the objective, the third selects activities and materials to be used, and the fourth verifies whether the objective has, in fact, been attained.

What do I want the students to be able to say (or do) at the end of the lesson?

What difficulties can I expect?

What can I do to help them overcome these difficulties?

What do the kids have to know how to say (or do) before they can reach the objective of my lesson?

Can they already do it? If not, how shall I teach this prerequisite?

(Subgoal: apply the strategy of objectives to this goal before aiming for larger goal.)

What resources do I have at my disposal to help the children learn to do (or say) what I want them to?

What can I include in my lesson?

Does this clearly take me toward my goal?

Have I remembered to include elements that appeal to all the sensory modalities of the students: visual, auditive, kinesthetic?

How will I know I have achieved my teaching goal?

How will I know the students can say (or do) what I want them to?

What will I have them do?

In what way will this prove that they have learned what I want them to learn?

FIGURE 1. Strategy of Objectives: Designing a Lesson

1. Review OLD STUFF (prerequisite for NEW STUFF)
2. Create LINK from OLD STUFF to NEW STUFF
3. Present NEW STUFF
   - Use and Review OLD GRAMMAR to teach NEW VOCAULARY
   - Use and Review OLD VOCABULARY to teach NEW GRAMMAR
   - Use and Review OLD VOCABULARY and OLD GRAMMAR to teach NEW COMMUNICATIVE FORMS
   - Use and Review OLD COMMUNICATIVE FORMS to teach NEW GRAMMAR and NEW VOCABULARY
4. Interact to practice NEW STUFF: teacher–student/student–student
5. Activities: oral, written, corporal, creative

   Prepare in the form of a scenario

   Teacher says: _____

   Student says: _____
6. Confirm whether the NEW STUFF has been learned

FIGURE 2. From Old Stuff to New Stuff

After teacher learners determine the objectives of their lessons, they must determine how to set up the lesson, present new elements, and continue to help the class progress from one element of language to the next. Teacher learners are taught to move the lesson in a spiral path that allows pupils to maintain what they have already learned as they acquire new concepts, as seen in Figure 2.

Guide Teacher Learners to Plan for Language Needs

If teachers with limited English proficiency are to be able to carry out successful English lessons, they must foresee what language they will need to use, learn that language, plan for how they will present new language forms, figure out how they will elicit children's productions, and have clear expectations as to what they want the children to say. Figure 3 shows a form containing specific guidelines for preparation to help teachers carry out this fundamental task.

Help Teacher Learners Prepare Activities for a Lesson

Obviously, knowing how to prepare for teaching must be accompanied by knowing what to prepare. Learning occurs in four stages. At first the concept is (1) unknown by the pupils; they then (2) go through a learning stage until the notion has been (3) learned. The teacher, however, should not stop here because learning experiments have shown that if studying does not continue, pupils will forget between one lesson and the next. Therefore, the teacher should continue to focus instruction on the concept. This stage is called (4) overlearning and ensures that the pupils remember the concept over time. Of course, if the teacher continues too long on a single concept, the pupils become bored. Before the pupils arrive at this point, the teacher should have moved on to new language forms. Different types of activities (e.g., pair

Please include the following on your preparation sheet:

OBJECTIVES: This should take the following form:

"The students will be able to say/do _____ at the end of the lesson."

ACTIVITIES: Note that activities are not objectives in themselves but are the means to attaining the objectives.

LANGUAGE: List main grammatical forms and vocabulary, noting what is

- **new**—that is, to be introduced, presented, taught, and then produced by the students
- **old**—that is, already known and serves as a handle to learn what is new

CLASS SCENARIO: The lesson plan should take the form of a scenario, with everything the teacher will say/do and the students' responses for each exercise. The scenario will include verbal instructions for introducing exercises and the body language to be used. The exact form of the sentences/questions that the teacher will use to elicit the desired response from the students should appear in the scenario. The teacher's turn should be followed by the form of the response expected from the students.

Check:

- ✔ whether the required response is compatible with the teacher's elicitation in normal language use
- ✔ whether the students possess the language forms required to respond correctly
- ✔ what must be taught beforehand
- ✔ whether the activities help the students attain the stated objectives

FIGURE 3. Lesson Preparation Form

work) are appropriate for each of these four stages. The relationship between learning stages and types of pedagogical activities can be shown on a learning curve, as in Figure 4.

Train Teacher Learners in Self-Improvement

Good teachers need not be perfect teachers; no one is perfect. Teachers become great by constantly improving with every class they teach. No one is accompanied by trainers at all times; therefore, excellence is achieved through self-training. After every class, teachers can reflect on what did and did not go well and store that information for further use. Teachers can improve exercises that did not achieve the objectives or drop them if they are totally inappropriate. It is important that teachers be trained to internalize self-improvement skills, and to this effect a follow-up form has been developed (see Figure 5). This form is used as a framework for discussions between teacher learners and the trainer after class to analyze the instruction and discuss ideas for improvement. The intent is for teacher learners to apply the same type of analysis once they are teaching English in their own classes.

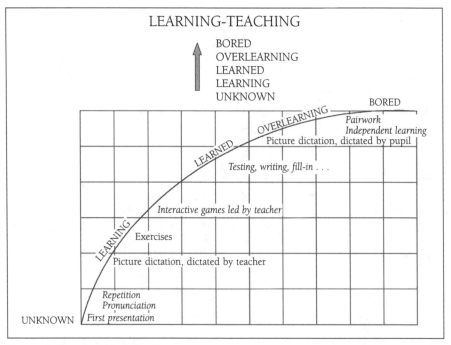

FIGURE 4. Learning-Teaching Curve

WHAT DID YOU DO RIGHT? Questions to analyze the lesson:

What have the pupils learned? What can they do (or say) now?

What went well? What took you toward your objectives?

Did you take into account pupils' different learning styles and sensory preferences: visual, auditive, kinesthetic?

Did the lesson make use of a maximum of listening/speaking, looking, moving?

How much speaking time did the pupils have?

HOW CAN YOU IMPROVE? Questions to improve after a problem:

Why did you choose that exercise?

What was the objective of the exercise?

Why did you choose to do that particular exercise at that particular moment in the progression of the lesson?

Were the pupils able to do it? If not, why not?

Why did the pupils have difficulties carrying out the exercise? (if they did)

Why were the pupils noisy? (if they were)

Why weren't the pupils listening? (if they weren't)

WHAT NEXT?

FIGURE 5. Follow-Up

◈ CONCLUSION

In response to France's serious need to improve the communicative abilities of French students in order to be a major player in the global community (Boissinot Education Ministry memo, April 1, 1998), and following recommendations by language experts, the Education Nationale has decreed an ambitious foreign language program for primary school. Its long-term vision is to incorporate the teaching of English into the primary classroom teacher's routine work.

Today, teaching English in primary school in France is caught between an ideal and reality: the ideal that all primary school teachers have the language ability and teaching techniques to teach a foreign language, and that they should be doing so now, and the reality that France lacks teachers with language competence and pedagogical tools to carry out its objectives. Faced with this dilemma, teachers' colleges all over the nation have implemented programs to work with teachers (both new and experienced) to aid them in including foreign language instruction in their weekly schedule. Given the number of children to teach, at this time it cannot be expected that all primary school teachers be fluent in English, especially considering that they must teach other subjects besides English. That the teacher's own language competence is limited goes against the intuitive feeling toward language teaching: that the teacher must be a fluent speaker of the language taught. Working with primary teachers in France to get the English program moving ahead means accepting that teachers who may not be fluent in English can start the pupils off in the basics of English communication as long as they have precise tools for planning and structuring their lessons.

Obviously, the next step is to offer teachers more opportunities to become competent users of English. This means the Education Nationale needs to plan for, budget, and offer many more hours of language study programs for primary teachers and offer teachers more opportunities to participate in exchange programs in English-speaking countries.

If France begins teaching foreign languages at earlier ages, and if French primary teachers constantly improve their language instruction, the product of this education will be better prepared teachers of tomorrow. This next generation of teachers will, in turn, help France become a nation whose people are better equipped to communicate with those outside its borders. With careful preparation and well-structured lessons, teachers can take their primary-level English classes a long way.

◈ CONTRIBUTOR

Marlene Dolitsky is an associate professor at the University of Paris's Teacher's College (Institut Universitaire de la Formation des Maîtres). Her main mission is to train teacher learners to teach English in their future primary school classes. One of her major research interests, and the subject of her doctoral thesis, is child bilingualism. She is coeditor of a volume on language acquisition called *Language Bases . . . Discourse Bases*, and a *Journal of Pragmatics* special issue on code-switching. She has also designed a set of cards and instructions (Happy English) to help primary school English teachers set up games in the classroom.

CHAPTER 13

EFL Teacher Training for South Korean Elementary School Teachers

Sung-Hee Park

◈ INTRODUCTION

In 1995, the South Korean Ministry of Education realized there was a need for official English language education in elementary schools and accepted the new educational policy suggested by the Globalization Steering Committee for teaching English as a required subject in elementary schools.

In 1997, the new policy was initiated with third-grade students, and it was projected that by 2000 all elementary school students from Grade 3 through Grade 6 would benefit from learning English in school (South Korea Ministry of Education, 1995). Now, more than 8 years have passed since the new education policy was implemented. English education in elementary schools, based on the Seventh National English Curriculum, has been practiced quite successfully, but there are still questions to consider: Who should teach young children in schools—regular classroom teachers or specialized English language teachers? How should teachers of elementary English be trained? How can level-based textbooks and teaching materials be developed?

◈ CONTEXT

When the new educational policy was suggested, there were several reasons to support it. One was globalization. The general public, along with politicians and educators, believed that it was necessary for Koreans to acquire cross-cultural understanding and leadership qualities (South Korea Ministry of Education, 1997). They also felt it was desirable to have an open-minded attitude toward the world, to behave in a globally acceptable manner, and to gain communicative ability in an international language. Furthermore, Koreans realized that they should learn English as an international language to survive in a global society and that the nation needed citizens with confidence in English language skills to make Korea competitively stronger. Therefore, a major emphasis was placed on instruction in English as a foreign language (EFL).

The public also raised the issue to revise English language education policies and to change English teaching methodologies. Even though people study English for more than 10 years in school, they still find that they have difficulties communicating in English in the real world.

A number of relevant studies published in South Korea indicate possible problems and major concerns that could occur in implementing the new educational policy. For example, Lee (1997) found that elementary school teachers and parents of elementary school students were most concerned about curriculum planning and implementation, acquisition of textbooks for the new subject in elementary schools, and last but not least, the increased demand for qualified English language teachers in elementary schools. Training for elementary teachers was considered the most urgent need because teacher quality greatly contributes to successful teaching (Scarbrough, 1976).

Min (1993) also found that most elementary schools rarely had English language teachers on their staff, and even when they did, these teachers had neither the appropriate command of the target language and culture nor the necessary teaching methods and skills for elementary English education. Many researchers have thus become concerned about providing elementary schools with qualified English language teachers (see Park, Jung, & Chun, 1991). Ko (1996) suggests that it is necessary to develop efficient and effective English teacher training programs and to provide the teachers with continuing retraining opportunities. To train qualified English language teachers, whether through pre- or in-service training, a program must be developed efficiently and systematically; correspond to the teaching context, objectives, and goals of the teacher learners; and offer appropriate content.

Investigating teacher learners' perceptions concerning their language teaching context and training program contributes to the development of better training programs. The general purpose of this case study was to identify and describe South Korean elementary school teachers' perceptions about the EFL teacher training program they participated in and the teacher learners' expectations and attitudes toward the program. This case study presents an analysis of teacher learners' needs in the training program and gives practical suggestions to improve the training program in the future.

◈ DESCRIPTION

To cope with the issue of teachers who did not major in English language education, each city or province board of education has offered English teacher training programs for elementary teachers to help them improve their English teaching skills and their proficiency in the language. The government and the Ministry of Education have also tried to provide qualified specialist English language teachers for elementary schools during the past several years through specific courses for elementary English teaching at national universities of education. However, when the new policy was implemented, there was still a shortage of English teachers. Therefore, as a short-term plan, the Ministry of Education decided to train regular elementary teachers to teach English in their classes.

The ministry established a guideline for designing a training program for elementary teachers (South Korea Ministry of Education, 1996), which detailed the program's purposes, principles, and total training hours. According to the guideline, the English teacher training program should serve three purposes: to raise teachers' awareness of the effectiveness of elementary English education, to improve teachers' communicative English language skills, and to educate elementary teachers nationwide in elementary English curriculum and teaching methodology. The program design must follow several principles:

- The curriculum is developed with a focus on communicative language teaching, which is the major methodology in the English education program.

- If a provincial board of education does not have the means to offer a training program, the board can select specific training centers attached to universities and ask them to organize a training program.

- The Ministry of Education will cover the training costs of every local board of education and that of the selected training centers.

- Each local board of education is in charge of planning the program and hiring trainers.

The guideline allows a certain amount of flexibility in designing the training program, depending on the ability of the training center to meet the demands of a local school district, the center's finances, the specific purpose of English teacher training, and the availability of teaching staff.

The guideline requires that 120 hours (see the appendix) should be divided into 84 hours of communicative competency, 34 hours of teaching methodology, and 2 class hours devoted to other unspecified curriculum items. The framework for syllabus planning includes 14 hours (11.7%) of lectures and 88 hours (73.6%) of practical work. Based on this guideline, the board of education in the province is authorized to organize the total training hours, training curriculum, training modes, and teaching staff, considering the local training center's facilities and teacher learners' English language proficiency. The Ministry of Education's guideline for elementary school English teacher training is realistic because it emphasizes improving teacher learners' communicative language skills as well as their teaching skills.

The teacher training program analyzed by this study was developed to train elementary teachers who plan to teach English. The program was offered by the Elementary School Teacher Training Center, which is attached to the National University of Education, located in Inchon, the third largest city in South Korea. Unlike other cities, which belong to provinces, Inchon is under the direct control of the government of South Korea. Whereas city boards of education are usually controlled by boards of education in the city's province, Inchon has an independent board of education, as do relatively larger cities such as Seoul, Pusan, Daejon, Daegu, and Kwangju. Elementary teacher training centers or language institutes for Inchon are attached to universities in the city, which offer English teacher training programs for elementary school teachers with the cooperation of the city board of education.

The Elementary School Teacher Training Center sessions occurred in January 1999, offering a total of 120 hours of training over the course of 20 days. No training occurred on Sundays or during the Chinese New Year break. All teacher learners were regular elementary school teachers. The training staff consisted of professors in the English language education department of the National University of Education, practicing English teachers at the elementary or secondary level, and qualified native speakers of English.

◈ DISTINGUISHING FEATURES

There were three specific objectives for this training program, which follows the guideline presented in the previous section. Elementary school teachers will (1) understand the curriculum for elementary school English and develop appropriate teaching methods and skills for teaching English to children, (2) improve their ability to use English as a medium of instruction, and (3) be able to teach basic communicative language skills. Most courses in the training program focused on practical teaching methods of English language education and introduced useful teaching techniques applicable to English classes in the elementary school. Also, more than two thirds of the training hours were devoted to two forms of speaking and listening. The course called Speaking and Listening A emphasized English speaking skills with native-speaking trainers, and Speaking and Listening B emphasized English listening skills with South Korean professors in the English language education department. In the former course, teacher learners learned communicative English language skills in a group, and in the latter course they practiced listening comprehension skills in the language laboratory.

Two hundred elementary school teachers followed this training program. They all taught at schools in the same school district. They had a variety of teaching experience with children in Grades 1–6, and most were regular classroom teachers who taught several required academic subjects. A large proportion of teacher learners was female, between the ages of 20 and 30, and had majored in elementary education at the national universities of education. Some of them had a specialization in a specific area, such as the South Korean language, education, social science, art, mathematics, music, science, early childhood education, English education, or physical education. Of the teacher learners who were expected to teach English in the elementary school, only one in the training program had followed courses in English language education, and only a few had previous experience (less than one year) teaching English. About 60% of the teacher learners had rarely used English on a regular basis. Their usual methods of learning and using the language were to attend English language institutes, to listen to or watch educational English language programs, or to use commercial teaching materials in English learning products. Seventy-eight percent of the teacher learners considered their English language level to be low or very low. No teachers thought their English language proficiency was high. These data suggest how important the English teacher training program was in educating novices about teaching English and in fostering successful English language education in elementary school.

Only a few teachers in the program had been trained in English teaching if their specific major was other than English or English language education. Most had been trained in the English training program for elementary school teachers, and some had taken English education courses as electives in the University of Education or had attended a private English language institute. Their past training varied from a minimum of 60 hours to a maximum of one year, but most had attended a 120-hour teacher training program similar to this one. Most of the teacher learners were participating in this training program for the first time, and a few had participated in an English teacher training program, including this one, more than twice. The teachers entered the program for different reasons: voluntarily, on the school dean's recommendation, as a requirement to teach English, or for a promotion.

◈ PRACTICAL IDEAS

Most teachers seemed to have positive attitudes toward the training program overall and believed the training courses would help them teach English to their students. They understood the difficulty of designing and managing a training program that satisfies every teacher learner and meets each one's needs. The teacher learner's questionnaire brought to the surface what different people needed from the training program as well as their suggestions for improvement of the program. The rest of this section discusses the practical ideas that teacher learners suggested for training other primary EFL teachers.

Organize the Training Courses in Suitable Teacher Training Centers

The teacher learners emphasized the need for an English-only teacher training center equipped with training staff, training facilities, and resources appropriate for training English teachers. Although it is difficult to establish such training centers in the current situation in South Korea, the teacher learners' suggestion should be taken seriously. For example, one option in South Korea could be to send teacher learners to English language institutes in English-speaking countries for at least 3 months, if not longer, to expose them to both the target language and the culture as much as possible. The government should be responsible for all, or at least half, of the expenses associated with such an effort.

The training center should offer special facilities to train English language teachers and to promote a better learning environment. As the teacher learners pointed out, the physical environment and educational facilities are important factors in effective teaching and learning. The teacher learners wanted adequate heating and air conditioning systems in every classroom, lounges in which to relax, a cafeteria, and an available photocopier. They also wanted various audiovisual materials, multimedia resources, and computers to practice teaching and to improve their own learning. Furthermore, the training center should offer facilities for a residential training course with native-English-speaking trainers to provide as many opportunities as possible for teacher learners to be exposed to the target language in a natural learning environment. One important and interesting suggestion by a teacher learner was to decorate lecture rooms like elementary school classrooms so the teacher learners could be trained in an environment similar to the one in which they were going to teach. The trainees also wanted participation in the courses to be voluntary. They felt that trainees who participated in the training program voluntarily would probably be more successful learners and active trainees and attain better results from the course.

Consider Training Schedules Carefully

In this program, teacher learners trained an average of 7–8 hours every day except Sundays for 20 days. This schedule was so tight that fatigue prevented them from being able to fully concentrate on lessons and review what they had learned. The teacher learners found that the emotional pressure might influence the effectiveness of the training program. Also, the content level of the training courses was quite high for most of the teacher learners who were participating in the program for the first time. It seems that the program was developed without sufficient information about the target population it was meant to train. Therefore, the teaching staff should investigate in advance the teacher learners' level of English proficiency, their background knowledge about tasks they are going to do, and their learning capacity so as to develop an effective training schedule for the prospective teacher learners.

Include Practical Training That Focuses on Teaching Methods and Skills

Through the South Korean training program, the teacher learners gained confidence in teaching English to their students and learned a variety of teaching methods and techniques applicable to real teaching situations: how to prepare teaching materials and classroom activities and how to improve their English speaking and listening skills. For example, the teacher learners considered observing model classes run by experienced elementary English teachers to be one of the most helpful aspects of the course. Practicing elementary English teachers knew the appropriate ways to teach English to children and possessed expertise in preparing teaching materials to be used for planned activities. The teacher learners also benefited from having opportunities to demonstrate their own lessons, observe other teacher learners' demonstrations, and engage in hands-on experiences using authentic teaching materials. Through such instructional practice, teacher learners exchanged feedback that helped them improve their own teaching.

Regarding course offerings, the teacher learners mostly wanted practical courses such as Speaking and Listening in English, Methods in Teaching English, Songs and Games for Teaching English to Children, Observations in Elementary English Classes, and Teaching English Pronunciation. That is, the teacher learners felt that all training should be directly centered on the everyday school situation and the target teachers' job so that teachers would immediately be able to see the relevance to their own classrooms (Hayes, 1995; Veenman, Tulder, & Voeten, 1994). As Hayes (1995, 1997b) argues, training courses should be essentially practical and give teacher learners an opportunity to put into practice what they have learned in a nonthreatening environment.

Offer an English Language Course

Teacher learners need to practice and use English to improve their English speaking and listening skills. Teaching staff should keep in mind that the course content, teaching methods, and text materials should relate to English classes in the elementary school. And the course should focus on teaching classroom English with the words and phrases used in elementary English classes, rather than those used in ordinary adult English classes. In this training program, the content of the English language course was very similar to adult English as a second language (ESL) classes, with a focus on teaching English communicative skills for daily life. However, most teacher learners wanted to learn classroom English so they could use the target language as a medium of instruction in their classrooms and to apply what they learned directly to their English classes. It was also suggested that the class size should be reduced to fewer than 10 teacher learners and that they should be grouped by their level of English proficiency, which would allow every class member to have more opportunities to use the target language during class.

Provide Information About Relevant Educational Policies and Curricula

Through the South Korean training program, the teacher learners gained a better understanding of the new policy and the new curriculum for elementary English language education. Courses like the ones offered in this program help teacher learners develop more positive attitudes toward policy implementation and increase their motivation.

Keep in Mind the Usefulness of Native-English-Speaking Trainers

South Korean teacher learners mentioned that native-English-speaking trainers played an important role in their training by helping the teacher learners reduce their anxieties and improve their English pronunciation and communicative skills. The teacher learners reported that they were no longer afraid to speak English to native speakers after working with native-English-speaking trainers. They also found learning about English language and English-speaking cultures through classes with native-speaking trainers to be a valuable experience. However, these trainers needed to develop their teaching methods, text materials, and lesson plans to match the teacher learners' level of English proficiency and the purpose of the training program. Some teacher learners, because of their low English proficiency level, had a difficult time understanding native-English-speaking trainers' instructions. Teacher learners should be placed in classes according to their competence, and native-English-speaking trainers should keep this in mind when developing lesson plans based on proficiency level and teaching their classes.

Improve Trainers' Teaching Skills and Provide Well-Prepared Lessons

In this training program, the text materials and resources some trainers used were useful and sufficient in training elementary teachers as English teachers; they used authentic teaching materials and demonstrated how to design them in detail. In fact, the teacher learners wanted to use such materials for their own teaching. However, some trainers' teaching methods or techniques did not satisfy the teacher learners. The learners preferred trainers who motivated them and taught them in vivid and interesting ways using various methods and materials. Trainers who did so got maximum participation from teacher learners, compared with trainers who bored teacher learners by reading the textbook. Responses on this topic indicate that learning is often effectively achieved if teacher learners experience the target approach, rather than simply hear about it (Bax, 1997). For these teacher learners, a one-sided lecture without their participation was useless. All trainers need to avoid lecture-based or transmission-style teaching methods, which do not help teacher learners acquire and understand the content of a lesson. Ibrahim (1991) and Hayes (1997b) also argue that such modes of training do little to encourage specific teaching or learning behavior. As the teacher learners suggested, the trainers should make efforts to interact with learners through different kinds of classroom activities, such as comprehension checks or discussions about the specific topic, rather than simply read the textbook.

Hire Trainers With Related Teaching Experience and Knowledge of Elementary English Language Education

Teacher learners also mentioned that most professors on the teaching staff did not know what it was like to teach English in elementary school. They felt that some teaching staff members had theoretical knowledge about teaching English to children, but they rarely had actual teaching experience with children. Their lectures, as a result, were often too superficial and not realistic. If the trainers had some teaching experience with children, they could offer more realistic and practical instructions and understand the difficulties that elementary teachers encounter in English classes.

In fact, the teacher learners preferred elementary school English teachers as trainers to experts from universities. Hayes (1995, 1997b) found that using practicing teachers as trainers was valuable to teacher learners because of the practicing teachers' classroom experience, whereas training given by "experts" from local universities was not as valued. Therefore, trainers in the teacher training program should be teachers who practice what they preach. If the South Korean trainers had practical teaching experience, or at least extensive observations of English classes in the elementary school, they would not only have a better understanding of children and the difficulties that teachers face, but also be able to offer more realistic and practical instructions.

Ensure That Assessments Correspond to the Objectives of the Training Program

In this program, the objectives were to develop teacher learners' teaching skills on the one hand and to improve their English language skills on the other. First, it is mainly the teacher learners' English teaching ability that should be evaluated, and standardized written tests should not be used. Written tests were not appropriate for assessing their competence or performance; they only measured how much the teacher learners were able to memorize, rather than what they learned from the training courses. One teacher learner commented,

> Standardized written tests are not necessary. Such type of tests assesses not the teacher learners' actual ability to teach English, but short-term memory—for example, how well teacher learners memorize theories. Teacher learners should be assessed by their performance in the training courses, not by written tests.

Teacher learners preferred a performance test that is more relevant to the purpose of the training course. Teaching staff should make efforts to develop an efficient and effective testing system, such as demonstration of a lesson, a listening comprehension test, an interview with native speakers, or comprehensive tests for theories in teaching English.

In addition, the training center should conduct a preassessment or placement test for teacher learners when they enter a training program in order to evaluate each teacher learner's level of English proficiency and knowledge of training. The results of such a test would offer trainers a better understanding of the teacher learners, and teacher learners could be placed in the most appropriate class.

Offer Professional Training Programs and Follow-Up Programs

The South Korean teacher learners wanted an independent professional training program designed for specific training purposes, which would permit them to select courses according to their preferences or needs. The teacher learners also requested as many opportunities as possible to participate in the English teacher training program and follow-up training programs regularly so that they could exchange new educational information and effective teaching methodologies, improve their communicative English language skills, and discuss problems they encounter in class.

◈ CONCLUSION

Since 1997, English has been taught in South Korea as a required subject to students beginning in the third grade in elementary school. When this new educational policy was implemented, there were very few English language teachers in the elementary schools because there had been no official program to educate English teachers for that level.

Because of the shortage of elementary school English teachers, the South Korean government and the Ministry of Education decided to train regular elementary school classroom teachers to teach English to their students. The government and the ministry have also supported provincial boards of education in setting up English teacher training programs for elementary teachers. Through these programs, many teachers have gained knowledge, improved their English language skills, learned English teaching methods, and gained confidence in teaching English. These English teacher training programs have played an important role in elementary school English language education.

Investigating South Korean teacher learners' opinions of their training program was very useful for them. It helped them strengthen their learning through critical reflection on their performance in the program, and it played a positive role in improving the quality of training (Gower, Phillip, & Walters, 1995). This study shows that the training program plays an important role in encouraging elementary school teachers to make personal efforts to improve their own teaching skills and English proficiency, and in helping teacher learners gain confidence in teaching English to children. Furthermore, analyzing the teacher learners' opinions provides suggestions for improving the quality of training in future programs.

It is true that there are various expectations, needs, and suggestions for any training program regarding the target teacher learners, the length of training, or the purpose of the training. It is important for training staff to accept teacher learners' demands, dissatisfaction, or suggestions and to analyze them and include what the teacher learners want to learn from the training program. Although some of the suggestions presented in this study might seem idealistic, anyone setting up a training center should consider such suggestions seriously and make a great effort to find ways to implement them.

◈ CONTRIBUTOR

Sung-Hee Park received her MA in teaching English to speakers of other languages (TESOL) from Southern Illinois University at Carbondale and is a doctoral candidate in TESOL at the University of Kansas. She is currently a lecturer in TESOL and English education at Sejong University and Chungang University in South Korea. Her research interests include second/foreign language learning strategies, second language acquisition, and teacher training.

◈ APPENDIX

Training Curriculum	Class Hours	Practical Test	Written Test	Points
1. Speaking and Listening A (native speaker trainers)	40	O		400
2. Speaking and Listening B (South Korean trainers)	12	O		100
3. Understanding the Elementary English Curriculum	2		O	
4. Theory of English Education	2		O	
5. Materials Preparation	2		O	100
6. Testing	2		O	
7. English Teaching Methodology	2		O	
8. Teaching Methods English Pronunciation	5		O	
9. Methods in Teaching Listening	5		O	
10. Methods in Teaching Speaking	4		O	200
11. Methods in Teaching Reading	2		O	
12. Methods in Teaching Writing	2		O	
13. Practice Teaching	10		O	100
14. Using Songs in the English Classroom	2			
15. Using Chants and Rhyme in the English Classroom	2			
16. Using Games in the English Classroom	2			
17. Language Instructions Through Open Education	2			
18. Storytelling in the English Classroom	2			
19. Using Role Play	2			
20. Multimedia in the English Classroom	2			
21. Creative Activities	2			
22. Using Audiovisual Tools	2			
23. Classroom English	2			
24. Using Overhead Projectors and Video	2			
25. Creative Activities in the English Classroom	2			
26. Special Lecture	2			
27. Assessment Test	2			
Registration and Orientation	2			
Total hours	**120**			

Note. O = Available test.

CHAPTER 14

Enabling Effective Practices in the Teaching and Learning of English in Hong Kong

Gertrude Tinker Sachs and Tony Mahon

◈ INTRODUCTION

Enabling learners in another language requires that educators and facilitators provide and create the setting, space, and opportunities in classroom teaching and curriculum design for learners to become spontaneous and creative users of the language. To enable learners requires scrutiny of the practices that educators adopt to help learners become risk takers in language learning. Enabling learners implies appreciating how educators assist them in becoming aware of how they claim the target language as their own, make sense of the language, find personal meaning and humor in the language, and learn how to manipulate the language with all its imperfections. These characteristics help learners appreciate their own language learning challenges. However, to enable learners, educators themselves need to be enabled so that they can accord learners' needs, interests, and cultural histories a primary place in their everyday teaching, in the development of their curriculum, and in their use of the textbook and other learning materials and resources. To enable educators means to provide a liberating setting for the enhancement of their knowledge, skills, and teaching attitudes and beliefs. Wilson and Berne (1999) argue that in teachers' professional development there is a strong need for insights into how teacher learning and its relationship to student learning are manifested. They contend that researchers have not demonstrated a clear connection between the two.

In this case study, we show how we facilitated the development of teachers' enabling practices and the general resultant impact on their pupils' English language learning. The central thrust of this study, therefore, is to present a description of some of the key teacher development and pedagogical approaches of a 3-year longitudinal investigation into the implementation of a literature-based approach in the teaching of English as a foreign language (EFL) in several primary schools in the Hong Kong Special Administrative Region of China (HKSAR). In so doing, we demonstrate how the nature of our work enabled Hong Kong primary EFL learners to personally engage in learning English. We describe the work of the project with a special emphasis on some of the enabling practices that teachers adopted, which resulted in students' improved performance on a range of assessment measures. The teachers' engagement in the project afforded them opportunities to change their mindset and their instructional strategies and, simultaneously, their students' overall general performance in what many students had previously called a difficult and boring subject (Tinker Sachs, 2001).

◈ CONTEXT

English in the HKSAR has a unique position because it functions both as a foreign language and as a second language (see Falvey, 1998; Li, 1999). Historically, English has been accorded second language status due to the influence of the British and the prominent role it plays in government, business, commerce, and higher education. Even after the departure of the British in 1997, English has not lost its status and continues to play a dominant role in different spheres of life in Hong Kong. English is also highly valued and sought after. Parents and students recognise its symbolic cultural value (Bourdieu, 1991) and the pragmatic importance of learning it (Li, 1999). However, for the vast majority of HKSAR residents, although they are surrounded daily by English in the media or on the streets and are able to easily access the language, English really functions as a foreign language in its impact on their everyday life. For most Hong Kong citizens, there is very little need to use English for daily transactions or personal communication. Ninety-eight percent of the population is ethnic Chinese, and the medium of communication is Cantonese, a dialect of southern China. The classroom, therefore, remains the principal setting for acquiring English for the majority of Hong Kong citizens.

Most students begin learning English in preschool, and all students learn English formally from Primary 1 through Form 5 and beyond.[1] Students in primary schools have at least seven 30- to 35-minute periods of English per week. In secondary schools, students take at least five periods of English per week, with the duration of each period similar to those in the primary setting. In all, most students in Hong Kong have at least 9–12 years of daily exposure to English in the classroom setting. Yet many in the community are dissatisfied with the level of English spoken by Hong Kong high school graduates, and usually the first to be accorded blame are the education system and the teachers who are a part of it. However, Halliday (1998) reminds that "teaching a foreign language effectively is one of the hardest pedagogical tasks there is" (p. 34). Li (1999) discusses some of the many social factors accounting for the public's perceptions of school leavers' level of English. Two of the main reasons for the perceived decline can be attributed to the fact that secondary and tertiary education has become less elitist over the years, thereby allowing students from a greater range of backgrounds to access English. A second factor is associated with increased language demands for more proficient users of English with the move from manufacturing to service-oriented jobs (Au, 1998; Choi, 1998).

In addition to society's demand for more proficient speakers of English, there has been persistent government pressure on teachers to change their pedagogical practices. During the past 20 years, the official government syllabi for teaching English have gone through dramatic changes; there has been a noticeable shift from an audiolingual focus on oral proficiency, to communicative language teaching of information-gap activities, to the current focus on task-based learning and the use of new technologies in English language teaching (Pang & Wong, 2000; Wong & Pang, 2000). However, although official documentation has evidenced significant changes over a relatively short period, the extent to which the official syllabi have been

---

[1] Children start formal education at age 6 in Primary 1, which is equivalent to Grade 1 in North America. Form 5 is equivalent to Grade 12. Many students study Forms 6 and 7 to attain A levels, which are required for admission to university.

translated into classroom practice is highly debatable. During the past decade, there has been a high degree of resistance not only to the rapidity of new curriculum initiatives but also to the content and degree of change required in teachers' classroom practices (Adamson, Kwan, & Chan, 2000; Carless, 1997, 1999) and ways of thinking (Mahon & Tinker Sachs, 1995). Similarly, during the past few years, there has been a surge in government demands for the increased professionalisation of teachers. Teachers are now expected to have a first degree and certification in the subjects taught, and teachers of English in particular are now required to demonstrate their ability to meet the standards of the Language Proficiency Assessment Test (LPAT) for teachers (Coniam, 1998) or face dismissal from their posts.

◈ DESCRIPTION

In response to the need to enhance students' exposure to English beyond the textbook in language-enriched contexts, the Primary English Reading Project (PERP) was formed in 1994.[2] The Project Team[3] conducted two interrelated studies on learning and teaching reading in English in a local primary school. The first study was a comprehensive baseline study of primary pupils' reading behaviour (Tinker Sachs & Mahon, 1997). The team discovered that pupils in Primary 1–6 demonstrated a weak foundation in English reading strategies and lacked exposure to a wide range of English texts. Pupils also demonstrated a strong reliance on memory when reading aloud words that they had been exposed to. However, when approaching unfamiliar words, students often made no attempt to read them. The second study examined the core reading in English instructional practices of teachers from 79 primary schools (Chow, Lee, & Murphy, 1996). This study revealed that teachers tended to adopt a narrow range of teaching strategies that were essentially defined by the course books they used. These strategies focused on teaching grammar and vocabulary and included limited, if any, explicit instruction in how to read or write effectively in English. Based on the results of these two studies, and the team's knowledge and experience from working with teachers, the Project Team applied for and received funding from the Hong Kong government to conduct a 3-year longitudinal investigation into the teaching and learning of reading in Hong Kong primary schools.[4]

The project included four core components. The first of these was support for schools in developing comprehensive English reading programmes that were appropriate to their needs and circumstances. The second important aspect of this development work was a monitoring and assessment component to evaluate children's performance and progress in a wide range of reading literacy skills. The third component was a strong school-based staff development strand that involved teachers and school principals in the design and ongoing development of the project.

---

[2] PERP was established by lecturers at the former Institute of Language in Education (ILE). The ILE was merged with the Hong Kong government's colleges of education in 1995 to form the Hong Kong Institute of Education.

[3] In addition to us, the two principal investigators, there were other team members who are acknowledged at the end of this chapter.

[4] The project was funded for HK$1.56 million (slightly more than US$200,000) by the Language Fund of the Hong Kong SAR government.

The final component involved dissemination of the project's findings, in terms of research on children's reading and on the effectiveness of particular strategies in other schools. The core components of the project are encapsulated in the following objectives:

- Investigate school-based practices in teaching and learning reading in English in Hong Kong primary schools.

- Collaborate with teachers and school administrators in developing comprehensive reading programmes designed to meet the needs and interests of pupils in Primary 4–6.

- Promote and encourage reading in English through the development of supportive reading environments, including the creation of classroom and schoolwide print-rich environments.

- Develop teachers' skills and expertise in explicit reading strategy instruction in reading in English.

- Monitor pupils' progress and attitudes toward reading in English for the duration of the project.

- Develop parental awareness and support for the reading programmes.

- Extend the project to other schools through the provision of supportive in-service packages and start-up kits.

All primary schools in Hong Kong received invitation packets to consider joining the project. But the Project Team was concerned about making an impact where it was most needed, so we agreed that PERP would select schools that were representative of the primary schools in Hong Kong and that did not possess well-developed reading programmes. Thus, schools that lacked well-developed school and class library systems would be given priority for admission to the project. It was also important that schools demonstrate their willingness to make a commitment to the project by providing time within the curriculum for the project to be conducted; hence, schools were required to commit one or two lessons a week to PERP. The Project Team also wanted a critical mass of four to six teachers from Primary 4 classes to join the project on a voluntary basis, so we asked school administrators to recruit only interested teachers for our project. The teachers were expected to remain with the project for 3 years and progress with their students to Primary 6. The purpose of all of these criteria was to ensure a project that was geared toward success by having willing participants and sufficient time in which to run the programme. After a careful selection process, five schools were invited to participate in the initial development phase of the project. In the final year of the project, eight additional schools were selected to participate in the extension phase.

A total of 17 teachers and approximately 680 Primary 4 students from the five core schools participated in the project. There was an average of 35 pupils in each class, with approximately equal numbers of boys and girls. In the final year of the project, the number of schools was expanded to include eight more for a total of 72 teachers, 83 classes, and approximately 3,000 pupils from a variety of Hong Kong districts representing a range of socioeconomic backgrounds. In general, students in the project classes had had 4 years of English language learning with about seven to nine 35-minute periods of English per week. They displayed the same reading weaknesses found in our baseline study (Tinker Sachs & Mahon, 1997) described previously. They had weak vocabulary and limited reading comprehension and word recognition strategies. Teacher participants also manifested a similar narrow range of instructional behaviours found in Chow et al.'s (1996) study.

◈ DISTINGUISHING FEATURES

Principles Underlying the Development of PERP

In determining the principles, key approaches, and instructional strategies underlying this pedagogical focus, the Project Team was influenced by the work of both reading theorists and reading educator practitioners. In particular, the thinking of the Project Team was informed by the perspectives of reading theorists whose work emphasised reading as an interactive or transactional meaning-making process, particularly, Anderson (1984); Paris, Lipson, and Wixson (1994); Pearson and Dole (1987); Ruddell and Ruddell (1994); Ruddell and Unrau (1994); and Rumelhart (1985). The Project Team was also influenced by the work of reading educators who had been engaged in the development of shared reading with big books and the use of children's literature as a strategy for teaching children to read, such as Holdaway (1979), Lynch (1986), and Slaughter (1993). We were also impressed with the success of different book flood projects in countries in the Asia Pacific region (Fiji, Singapore, and Brunei), in particular Elley (1997), Elley and Manghubai (1983), Ng (1994), and Ng and Soh (1986). Exposure to quality children's literature had been an important aspect of each of these projects. We also recognised the importance of attention to explicit instruction of skills in, for example, phonological awareness and drew on the work of Adams (1990, 1994) and Goswami and Bryant (1990).

Our teacher development strand was underpinned by research and literature in the areas of teacher development and curriculum change (Fullan & Hargreaves, 1996; Fullan & Steigelbauer, 1991; Grimmett & Crehan, 1992; Guskey, 1986; Hargreaves, 1992, 1994; Hargreaves & Fullan, 1992; Leithwood, 1992; Little, 1987, 1990); teacher beliefs (Datnow & Castellano, 2000; Richardson, 1994, 1996; Richardson, Anders, Tidwell, & Lloyd, 1991); and constructivist teacher education (Richardson, 1997). The Project Team was particularly influenced by the Reading Instruction Study, which adopted a school-based model of teacher development (Richardson, 1994; Richardson & Anders, 1994).

At the heart of all of these principles was the concept of collaboration. Collaboration involved all parties working closely together to decide on directions, responsibilities, and roles as well as a mutual definition of shared visions of what the project would mean in individual schools. It was conceived as conceptually different from cooperation, which often tends to rely mainly on following the vision of a leader (Hargreaves, 1994; Tinker Sachs & Mahon, 1998). The next section provides a description of some of the strategies the team used to enable effective practices in the teaching and learning of English.

Effective Teacher Practices

The following five main strategies were adopted to support teachers in their professional development in PERP (Mahon & Tinker Sachs, 1995, 1996):

- offer across-school and within-school teacher development workshops
- provide resources—namely, big books, class library books, and teacher development booklets—and develop curriculum units
- assess, report, and discuss pupils' progress
- conduct school visits
- produce a newsletter

In addition to supporting teachers in developing further knowledge, understandings, and skills about reading literacy, these strategies were adopted to help teachers develop a sense of identity with and ownership of the project. The strategies were also utilised to promote teacher efficacy in assuming leadership to facilitate the development of a literature-based approach to teaching English in their schools. In the next section, we describe the major features of the first two of the five key teacher development strategies: offering across- and within-school workshops, and providing big books and developing curriculum units. We also provide insights into a typical PERP lesson by commenting on teachers' perceptions.

Commentary on the PERP Lesson

Through key strategies, PERP afforded students an opportunity to enjoy learning English. The enjoyment factor featured prominently in students' responses when they were questioned about the PERP lessons, and it was also a dominant feature of the teacher data. Before PERP, students viewed English as boring and difficult. With active engagement of pupils, as can be seen in the lesson transcriptions in the next section, students experienced the opportunity to savour learning English in a setting that was conducive to learning. Through their personal response (see Rosenblatt, 1938/1976), students had an opportunity to become personally involved in learning English, thereby reducing many of their language learning anxieties (Tsui, 1996). The following comments made by PERP teachers and students illustrate the enjoyment factor as a dominant response of PERP participants:

> They enjoy it because there's a lot of activity, a lot of chances to . . . express themselves and more chances than in the usual . . . er . . . English lessons. More predictions and more activities. And in the big books, some of the characters do some funny things and they laugh a lot. That's another bit of enjoyment for them. (Teacher C)

> They have become more confident when they read. They will think about the story, what does it mean, think about the cause and the problem. In the regular English lesson, they won't because they know it is only part of the textbook. (Teacher D)

> They know more about English. Before it's too boring. Maybe the teacher didn't tell them English is interesting. They just teach it as a subject but this time English is a language. I think this is a change for them. It's emotional. They are more eager to learn. (Teacher E)

> In my opinion the best book is *Sloppy Tiger* because the content is very interesting and there are many funny things happening to him. We all smiled and laughed during the lesson. We raised up our hands more often and answered more questions than the other lessons. The words and the pictures

of the big books are large. The stories are funnier. Some boring stories have many words and I think it's troublesome and difficult to read but the big books have few words and they are easier to understand. (Primary 6, Student A, translation)

I like big books because reading is very interesting. There is a chance for us to have our teacher telling stories and we do not have to read by ourselves, especially when I do not know some words. In this lesson, we can read a lot of story books and learn a lot of new words. (Primary 6, Student B, translation)

During our initial workshops, many teachers often expressed amazement at the answers the students could generate during the PERP lessons and particularly during the prediction stages of the lessons. At all stages of the project, however, teachers were concerned about project demands on their limited time and the fact that the syllabus content was not reduced to accommodate the two periods for the project. In many instances, the two lessons for PERP became a casualty when the regular syllabus demands were overwhelming, and teachers felt they were lagging far behind their nonproject teachers of the same teaching level. The project was added to the existing teaching content and created unusual stress and challenges for teachers whose students had to take form or grade-level exams at the end of the year along with the nonproject students.

◈ PRACTICAL IDEAS

PERP teachers attended numerous large, across-school and small, within-school workshops led by the Project Team. One of the first workshops dealt with the shared-reading approach. Team members modeled, practiced, and discussed the rationale and procedures for using big books (Slaughter, 1993). Later, they worked with teachers in their classes to assist them in developing shared-reading instructional skills and practices. In the following sections, we provide more information on procedures and offer recommendations for implementation in a variety of classroom settings.

Select Suitable Books for Learners

During the course of the project, the 13 project schools received 289 big books. The number of big books supplied to individual schools ranged from 13 to 42, with an average of 22 books per school (see the appendix for a sample list of the books provided). In the initial stages, a selection of big books was made by the Project Team and later endorsed by the teachers for use with their respective groups of learners. The final selection was based on interests of and appeal to learners, illustrations, repetitive language patterns, rhyming words, and vocabulary load. Above all, when selecting appropriate big books from the wide range of those available, teachers need to keep in mind their learners' experiences and literacy needs and the kinds of after-reading experiences they want to afford them.

After selecting appropriate books to use with a particular class, it is important to rehearse before meeting the students to determine how the story will be read to promote student interest and enjoyment and also to decide on the focus of the literacy skills to be developed in the after-reading activities.

Prepare for Shared Reading

Teachers need to create a warm socioemotional setting for listening and responding to the story. They can do this by allowing students to move from their regular seats to sit on the floor or to sit in a semicircle so they can all see the book and the teacher. Setting is important in fostering the development of community and the shared experience of reading.

In creating a setting conducive to a shared-reading experience, many project teachers were concerned with classroom management in moving students from their traditional seating in rows. Because of the small size of classrooms and the large number of students, team members recommended encouraging students who sat at the back to move their chairs into the aisles to bring the back half of the class closer to the front. The teachers were also concerned about where to place the book and how to hold it. Team members recommended that teachers find what is comfortable for them. Some teachers liked to place the book on a stand or chair and sit at the side, whereas others were more comfortable holding the book. Whatever choice is made, it is important to ensure that students can see the book easily and that the teacher is comfortable making appropriate hand movements, which may involve tracking the words with a pointer or with the hand as well as making gestures to dramatise the reading of the story.

Stimulate Interest in the Story Before Reading

Before reading the story, teachers need to help students develop interest in the story. One way to do this is to discuss the illustrations or the book cover and ask students to predict what they think the story is about. Students can also look at the title of the book and guess what will happen in the story. Their predictions and ideas can be written on the board (which can take the form of a semantic map, as illustrated in Figure 1) so that they can be referred to later.

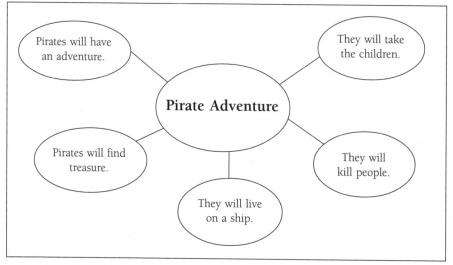

FIGURE 1. Semantic Map

Would you like to be a pirate?							
Yes							
No							

Reasons

Yes No

Figure 2. Building Expectations

K What I already know	W What I want to find out	L What I learned

Figure 3. KWL Framework

To build their expectations about the story, another prereading activity can focus on the main character(s). For example, in the story *Pirate Adventure* (Hunt, 1988), teachers can ask the students to look at the cover and describe the pirate they see. Related questions such as "Would you like to be a pirate?" may help children form more connections before reading. Teachers can then ask students for their reasons, which can be recorded on the chalkboard (see Figure 2).

Another prereading activity that taps into students' background knowledge and develops their interest in the theme of the story is to use a Know-Want-Learned (KWL) framework (Ogle, 1986). This framework can be revisited at the end of the story so that students can tell what they learned. It can be extended even further by adding another column to develop independent reading and research habits: What I still want to learn. Figure 3 shows an example of a KWL chart.

Solid background knowledge of a topic supports comprehension of the text. When stories contain less familiar topics, teachers can use strategies in addition to KWL at the prereading stage to help children develop or extend their background knowledge. The following excerpt demonstrates how one teacher (T) helped her Primary 5 students (Ss) determine the meaning of a word by drawing on their background knowledge of pirates in the story *The Wicked Pirate* (Eggleton, 1998).

Excerpt 1

T: Let's see the title of the book: *The*— . Do you know this word? (pointing to the word *wicked* in the book's title)

Ss: No.

T: You don't know this word? (writing the word *wicked* on the chalkboard)

T: It's an adjective. OK. You know this part of the word. (pointing to the first syllable in the word) OK, try . . . Jacky?

S1: /wĭk'/.

T: /wĭk'/ . . . Margaret?

S2: /wĭkėd/

T: Yes, /wĭkėd/. OK. Now, try to guess its meaning. Adjective for *pirate,* an adjective.

S: Brave.

T: Brave, OK. You think it's brave? That word means brave? But no, not brave, can you guess? (S looking in the dictionary) No, no need to have the dictionary, just guess. Any ideas? No ideas? (drawing the outline for a semantic map on the board)

T: OK. Can you tell me anything about pirates? After this part you can guess the meaning of this word. OK. Tell me anything you know about pirates. Any ideas? Any words you know? (S raises his hand)

T: William?

S4: Some of the pirates is . . . are ugly.

T: Ugly. OK. Some of them, not all of them, some are ugly. Am I right? OK. Any more ideas? (writing *ugly* on the semantic map). Bernard?

S5: The police want to catch them.

T: OK. OK. The police want to catch them. Policemen want to take all of them into prison. You know prison? (writing on the board)

Ss: *Gàam yuhk* [prison].

T: Right. Any ideas? Do you think pirates are good or bad?

Ss: Bad.

T: You think they are bad.

Ss: Yes.

T: OK. Some of them, most of them are bad. OK. What did they do? What do they do?

Ss: Kill, take money. (shouting out answers)

T: Get money. They want to get money. OK. Kill others. (writing on the board)

T: OK. Anything else?

S6: Steal things.

T: Yes, they stole. Maybe they rob. They rob things from the sea. OK. Can you get this word now? Wicked? Yes?

Ss: Bad.

T: Yes, that means bad, very bad, very, very bad. (emphasizing *very*; Ss laugh) Very, very bad. OK. OK. Let's read the story together. You know a lot of things about pirates. Now you can read the story to see what the wicked pirates did. The wicked pirates, the very, very bad pirates, very, very bad. Story by Jill Eggleton.

Carry Out the First Reading

After preparing the students, it is time for the first reading of the story, which provides a model of reading aloud. The teacher should read the story in an animated and enthusiastic manner with appropriate facial expressions, intonation, emphasis, and gestures to enliven the telling of the story. A pointer or finger may be used to track the words. The pointer should not jerk or bounce because it could disturb the students who are following the words.

Stop and Ask Students to Predict

During the first reading, teachers may stop at interesting and exciting parts and, before turning the page, ask students to predict what will happen next. Teachers should be careful about the number of prediction questions they ask because too many could lessen students' enjoyment of the story. Prediction is an important part of the reading process. It requires the reader to use semantic, syntactic, and graphophonic knowledge and cues in the text to anticipate and predict what language or events will occur. The following excerpt from a Primary 4 lesson illustrates this strategy. The teacher is reading from the big book *Pirate Adventure* (Hunt, 1988). In the excerpt, the teacher is eliciting students' views on what will happen next. During prediction, students often use their first language as a resource to supplement their second language. The teacher accepts all of their first language responses to maintain the flow of the storytelling.

Excerpt 2

T: (reading from the story) "What an adventure!" said Biff. "What an adventure!" What an exciting story. OK. So who comes? Who comes?

Ss: Pirate.

T: Pirates come?

Ss: Yes.

T: Yes, let see. (turning the page) Well, a pirate . . . .

S1: *Daaih gauh sèui* [a big guy].

T: OK, is this one the same as our book cover? Is this one the same as our cover?

S1: Yes, *gó go daaih gauh sèui* [that big guy].

T: He . . . .

Ss: *Daaih gauh sèui a, daaih gauh sèui a* [oh, that big guy, that big guy].

T: Are they the same? (showing the picture of the book cover and the one in the story)

Ss: Yes.

T: Yes, this pirate comes. He had a sword. What did he do? What did he do? Can you read it out please? "He" . . . .

Ss: "He looked at the children." (reading the text)

T: And what did the pirate say?

Ss: Children. (reading the text)

T: Children! (in a dramatic tone)

Ss: *Daaih gauh sèui a* [oh, that big guy].

T: Well, why did he want the children? Why did he want the children? Yes, Tammy?

S2: Kill them.

T: Kill them.

S3: *Jáam kéuih sahp baat lūk* [cut them into 18 pieces].

T: Cut them into parts. Yes, Felix?

S4: Dump, *kéuih deih lohk hói* [throw them into the sea].

T: Throw them into the sea.

S5: *Lòh kéuih deih làih bòu tòng* [use them to make a soup].

T: Yes, what about Tony?

S6: *Jūk kéuih deih lohk sí hàang* [throw them into rubbish bin].

T: It's smelly there. Yes. OK, let's see. OK. (turning the page)

After the first reading, teachers should return to the initial predictions that students made about the cover and/or title of the story. Teachers should encourage students to confirm or modify their initial predictions and ideas.

Do the Second Reading

When it is time to read the story a second time, teachers invite students to join the teacher in reading the text (not repeating after the teacher) so that they can emulate and follow the teacher's intonation and phrasing. Children at different levels of understanding may respond to participating in the second reading differently: Some may join in and read along, some may only join in the repetitions, and others may just follow the pictures and listen. It is therefore important to use the pointer or a finger to facilitate the tracking and reading of the story by slower readers. Reluctant readers will also find it easier to join in if the story has a lot of repetitive patterned language and rhyming words. Pause before the patterned words or phrases and let the pupils read the words alone. After the second reading, encourage them to share their feelings and ideas about some of the events and characters in the story.

Create Follow-Up Activities

After students have participated in shared reading, teachers should create follow-up activities to provide explicit instruction in reading skills and strategies. In the PERP lessons, the postreading activities focused on sequencing and retelling the story, developing sight vocabulary, developing phonological awareness, engaging in repeated readings, and getting students to respond in a personal way to the stories. Some examples and ideas of how the team used these strategies follow. These examples, as in the previous ones, come from the project's curriculum units and teachers' handbooks. The examples are also illustrative of how *Pirate Adventure* was used (it was the most popular of all the big book stories).

Extend Sequencing Activities

Sequencing activities can help students recall the events of the story and reinforce the concept of story structure or story grammar (Tierney, Readence, & Dishner, 1995). Reading comprehension and narrative writing skills can also be enhanced when children have an understanding of story structure, which involves knowing the setting, characters, problem, episodes, and resolution of the problem. When introducing story structure to students, teachers can begin by modeling the process with the whole class. Select four key events from the big book story and create sentence strips on separate sheets of paper for each event. Similarly, teachers can create pictures on separate pieces of paper for the main events and ask students to come to the front of the classroom and hold them so that the rest of the class can see. The pictures are not in sequence, and the class must place them in the correct order and then place each one on the board until all are posted in the correct order. Afterward, teachers can ask another group of students to do the same ordering with the sentence strips and then place each sentence strip under the appropriate picture (see Figure 4). When the sentence strips are in place, teachers can ask the whole class, or groups of students, to read the story.

To develop pupils' initial skills in retelling the story without help, teachers can remove one or more of the captions and ask pupils to read the remaining captions

Picture 1	Picture 2	Picture 3	Picture 4
Sentence 1	Sentence 2	Sentence 3	Sentence 4
_____	_____	_____	_____
_____	_____	_____	_____
_____	_____	_____	_____

FIGURE 4. Sequencing a Story

and fill in the missing caption(s) in their own words. If this is too challenging, cover only part of each caption. After participating in whole-class activities, students can be given smaller pictures and captions and work in pairs to sequence and match. They may then retell to each other. When pupils are proficient at sequencing, they can then engage in a variety of story structure activities, such as oral or written retelling of the story (Figure 5) and identification of key story elements (Figure 6), which are all supported by their original rewriting of the story. Students may also construct their own story endings (Figure 7) or explore character traits (Figure 8).

Have Students Retell Stories Orally

Being able to retell a story in one's own words in a foreign language is quite a challenging task for children. PERP students were supported in developing their confidence in this area through a range of scaffolded activities, which extend the story structure tasks, examples of which were given earlier.

Work on Developing Students' Sight Vocabulary

Research is very clear on the importance of a strong sight vocabulary for fluent reading (see, e.g., Adams, 1990). Weak sight vocabulary also affects comprehension of text and consequently the ability to talk and write about what has been read. To develop a strong sight vocabulary, pupils need repeated exposure to key words and phrases and, most of all, numerous opportunities to use them in speaking and writing and in individual and pair or group activities. The following sections offer suggestions for developing sight vocabulary and building fluency.

Use Word Charts

Teachers can select 5–10 words and phrases from the story that they would like their pupils to learn to recognise on sight. These may be content words related to a particular topic, such as nouns, adjectives, and adverbs, or they may be function words that are easily confused, such as *they, there,* and *them.* These words can be written on a large chart and displayed in a prominent place in the classroom. Teachers should read the words aloud to the class and ask pupils to repeat them as a class or individually. This should be done for a few minutes as often as possible and should be incorporated into the daily classroom procedures. During the work with words, students should be encouraged to tell what they know about the word or phrase and where they saw it and then asked to use the word or phrase in a sentence.

For concrete nouns, teachers may use pictures and labels to support recognition.

Three Billy Goats Gruff

In this story the problem starts when the three Billy Goats Gruff ate all the grass in their valley. The bridge lived a great troll.

After that, the little Billy Goat Gruff crossed the bridge. The troll wanted to eat him. The troll let him go because he was too small.

Next, middle Billy Goat crossed the bridge. The troll let him go because he wanted to eat the bigger one.

Then, the Great Billy Goat Gruff crossed the bridge. The troll wanted to eat him. The Great Billy Goat Gruff poked him and kicked him and scared him.

The problem is finally solved when The troll tumbled off the bridge, own into the deep water under the bridge. The Great Billy Goat Gruff crossed the bridge.

The story ends with the three Billy Goat Gruff, had plenty to eat and lived happily even after. No one has ever seen the troll again.

FIGURE 5. Write a Retelling of the Story

Students' sight vocabulary may also be developed using games such as bingo and other board games.

Use Vocabulary Books

Active involvement in the creation of individual vocabulary books with all the words and phrases students are learning can also help to build sight vocabulary. In the vocabulary books, students can be asked to give the key word or phrase and, amongst other aspects, the meaning(s), the translation, a drawing of the word or phrase, and a sentence using the word or phrase. It is also important for teachers to

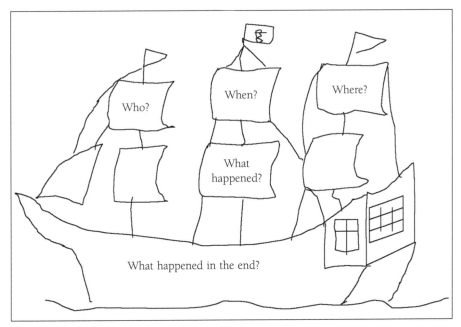

FIGURE 6. Identify the Key Story Elements

allow time in class for sharing the vocabulary books, and the new words contained in them, at least once a week. The vocabulary books and the word charts can form the basis of a print-rich literacy environment. As pupils work with stories and engage in the activities, their work can be posted to promote sight recognition and vocabulary development.

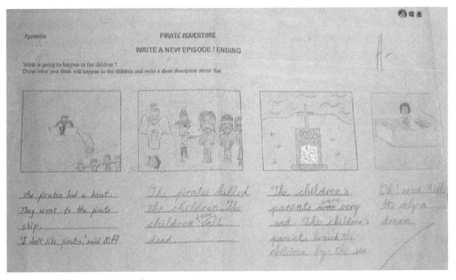

FIGURE 7. Write a New Ending

POLICE INFORMATION FORM

Name: _____

Age: _____

Appearance: _____

_____

_____

Special Features: _____

_____

Crime: _____

Reward: _____

FIGURE 8. Identify Character Traits Using a Wanted Poster

TABLE 1. ONSETS AND RIMES

Word	Syllable	Onset and Rime	Phoneme
bag	bag	b-ag	b-a-g
string	string	str-ing	s-t-r-I-n-g
peanut	pea-nut	p-ea/n-ut	p-ea-n-u-t

Work on Students' Phonological Awareness

In addition to developing sight vocabulary, the ability to decode and encode written language is another essential aspect of the reading process. Students need to be able to work out how to read new words that they come across when reading. PERP teachers were introduced to different strategies to foster phonological awareness in their pupils through teaching phonics within the context of the big book stories. One of the easiest strategies is helping pupils become aware of the onsets and rimes in words. Words contain syllables, and each syllable can be divided into an onset and rime. The onset is the beginning sound of the syllable, and the rime is the rest of the syllable (Adams, 1990). This is a rather different concept from traditional phonics, which focuses on learning individual phonemes or sounds. Table 1 helps to make the distinction clear.

In the following excerpt, a project teacher uses onsets and rimes to help Primary 4 students with the pronunciation of some words in the story *Pirate Adventure* (Hunt, 1988).

Excerpt 3

T: Now, another word, l-o-c-k, *lock*. This is the word from the storybook. Lock. Say, l, /l/.
Ss: /l/.
T: /l/.
Ss: /l/.
T: o-c-k, /ɔk/.
Ss: /ɔk/.
T: Lock.
Ss: Lock.

T: Now, can you suggest another word?

S1:   R-o-c-k. (spelling the word)

T: Good. R-o-c-k. Can you pronounce this word?

S1:   Co . . . .

T: R-o-c-k. You don't know? Can you read the word? (S4 shakes his head.)
      No? Try.

S2:   Rock.

T: Rock! Good. Say it again. Rock.

Ss: Rock.

T: Rock.

Ss: Rock.

T: /r/.

Ss: /r/.

T: /r/.

Ss: /r/.

T: /r/.

Ss: /r/.

T: /ɔk/.

Ss: /ɔk/.

T: Rock.

Ss: Rock.

T: Now, can you give me another word, another letter to form another
      word.

S3:   Clock.

T: Can you spell it?

S3:   C-l-o-c-k.

T: Good. C-l-o-c-k. Clock.

Ss: Clock.

T: c, l, /kl/.

Ss: /kl/.

T: Clock.

Ss: Clock.

T: One o'clock. Two o'clock. Clock.

Ss: Clock.

The teacher in Excerpt 3 selected a word from the story that begins with an initial consonant, blend, or digraph and has a high frequency rime (e.g., *book*) and wrote it on the board. She asked pupils to say it aloud. Then she divided the word into its onset and rime and asked pupils to read first the onset and then the rime. Under the onset, she made a list of consonant or consonant blends. She asked the pupils to read each onset and rime and then the whole word. Then she invited the pupils to generate other words containing the same rime to add to the list. She let the pupils practice pronouncing all of the words. The following example of the presentation format is given with the "ook" family illustration:

The OOK Family

B ook

C

L

H

Sh

Cr

Have Students Repeat Readings

An important goal of many reading programmes is for readers to develop automaticity, which involves developing a comprehensive sight vocabulary of both function and content words. Research has shown that repeated reading of the same extended text in different situations and for different purposes can be a particularly effective strategy for learners whose first language is not English (see, e.g., Denton, 2001; Samuels, 2002). All of the students involved in PERP received copies of the story text after every shared reading experience. They were given a few minutes to read the text silently in the lessons, then they were encouraged to take turns reading to each other in class and to take the story text home to read to their parents or siblings. Although teachers should not devote a great deal of class time to repeated reading, they should allow a few minutes for students to read silently or to a partner at least once a week.

An extended activity and reinforcement of the repeated reading text was the reading of poems written by one of the team members, Michael Murphy. The poems were based on the story that was just read and gave the students added exposure to the rhythm, rhyme, and vocabulary of English in the context of the big book story. The following poem is one of the original poems used to follow the story *Pirate Adventure* (Hunt, 1988). The poem also reinforces onsets and rimes as illustrated in the rhyming couplets.

> Pirates big, pirates small
> Pirates who are very tall
>
> Pirates weak, pirates strong
> Pirates singing all day long
>
> Pirates fat, pirates thin
> Pirates always like to win
>
> Pirates young, pirates old
> Pirates counting lots of gold
>
> Pirates friendly, pirates kind
> Pirates who are hard to find
>
> Pirates fight, pirates sleep
> Pirates clean and pirates sweep
>
> Pirates work, pirates play
> Pirates come, then go away
>
> Pirates happy, pirates sad
> Pirates are not always bad
>
> So, hand up if you'd like to be
> With these pirates on the sea!
>
> Come then, let us take a trip
> With these pirates in their ship!

Design Activities That Invite Students to Respond

Activities involving personal response allow pupils to relate what they read in the story to their own experiences and background knowledge (McMahon & Raphael,

1997; Rosenblatt, 1938, 1976). This is a very important aspect of helping students appreciate and engage with reading in a second language. Deeper levels of comprehension involve going beyond simple recognition and recall of explicitly stated information to reading between and beyond the lines. In other words, to infer meaning that is implicit, one must draw conclusions, give opinions, and consider how the text relates personally to oneself, which are important aspects of the process of constructing meaning and contribute to the development of critical thinking. In PERP, as in all activities, students were encouraged to respond to personal response questions in English. If they were unable to or felt very uncomfortable, they could use the mother tongue. The following activities and questions were generated in English to develop pupils' written and oral personal responses:

- Draw and write about your favourite character and explain why he or she is your favourite.

- Create a new ending to the story.

- Create a story based on the story you read.

- Write a letter to one of the characters telling him or her how you feel about what happened.

- Describe an experience you had that is similar to the one in the story.

- What would you do if you were one of the characters in the story?

- What do you think? What would you do? How would you feel if you were this character?

Provide Class Library Lessons

The PERP lesson provided explicit teaching in specific reading strategies, and the PERP class library lesson provided opportunities for children to apply those strategies naturally by independently reading an extensive range of interesting, high-quality books. These books included both narrative and nonfiction stories. Class library sessions were held once a week for a single, 35-minute lesson, during which students read the books provided by the project and the school and retold the stories to their classmates.

Develop Curriculum Units

In collaboration with teachers, the Project Team developed 38 curriculum units. Following the workshops, teachers tried out ideas in their lessons, and successful ones were then drafted by teachers and edited by the Project Team. Ideas from various schools were shared and compiled into draft curriculum units and distributed to all project schools. Each unit was related to a specific big book story and contained a range of activities that exemplified the key pedagogical strategies, which were described with examples from earlier curriculum units. The units also played a key role in introducing the project to the new schools. Eighteen of the units were subsequently selected for more detailed development and published as *Using Big Books to Teach English: Units of Work from the Primary English Reading Project* (Mahon, 1999), which was distributed to all primary schools in Hong Kong and remains an invaluable resource for teachers.

◈ CONCLUSION

As outlined in project reports and journal articles (e.g., Lee, Lee, & Murphy, 1998; Mahon & Tinker Sachs, 1995, 1996; Shum & Tinker Sachs, 1999; Tinker Sachs & Leung, 2001) and as described in our final report (Mahon & Tinker Sachs, 2001), the results our students achieved on a range of tasks involving assessment of oral reading, oral retelling, reading comprehension, vocabulary, phonological awareness, and attitude surveys show that

> the Project has made a positive impact upon the reading progress and performance of upper primary school pupils. The results also indicate that the gains achieved during Year One were sustained and further consolidated in Year Two. Finally, the results suggest that greater benefits may be achieved when this type of programme is started earlier. (Mahon & Tinker Sachs, 2001, p. 4)

Teachers who participated in the project experienced a great deal of professional growth and development in many aspects, as evidenced in their participation in in-school and across-school sharing sessions and also in presentations at local seminars and international conferences. From the analyses of team members' annual interviews with teachers and of teacher questionnaire data, results also show that teachers who participated in PERP experienced a wide variety of positive changes in their knowledge, beliefs, and instructional practices. These changes included

- increased knowledge of specific strategies to develop various aspects of literacy
- increased knowledge of a wider range of resources
- more critical understanding of resources for teaching reading
- increased knowledge of how to use storybooks to teach reading
- recognition of the limitations of the course book as a resource for teaching children to read in English
- recognition that they could develop pupils' language ability through the use of big books in ways that they could not with the course book
- change from a belief that the course book was the most appropriate reading material, to a belief that the course book was useful only for teaching grammar and vocabulary, not for developing reading ability
- emergence of the belief that using storybooks and big books was effective for helping children develop as readers
- emergence of a definite purpose and objectives for teaching reading
- emergence of a belief that they had improved as teachers of reading because of PERP
- change from using traditional instructional practices based almost exclusively on the course book to using a range of resources including big books, storybooks, informational books, poems, and rhymes to develop literacy
- development of expertise in using big books for shared reading

- development of expertise in a wider repertoire of skills and strategies for teaching reading
- change from negative to mainly positive perceptions of their pupils' reading ability
- emergence of the belief that their pupils had developed greater interest in reading as a result of PERP
- increased professionalism and efficacy (Mahon & Tinker Sachs, 2001, p. 4)

There were many successes in PERP, but also many constraints for teachers and researchers. Constraints were related mainly to class size and space, resources, workload and time, and the general lack of integration of PERP with the mainstream English curriculum. However, the project has been successful in enabling considerable improvement in pupils' progress and performance as readers in English, and it has had a tremendous impact on the professionalism of many primary teachers of English, who have been enabled in their teaching strategies and teaching efficacy through PERP. We believe that all of this was possible through the project's model of teacher development, which was long term, teacher focused, school based, and founded on varied modes of collaboration.

Since the completion of the project, the instructional strategies have been disseminated widely, and teachers in a number of other schools have started to adopt many of these strategies, particularly the strategy of shared reading with big books. The efficacy of a literature-based approach to English reading literacy has been tried, tested, and validated by this project. A literature-based approach therefore appears to provide a valuable and viable alternative to the current instructional practices typically used to teach reading in English as a second or foreign language in Hong Kong's local primary schools.

◈ ACKNOWLEDGMENTS

We would like to acknowledge our colleagues on the PERP team: Alice Chow Wai Kwan, Ina Lam Siu Yuen Mei, Icy Lee Kit Bing, May Lee Mee To, Michael Murphy, Sandy Shum So Po, and Winnie Wong Shiu Yu.

◈ CONTRIBUTORS

Gertrude Tinker Sachs has been a primary and secondary school teacher and has worked as a teacher of teachers in the Bahamas, Hong Kong, and the United States. She is a professor of language and literacy at Georgia State University in the United States.

Tony Mahon is senior lecturer in the Faculty of Education at Canterbury Christ Church University College in the United Kingdom.

◈ APPENDIX

Name of Big Book Story	Publisher	Author
The Humongous Cat	Sunshine	Joy Cowley
Birthday	Sunshine	Joy Cowley
Dippy Dinner Drippers	Sunshine	Joy Cowley
Mrs. Muddle Mud-Puddle	Sunshine	Joy Cowley
Don't You Laugh at Me	Sunshine	Joy Cowley
Greedy Cat	Troll Associates	Joy Cowley
Castle Adventure	Oxford University Press	Roderick Hunt
Pirate Adventure	Oxford University Press	Roderick Hunt
A New Dog	Oxford University Press	Roderick Hunt
The Secret Room	Oxford University Press	Roderick Hunt
The Dragon Tree	Oxford University Press	Roderick Hunt
Rosie's Walk	Scholastic	Pat Hutchins
Old Man's Mitten	Scholastic	Unknown
The Three Billy Goats Gruff	Scholastic	Ellen Appleby
The Little Red Hen	Addison Wesley	Seddon Kelly
The Rabbit and the Turnip	Addison Wesley	Seddon Kelly
The Farmer and the Beet	Addison Wesley	Seddon Kelly
Goldilocks and the Three Bears	Addison Wesley	Unknown
The Wicked Pirate	Heinemann	Sue Eggleton

Note. The Oxford University Press titles listed here are part of the Oxford Reading Tree Series.

References

Abe, K. (1996). Teaching English to children in an EFL setting. In T. Kral (Ed.), *Teacher development—Making the right moves* (pp. 264–268). Washington, DC: English Language Programs Division, United States Information Agency.

Adams, M. J. (1990). *Beginning to read: Thinking and learning about print.* Cambridge, MA: MIT Press.

Adams, M. J. (1994). Modeling the connections between word recognition and reading. In R. B. Ruddell, M. R. Ruddell, & H. Singer (Eds.), *Theoretical models and processes of reading* (4th ed., pp. 838–863). Newark, DE: International Reading Association.

Adamson, B., Kwan, T., & Chan, K. K. (Eds.). (2000). *Changing the curriculum: The impact of reform on primary schooling in Hong Kong.* Hong Kong: Hong Kong University Press.

Alexander, R. J. (1984). *Primary teaching.* London: Holt, Rinehart & Winston.

Altwerger, B., Edelsky, D., & Flores, B. M. (1989). Whole language: What's new? In G. Manning & M. Manning (Eds.), *Whole language: Beliefs and practice, K–8* (pp. 9–12). Washington, DC: National Education Association.

Anderson, R. C. (1984). Role of the reader's schema in comprehension, learning and memory. In R. C. Anderson, J. Osborn, & R. J. Tierney (Eds.), *Learning to read in American schools: Basal readers and content texts* (pp. 243–258). Hillsdale, NJ: Lawrence Erlbaum.

Anthony, E. M. (1963). Approach, method, technique. *ELT Journal, 17,* 63–67.

Au, A. (1998). Language standards and proficiency (an employer's viewpoint). In B. Asker (Ed.), *Teaching language and culture: Building Hong Kong on education* (pp. 179–183). Hong Kong: Addison Wesley Longman.

Bada, E. (1999). In-service teacher training in ELT: Capturing efficiency. *Language, 75,* 24–33.

Baetens-Beardsmore, H. (1982). *Bilingualism: Basic principles.* Clevedon, England: Multilingual Matters.

Bagby, K., Basile, L. J., McClay, J., & Wallace, A. H. (1996). *How to manage learning centers in the classroom.* Huntington Beach, CA: Teacher Created Materials.

Baker, C. (1993). *Foundations of bilingual education and bilingualism.* Clevedon, England: Multilingual Matters.

Baker, C. (1996). *Foundations of bilingual education and bilingualism* (2nd ed.). Clevedon, England: Multilingual Matters.

Baker, C., & Garcia, O. (Eds.). (1995). *Policy and practice in bilingual education.* Clevedon, England: Multilingual Matters.

Balboni, P. (1993). Lingue straniere alle elementari: Una prospettiva Italiana [Foreign languages in primary school: An Italian perspective]. *Biblioteca di Quaderni di Italianistica, 13.* Ottawa, Canada: Canadian Society for Italian Studies.

Balkcom, S. (1992). *Cooperative learning.* Washington, DC: Office of Research Education. (ERIC Document Reproduction Service No. ED346999).

Bax, S. (1997). Roles for a teacher educator in context-sensitive teacher education. *ELT Journal, 51,* 232–241.

Benvenuto, G., & Lopriore, L. (1999). *La valutazione delle competenze in lingua straniera nella scuola elementare. Rapporto di ricerca* [Foreign language assessment at primary level. Research report]. Rome: Italian Ministry of Education.

Benvenuto, G., & Lopriore, L. (2000). *La lingua straniera nella scuola materna ed elementare* [Foreign languages at kindergarten and primary school]. Rome: Anicia.

Bishop, G. (1986). *Education: An innovation.* Basingstoke, England: Macmillan.

Block, D., & Cameron, D. (Eds.). (2002). *Globalization and language teaching.* London: Routledge.

Blondin, C., Candelier, M., Edelenbos, P., Johnstone, R., Kubanek-German, A., & Taeschner, T. (1998). *Foreign languages in primary and preschool education: A review of recent research within the European Union.* London: CILT.

Boletín Oficial del Estado. (1970). *General de educación y financiamiento de la reforma educativa* [General Law 14/1970 on education and financing of educational reform]. Madrid, Spain: Ministerio de la Presidencia.

Boletín Oficial del Estado. (1985). *Reguladora del derecho a la educación* [Organic law 8/1985 on the right to education]. Madrid, Spain: Ministerio de la Presidencia.

Boletín Oficial del Estado. (1990). *Ordenación general del sistema educativo* [Organic Law 1/1990 on the general organization of the education system]. Madrid, Spain: Ministerio de la Presidencia.

Boletín Oficial del Estado. (1991a). *Real Decreto 1006/1991, de 14 de junio (BOE de 26 de junio), por el que se establecen las enseñanzas mínimas correspondientes a la educación primaria* [Royal decree 1006/1991 that established the curriculum for primary education]. Madrid, Spain: Ministerio de la Presidencia.

Boletín Oficial del Estado. (1991b). *Real Decreto 1344/1991, de 6 de septiembre (BOE de 13 de septiembre), por el que se establece el currículo de educación primaria* [Royal Decree 1344/1991 that established the curriculum for primary education]. Madrid, Spain: Ministerio de la Presidencia.

Boletín Oficial del Estado. (1995). *Ley org·nica 9/1995, de 20 de noviembre (BOE de 21 de noviembre), de la participación, la evaluación y el gobierno de los centros docentes* [Organic law 9/1995 on the participation, evaluation and management of schools]. Madrid, Spain: Ministerio de la Presidencia.

Bourdieu, P. (1991). *Languages and symbolic power* (G. Raymond & M. Adamson, Trans.). Cambridge, MA: Polity Press.

Bradman, T., & Hawkins, C. (1986). *See you later, alligator.* New York: Penguin Books.

Brown, H. D. (2000). *Principles of language learning and teaching* (4th ed.). Englewood Cliffs, NJ: Prentice Hall.

Brumfit, C., Moon, J., & Tongue, R. (Eds.). (1991). *Teaching English to children.* London: HarperCollins.

Cameron, L. (2001). *Teaching languages to young learners.* Cambridge, England: Cambridge University Press.

Carless, D. R. (1997). Managing systemic curriculum change: A critical analysis of Hong Kong's target-oriented curriculum initiative. *International Review of Education, 43,* 349–366.

Carless, D. R. (1999). Perspectives on the cultural appropriacy of Hong Kong's target-oriented curriculum (TOC) initiative. *Language, Culture and Curriculum, 12,* 238–254.

Centro de Información y Documentación Educativa. (n.d.). *Hours for core curriculum in primary education by cycle in the Valencian community.* Retrieved November 7, 2005, from http://www.mec.es/cide/

Cerini, G., & Gianferraro, L. (Eds.). (2005). Do you speak English? *Notizie della scuola, 4,* 1–80.

Chapman, C., & Freeman, L. (1996). *Multiple intelligences: Centers and projects.* Arlington Heights, IL: IRI/Skylight Training and Publishing.

Charbonnel, P. (2002, June). Le point sur. . . . L'apprentissage des langues vivantes [Reviewing and taking stock of foreign language learning]. *Mensuel de l'observatoire de l'enfance en France,* 52. Retrieved March 1, 2005, from http://www.observatoiredelenfance .org/pdf/Numero_52.pdf

Choi, C. C. (1998). Language standards: An HKEA perspective. In B. Asker (Ed.), *Teaching language and culture: Building Hong Kong on education* (pp. 184–192). Hong Kong: Addison-Wesley Longman.

Chow, A., Lee, I. K. B., & Murphy, M. (1996). EFL reading in the primary classroom: Teachers' perceptions and practices. In G. Tinker Sachs, M. Brock, & R. Lo (Eds.), *Directions in second language teacher education* (pp. 123–146). Hong Kong: City University of Hong Kong.

Chupin, J. (2005, February). *Apprentissage précoce: oui, mais comment?* [Early (language) learning: Yes, but how?]. *Le Monde de l'education, 333,* 24–26.

Clyne, M., Jenkins, C., Chen, I. Y., Tsokalidou, R., & Wallner, T. (1995). *Second language from primary school: Models and outcomes.* Canberra: National Languages and Literacy Institute of Australia.

Coelho, E. (1992). Cooperative learning: Foundation for a communicative curriculum. In C. Kessler (Ed.), *Cooperative language learning* (pp. 31–50). New York: Pearson.

Coleman, H. (Ed.). (1996). *Society and the language classroom.* Cambridge, England: Cambridge University Press.

Coleman, H. (2002). *Project impact assessment report, 2002.* Colombo, Sri Lanka: The British Council/Department for International Development.

Collier, V., & Thomas, W. (1999). Making U.S. schools effective for English language learners: Part 3. *TESOL Matters, 9*(6), 1, 10.

Coniam, D. (1998). Establishing minimum-standard qualifications in Hong Kong for English language teachers. In B. Asker (Ed.), *Teaching language and culture: Building Hong Kong on education* (pp. 193–205). Hong Kong: Addison-Wesley Longman.

Cook, V. (1996). *Second language learning and language teaching* (2nd ed.). London: Edward Arnold.

Council of Europe. (1997). *The European language portfolio.* Strasbourg, France: Author.

Council of Europe. (1998a). *Communication in the modern languages classrooms.* Strasbourg, France: Author.

Council of Europe. (1998b). *Plurilingual and multicultural competence.* Strasbourg, France: Author.

Council of Europe. (2001). *A common European framework of reference for languages: Learning, teaching, assessment.* Cambridge, England: Cambridge University Press. Retrieved April 19, 2005, from http://www.culture2.coe.int/portfolio/documents_intro /common_framework.html

Cummins, J. (1979). Linguistic independence and the educational development of bilingual children. *Review of Educational Research, 49,* 222–251.

Datnow, A., & Castellano, M. (2000). Teachers' responses to Success for All: How beliefs, experiences and adaptations shape implementation. *American Educational Research Journal, 37,* 775–799.

de Gaudemar, J. P. (2001, November 8). Habilitation des personnels chargés de l'enseignement des langues vivantes à l'école primaire [Certifying personnel to teach foreign languages in primary school]. *Bulletin Officiel de l'Education Nationale, 41.* Retrieved September 25, 2005, from http://www.education.gouv.fr/botexte/bo011108 /MENE0102337C.htm de Gaudemar, J. P. (2002, August 29). Programme transitoire d'enseignement des langues étrangères ou régionales au cycle des approfondissements de l'école primaire [Transition curriculum for teaching foreign languages or regional languages in primary school, grades 4 and 5]. *Bulletin Officiel de l'Education Nationale, 31.* Retrieved September 25, 2005, from http://www.education.gouv.fr/botexte/hs04020829/MENE0201503A.htm

De Mauro, T. (1963). *Storia linguistica dell'Italia unita* [Linguistic history of united Italy]. Bari, Italy: Laterza.

Debbasch, R. (2006, June 8). Enseignment des langues vivantes: Renovation de l'enseignement des langues vivantes etrangeres [Teaching foreign languages: Renovating the teaching of foreign languages]. *Bulletin Officiel de l'Education Nationale, 23.* Retrieved July 28, 2006, from http://www.education.gouv.fr/bo/2006/23/MENE0601048C.htm

Dede, M., & Emre, M. (2002). *Spotlight on English 1: Teacher's book—Primary grade 6.* Ankara, Turkey: Özgün.

Densky, A. B., & Reese, M. (1993). *Programmers pocket summary.* Indian Rocks Beach, FL: Southern Institute Press.

Denton, C. A. (2001). The efficacy of two English reading interventions in a bilingual education program. *Dissertation Abstracts International, 61*(11), 4325–4326.

Department for International Development. (2002). *Primary English Language Project (PELP). Project memorandum—Extension addendum.* Unpublished paper.

Department for International Development and World Bank. (2000). *Towards social harmony in education.* Unpublished report.

Department of Education, Government of India. (1993a). *Statewise number of schools according to area and category.* Retrieved October 3, 2005, from http://www.ncert.nic.in/sites/educationalsurvey/sch.htm

Department of Education, Government of India. (1993b). *Statewise teachers in different category of schools.* Retrieved October 3, 2005, from http://www.ncert.nic.in/sites/educationalsurvey/sch.htm

Duhamel, M. (1995, May 11). Orientations pédagogiques et modalités de mise en oeuvre [Pedagogical orientations and how to implement them]. *Bulletin Officiel de l'Education Nationale, 19,* 1649–1671.

Dunn, O. (1985). *Beginning English with young children.* London: Macmillan.

Duwoye, P. Y., & Le Bihan-Graf, C. (2005, May 26). Concours [Entrance exams for teachers' colleges]. *Bulletin Officiel de l'Education Nationale, 21.* Retrieved July 28, 2006, from http://www.education.gouv.fr/bo/2005/21/MENP0500879A.htm

Eastman, P. D. (1976). *Are you my mother?* New York: Random House.

Edelsky C., Altwerger, B., & Flores, B. (1991). *Whole language: What's the difference?* Portsmouth, NH: Heinemann.

Eggleton, J. (1998). *The wicked pirate.* Portsmouth, NH: Heinemann.

El Naggar, Z. (2004, March). *The first standards-based English textbook for Egyptian primary one students: The agony and the ecstasy.* Paper presented at the annual convention of TESOL Arabia, Dubai, United Arab Emirates.

El Naggar, Z., Fadel, R., Hanna, R., McCloskey, M. L., & Thornton, B. (2001, February). *SPEER: An empowering primary EFL resource.* Paper presented at the 35th Annual TESOL Convention and Exhibit, St. Louis, MO.

El Naggar, Z., Fadel, R., Hanna, R., McCloskey, M. L., & Thornton, B. (Eds.). (2002). *Spotlight on primary English education resources (SPEER).* Washington, DC: Academy for Educational Development.

Elley, W. B. (1997, March). *Lifting literacy levels with storybooks: Evidence from the South Pacific, Singapore, Sri Lanka and South Africa.* Paper presented at the World Conference on Literacy, Philadelphia.

Elley, W. B., & Manghubai, F. (1983). The impact of reading on second language learning. *Reading Research Quarterly, 19,* 53–67.

Enright, D. S. (1991). Supporting children's English language development in grade-level and language classrooms. In Celce-Murcia, M. (Ed.), *Teaching English as a second or foreign language* (pp. 386–402). Boston: Heinle & Heinle.

Evaluation des compétences en anglais des élèves de 15 ans à 16 ans dans sept pays européens [Assessing English language competence in 15- and 16-year-old students in seven countries]. (2004). Retrieved December 27, 2004, from ftp://trf.education.gouv.fr/pub /edutel/dpd/noteeval/eva0401.pdf

Falvey, P. (1998). ESL, EFL and language acquisition in the context of Hong Kong. In B. Asker (Ed.), *Teaching language and culture: Building Hong Kong on education* (pp. 73–85). Hong Kong: Addison-Wesley Longman.

Farr, R., & Tone, B. (1998). *Portfolio and performance assessment: Helping students evaluate their progress as readers and writers.* Orlando, FL: Harcourt Brace.

Fisher, R. (1990). *Teaching children to think.* New York: Blackwell.

Froese, V. (1991a). Introduction to whole-language teaching and learning. In V. Froese (Ed.), *Whole language: Practice and theory* (pp. 1–16). Needham Heights, MA: Allyn & Bacon.

Froese, V. (1991b). Assessment: Form and function. In V. Froese (Ed.), *Whole language: Practice and theory.* Needham Heights, MA: Allyn & Bacon.

Fullan, M., & Hargreaves, A. (1996). *What's worth fighting for in your school?* New York: Teachers College Press.

Fullan, M. G., & Stiegelbauer, S. (1991). *The new meaning of educational change* (2nd ed.). London: Cassell.

Galambos, S. J., & Goldin-Meadow, S. (1990). The effects of learning two languages on levels of metalinguistic awareness. *Cognition, 34,* 1–56.

Gardner, H. E. (1993). *Multiple intelligences.* New York: Basic Books.

Genesee, F. (1995). The Canadian second language immersion program. In O. Garcia & C. Baker (Eds.), *Policy and practice in bilingual education* (pp. 118–133). Clevedon, England: Multilingual Matters.

Gokak, V. K. (1963). The teaching of English in India. *Report of the conference on the teaching of English in schools April 15–20, 1963.* New Delhi, India: National Council of Educational Research and Training.

Goodman, Y. M. (1989). Kid watching: An alternative to testing. In G. Mann & M. Manning (Eds.), *Whole language: Beliefs and practices, K–8* (pp. 115–123). Washington, DC: National Education Association.

Goswami, U., & Bryant, P. E. (1990). *Phonological skills and learning to read.* Mahwah, NJ: Lawrence Erlbaum.

Goutallier, M. (1993). Notes sur l'enseignement précoce des langues vivantes [Notes on teaching foreign languages to young pupils]. *Enseigner les langues vivantes à l'école elémentaire* (pp. 59–62). Paris: Centre National de Documentation Pédagogique.

The Government of Andhra Pradesh. (2002). *My English workbook class III and class IV.* Hyderabad, India: Author.

Gower, R., Phillips, D., & Walters, S. (1995). *Teaching practice handbook.* Oxford, England: Heinemann.

Grimmett, P. P., & Crehan, E. P. (1992). The nature of collegiality in teacher development. In M. Fullan & A. Hargreaves (Eds.), *Teacher development and educational change* (pp. 56–85). London: Falmer Press.

Guskey, T. R. (1986). Staff development and the process of teacher change. *Educational Researcher, 15*(5), 5–12.

Halliday, M. A. K. (1998). Where languages meet: The significance of the Hong Kong experience. In B. Asker (Ed.), *Teaching language and culture: Building Hong Kong on education* (pp. 27–37). Hong Kong: Addison-Wesley Longman.

Halliwell, S. (2000). *Teaching English in the primary classroom* (10th ed.). Essex, England: Longman.

Hargreaves, A. (1992). Cultures of teaching: A focus of change. In A. Hargreaves & M. Fullan (Eds.), *Understanding teacher development* (pp. 216–240). London: Cassell.

Hargreaves, A. (1994). *Changing teachers, changing times: Teachers' work and culture in the postmodern age.* London: Teachers College Press.

Hargreaves, A. (2000). Four ages of professionalism and professional learning. *Teachers and Teaching: Theory and Practice, 6,* 151–182.

Hargreaves, A., & Fullan, M. (Eds.). (1992). *Understanding teacher development.* London: Cassell.

Harley, B. (1986). *Age in second language learning.* London: Edward Arnold.

Hayes, D. (1995). In-service teacher development: Some basic principles. *ELT Journal, 49,* 252–261.

Hayes, D. (1997a). Articulating the context: INSET and teachers' lives. In D. Hayes (Ed.), *In-service teacher development: International perspectives* (pp. 74–85). Hemel Hempstead, England: Prentice Hall.

Hayes, D. (1997b). Helping teachers to cope with large classes. *ELT Journal, 51,* 106–116.

Hayes, D. (2004). Inside INSET: Trainers' perceptions. In D. Hayes (Ed.), *Trainer development: Principles and practice from language teacher training* (pp. 63–79). Melbourne: Language Australia.

Hillert, M., & Wilde, I. (1984). *Three little pigs.* Cleveland, OH: Modern Curriculum Press.

Holdaway, D. (1979). *The foundations of literacy.* Sydney, Australia: Ashton Scholastic.

Holliday, A. (1996). *Appropriate methodology and social context,* Cambridge, England: Cambridge University Press.

Holliday, A. R. (1992). Tissue rejection and informal orders in ELT projects: Collecting the right information. *Applied Linguistics, 13,* 404–424.

Holliday, A. R. (1994). *Appropriate methodology and social context.* Cambridge, England: Cambridge University Press.

Houwer, A. D. (1999). *Two or more languages in early childhood: Some general points and practical recommendations.* Washington, DC: Center for Applied Linguistics. Retrieved April 26, 2005, from http://www.cal.org/resources/digest/earlychild.html

Hudelson, S. (1996). EFL teaching and children: A topic-based approach. In T. Kral (Ed.), *Teacher development: Making the right moves* (pp. 255–263). Washington, DC: United States Information Agency, English Language Programs Division.

Huie, K., & Yahya, N. (2003). Learning to write in the primary grades: Experiences of English language learners and mainstream students. *TESOL Journal, 12*(1), 25–31.

Hunt, R. (1988). *Pirate adventure.* Oxford, England: Oxford University Press.

Hyltenstam, I., & Abrahamson, N. (2001). Age and L2 learning: The hazards of matching practical "implications" with theoretical "facts." *TESOL Quarterly, 35,* 151–170.

Ibrahim, N. A. (1991). In-service training in Malaysia for the New Primary Curriculum (KBSR). In K. M. Lewin & J. S. Stuart (Eds.), *Educational innovation in developing countries: Case studies of changemakers* (pp. 95–126). London: Macmillan.

INDIRE. (2005). *INDIRE main page.* Retrieved February 23, 2005, from http://www.indire.it

Ingraham, P. B. (1997). *Creating and managing learning centers: A thematic approach.* Peterborough, NH: Crystal Springs Books.

Inspection Générale de l'Education National. (1993). *L'Enseignement des langues vivantes à l'école élémentaire* [Teaching foreign languages in elementary school]. Paris: Author.

Italian Ministry of Education. (1985a). *Programmi didattici per la scuola elementare* [Teaching programs for primary school]. Rome: Author.

Italian Ministry of Education. (1985b). *Il Progetto ILLSE e l'insegnamento della lingua straniera nella scuola elementare* [The ILLSE Project and foreign language teaching at the primary level]. Rome: Author.

Italian Ministry of Education. (1994). *DIRELEM, L'insegnamento delle lingue francese, inglese, spagnolo e tedesco nella scuola elementare 1993/94* [DIRELEM, French, English, Spanish and German language instruction in 1993/94 elementary school]. Rome: MPI.

Italian Ministry of Education. (2001). *Progetto Lingue 2000. Atti dei Seminari per i nuovi formatori di lingue straniere* [Progetto Lingue 2000. Actions of the seminaries for the new makers of foreign languages]. Fiuggi, Italy: MPI.

Kagan, S. (1995). *We can talk: Cooperative learning in English reading.* (ERIC Document Reproduction Service No. 382035)

Kandiah, T. (2000). *Re-visioning, revolution, revisionism: English and the ambiguities of post-colonial practice.* Unpublished paper.

Kemmis, S., & McTaggart, R. (1982). *The action research planner.* Victoria, Australia: Deaken University Press.

Kennedy, C. (1987). Innovating for a change: Teacher development and innovation. *ELT Journal, 41,* 163–170.

Kher, B. G. (1957). *Report of the official language commission 1956.* New Delhi: Government of India.

Klein, K. (1993). Teaching young learners. *English Teaching Forum, 31*(2), 14–17.

Ko, K. S. (1996). The direction of teacher training program for primary school English. *Primary English Education, 2,* 26–51.

Kocaoluk, F., &. Kocaoluk, M. Ş. (2001). *İlköğretim Okulu programı 1999–2000* [Primary Education Curriculum 1999–2000]. Istanbul, Turkey: Author.

Krashen, S. D., Scarcella, P. C., & Long, M. (1982). *Child-adult differences in second language acquisition.* Rowley, MA: Newbury House.

Lamb, M. (1996). The consequences of INSET. In T. Hedge & N. Whitney (Eds.), *Power, pedagogy and practice* (pp. 139–149). Oxford, England: Oxford University Press.

Lang, J. (2001). *Séminaire sur l'enseignement des langues vivantes à l'école primaire* [Seminar on teaching foreign languages in primary school]. Retrieved February 6, 2005, from http://www.education.gouv.fr/discours/2001/langviv.htm

Laronche, M. (2004, October 22). *Déjà faible, le niveau des élèves français a baissé entre 1996 et 2002* [Already weak, French students' (English) level declined between 1996 and 2002]. *Le Monde,* p. 11.

Last but not least. (2004, October 22). *Le Monde,* p. 22.

Lee, I., Lee, M., & Murphy, M. (1998, April). *Primary pupils' profiles in reading and their implications.* Paper presented at the International Language in Education Conference, Hong Kong.

Lee, J. H. (1997). *The current status of teaching English in elementary schools and its problems.* Paper presented in the conference of the Korean English Education Institution, Seoul, South Korea.

Legendre, J. (2003, November 12). *L'enseignement des langues étrangères en France* [Teaching foreign languages in France]. *Rapport d'information, 63.* Retrieved January 23, 2005, from http://www.senat.fr/rap/r03-063/r03-063_mono.html

Leithwood, K. A. (1992). The principal's role in teacher development. In M. Fullan & A. Hargreaves (Eds.), *Teacher development and educational change* (pp. 86–103). London: Falmer Press.

Let's Go! (1993). Oxford, England: Oxford University Press.

Li, D. C. S. (1999). The functions and status of English in Hong Kong: A post-1997 update. *English World-Wide, 20,* 67–110.

Little, J. W. (1987). Teachers as colleagues. In V. Richardson-Koehler (Ed.), *Educators' handbook: A research perspective* (pp. 491–518). New York: Longman.

Little, J. W. (1990). The persistence of privacy: Autonomy and initiative in teachers' professional relations. *Teachers College Record, 91,* 509–536.

Lo, Y. H. (2000). Incorporating learning centers into EFL curricula in elementary schools. *The ETA-ROC Newsletter, 4*(1), 3–6.

Lo Bianco, J. (1999). A syntax of peace? Pragmatic constraints of language teaching and pragmatics in language learning. In J. Lo Bianco, A. J. Liddicoat, & C. Crozet (Eds.), *Striving for the third place: Intercultural competence through language education* (pp. 51–63). Melbourne: Language Australia.

Lopriore, L. (1997). Evaluating innovative TEFL at primary level. In *Papers from the First Euroconference on Young Learners* (pp. 159–163). Warwick, England: University of Warwick.

Lopriore, L. (1998). A pioneering teacher education program. *TESOL Quarterly, 32,* 510–517.

Lopriore, L. (2001). La valutazione degli apprendimenti delle lingue straniere nella scuola elementare [The evaluation of foreign language learning at primary level]. In F. Gattullo (Ed.), *La valutazione in lingua straniera* [The evaluation of foreign language learning] (pp. 215–244). Florence, Italy: Quaderni LEND, La Nuova Italia.

Lopriore, L. (Ed.). (2002). *PERSPECTIVES: A Journal of TESOL Italy, 29.*

Lotherington, H. (1996). A consideration of the portability and supportability of immersion education: A critical look at English immersion in Melanesia. *Journal of Multilingual and Multicultural Development, 17,* 349–359.

Lynch, P. (1986). *Using big books and predictable books.* Richmond Hill, Ontario: Scholastic Canada.

Mahon, T. (Ed.). (1999). *Using big books to teach English: Units of work from the Primary English Reading Project.* Hong Kong: Hong Kong Institute of Education.

Mahon, T., & Tinker Sachs, G. (1995). A collaborative approach to developing the teaching of reading in English as a foreign language. In University of Hong Kong Department of Curriculum Studies (Ed.), *Proceedings of Teacher Education in the Asian Region: An International Teacher Education Conference* (pp. 242–251). Hong Kong: University of Hong Kong.

Mahon, T., & Tinker Sachs, G. (1996). Constructing a blueprint for innovation in reading. In C. Zaher (Ed.), *New directions in reading: Proceedings of the 2nd EFL Skills Conference* (pp. 67–76). Cairo, Egypt: Center for Adult & Continuing Education, American University in Cairo.

Mahon, T., & Tinker Sachs, G. (2001). *Improving English reading in Hong Kong primary schools: Final report of the primary reading project.* Hong Kong: Hong Kong Institute of Education.

Malingre, V. (2004, October 22). Faut-il rendre l'apprentissage de l'anglais obligatoire dès le CE2? [Should English become an obligatory subject as of 3rd grade?]. *Le Monde,* pp. 1–11.

Marinova-Todd, S. H., Marshall, D. B., Snow, C. E. (2000). Three misconceptions about age and L2 learning. *TESOL Quarterly, 34,* 9–34.

Markee, N. (1997). *Managing curricular innovation.* Cambridge, England: Cambridge University Press.

Marsh, D., & Langé, G. (Eds.). (1999). *Implementing content and language integrated learning.* Jyväskylä, Finland: Continuing Education Centre, University of Jyväskylä.

McClay, J. L. (1996). *Learning centers.* Westminster, CA: Teacher Created Materials.

McCloskey, M. L. (2003, March). *Change that lasts.* Plenary address at the 37th Annual TESOL Convention and Exhibit, Baltimore.

McCloskey, M. L. (2004, March). *Standards for teaching in English: What, why, how?* Plenary address at the annual TESOL Arabia convention, Dubai, United Arab Emirates.

McCloskey, M. L., Thornton, B., El Naggar, Z., Touba, N., Mohasseb, M., & Ganem, E. (2003, March). *Home-owned, home-grown standards for teachers.* Paper presented at the 37th Annual TESOL Convention and Exhibit, Baltimore.

McDonell, W. (1992). Language and cognitive development through cooperative group work. In C. Kessler (Ed.), *Cooperative language learning* (pp. 51–64). New York: Simon & Schuster.

McMahon, S. I., & Raphael, T. E. (1997). The book club program: Theoretical and research foundations. In S. I. McMahon & T. E. Raphael (Eds.), *The book club connection. Literacy learning and classroom talk* (pp. 3–25). New York: Teachers College Press.

MEB. (2001). *2001 Yılı başında milli eğitim* [National education at the beginning of 2001]. Retrieved April 26, 2005, from http://www.meb.gov.tr/english/indexeng.htm

Min, C. K. (1993). The study of elementary English education in Korea. *English Teaching, 46,* 190–194.

Ministry of Education, Egypt. (1995). *Conference on the development of primary education curricula: Recommendations.* Cairo, Egypt: Author.

Ministry of Education, Egypt. (2003a). *CDIST resources center.* Retrieved May 11, 2006, from http://www.emoe.org/departments/cdist/resources.html

Ministry of Education, Egypt. (2003b). *Hand in hand 1.* Cairo, Egypt: Author.

Moon, J. (2000). *Children learning English.* London: Macmillan.

Moon, J., & Boullón, R. L. (1997). Reluctance to reflect: Issues in professional development. In D. Hayes (Ed.), *In-service teacher development: International perspectives* (pp. 60–73). Hemel Hempstead, England: Prentice Hall.

Murphey, T. (1992). *Music and song: Resource book for teachers.* London: Oxford University Press.

Murphey, T. (2003). NNS primary school teachers learning English with their students. *TESOL Matters, 13*(4), 1, 6.

National Council of Educational Research and Training. (2000). *National curriculum framework for school education.* Retrieved April 16, 2006, from http://www.ncert.nic.in /sites/publication/schoolcurriculum/cfcontents.htm

National Education Commission. (1992). *First report of the National Education Commission.* Colombo, Sri Lanka: Author.

National Education Commission. (1997). *Reforms in general education.* Colombo, Sri Lanka: Author.

National Education Commission. (2002). *National policy and action plan to promote English education.* Colombo, Sri Lanka: Author.

Newman, J. (1999). Notes on English teaching in Ethiopia. *TESOL Matters, 9*(6), 7.

Newman J. M. (1991). Whole language: A changed universe. *Contemporary Education, 62*(2), 70–73.

Ng, S. M. (1994). Improving English language learning in the upper primary levels in Brunei Darussalam. In M. L. Tickoo (Ed), *Research in reading and writing: A Southeast Asian collection* (pp. 41–54). Singapore: SEAMEO Regional Language Centre.

Ng, S. M., & Soh, O. (1986). The implementation of an English language programme for young Singapore children. In V. Bickley (Ed.), *Future directions in English language teacher education: Asia and Pacific perspectives* (pp. 148–160). Hong Kong: Institute of Language in Education.

Nicholas, H. (1983). But what do we mean by "bilingual"? *Polycom, 34,* 2–9.

Nunan, D. (1992). *Research methods in language learning.* Cambridge, England: Cambridge University Press.

Nunan, D. (1999). Does younger = better? *TESOL Matters, 9*(1), 3.

Nunan, D. (2003). The impact of English as a global language on educational policies and practices in the Asia-Pacific region. *TESOL Quarterly, 37,* 589–613.

Nye, B. A., Cain, V. A., Zaharias, J. B., Tollett, D. A., & Fulton, B. D. (1995, April). *Are multiage/non-graded programs providing students with a quality education? Some answers from the school success study.* Nashville, TN: Center of Excellence for Research in Basic Skills. (ERIC Document Reproduction Service No. ED384998)

O'Sullivan, M. C. (2001). The inset strategies model: An effective model for unqualified and underqualified primary teachers in Namibia. *International Journal of Educational Development, 21,* 93–117.

Ogle, D. (1986). K-W-L: A teaching model that develops active reading of expository text. *The Reading Teacher, 39,* 564–570.

Pang, M. Y. M., & Wong, W. S. Y. (2000). Reviewing the primary English language syllabi (1976–1997): Implications for curriculum study. In Y. C. Cheng, K. W. Chow, & K. T. Tsui (Eds.), *School curriculum change and development in Hong Kong* (pp. 201–225). Hong Kong: Hong Kong Institute of Education.

Paris, S. G., Lipson, M. Y., & Wixson, K. K. (1994). Becoming a strategic reader. In R. B. Ruddell, M. R. Ruddell, & H. Singer (Eds.), *Theoretical models and processes of reading* (4th ed., pp. 788–810). Newark, DE: International Reading Association.

Park, H. K., Jung, K. J., & Chun, J. Y. (1991). The study of English teacher-training models. *English Teaching, 41,* 3–50.

Pavan De Gregorio, G. (Ed.). (1999). *L'insegnamento delle lingue straniere in Italia* [Foreign language teaching in Italy]. Milan: CEDE.

Pearson, P. D., & Dole, J. A. (1987). Explicit comprehension instruction: A review of research and a new conceptualisation of knowledge. *Elementary School Journal, 88*(2), 151–165.

Pennycuick, D. (1993). *School effectiveness in developing countries: A summary of the research evidence.* London: Overseas Development Administration.

Pham, D. B. (1998). *English for primary school children, Book 2.* Ho Chi Min City, Vietnam: Nha Xuat ban Giao Duc.

Phillips, S. (1993). *Young learners.* Oxford, England: Oxford University Press.

Pica, T. (1994). Questions from the language classroom: Research and perspectives. *TESOL Quarterly, 28,* 49–79.

Pienemann, M., & Johnston, M. (1987). Factors influencing the development of language proficiency. In D. Nunan (Ed.), *Applying second language acquisition research* (pp. 45–141). Adelaide, Australia: National Curriculum Resource Centre.

Piper, T. (1993). *And then there were two: Children and second language learning.* Don Mills, Ontario, Canada: Pippin.

Porcelli, G., & Balboni, P. (1985). *Lingue straniere alle elementari: I risultati del progetto veneziano* [Foreign languages at primary level. The Venetian Project: Results]. Padova, Italy: CLUEP.

Pour la réussite de tous les élèves [Ensuring that all pupils achieve their full potential]. (2004). Retrieved December 27, 2004, from http://www.debatnational.education.fr /index.php?rid=87

Primary Education Planning Project. (2000). *Guidelines for the implementation of the primary education reform.* Colombo, Sri Lanka: Ministry of Education and Higher Education.

QKids. (1999). *QSteps 1.* Taipei, Taiwan: Studio Classroom.

Report of the English Review Committee. (1965). New Delhi, India: University Grants Commission.

Richards, J. C., Platt, J., & Platt, H. (Eds.). (1992). *Longman dictionary of language teaching and applied linguistics.* Edinburgh, Scotland: Longman.

Richards, J. C., & Rodgers, T. S. (2001). *Approaches and methods in language teaching* (2nd ed.). Cambridge, England: Cambridge University Press.

Richardson, V. (1994). The consideration of teachers' beliefs. In V. Richardson (Ed.), *Teacher change and the staff development process: A case in reading instruction* (pp. 90–108). New York: Teachers College Press.

Richardson, V. (1996). The role of attitudes and beliefs in learning to teach. In J. Sikula, T. J. Butteryj, & E. Guyton (Eds.), *Handbook of research on teacher education: A project of the association of teacher educators* (2nd ed., pp.102–119). New York: Simon & Schuster.

Richardson, V. (1997). Constructivist teaching and teacher education: Theory and practice. In V. Richardson (Ed.), *Constructivist teacher education: Building a world of new understandings* (pp. 3–14). London: Falmer Press.

Richardson, V., & Anders, P. L. (1994). The study of teacher change. In V. Richardson (Ed.), *Teacher change and the staff development process: A case in reading instruction* (pp. 159–180). New York: Teachers College Press.

Richardson, V., Anders, P., Tidwell, D., & Lloyd, C. (1991). The relationship between teachers' beliefs and practices in reading comprehension instruction. *American Educational Research Journal, 28,* 559–586.

Rixon, S. (1992a). English and other languages for younger children. *Language Teaching, 25,* 73–79.

Rixon, S. (Ed). (1992b). *Young learners of English: Some research perspectives.* London: Longman.

Rosenblatt, L. M. (1976). *Literature as exploration.* New York: Noble & Noble. (Original work published 1938)

Rosenblum, T., & Pinker, S. A. (1983). Word magic revisited: Monolingual and bilingual children's understanding of the word-object relationship. *Child Development, 54,* 773–780.

Rosenbusch, M. (1995). *Guidelines for starting an elementary school foreign language program.* Washington, DC: Center for Applied Linguistics. Retrieved April 26, 2005, from http://www.cal.org/resources/digest/rosenb01.html

Ruddell, R. B., & Ruddell, M. R. (1994). Language acquisition and literacy processes. In R. B. Ruddell., M. R. Ruddell, & H. Singer (Eds.), *Theoretical models and processes of reading* (4th ed., pp. 83–103). Newark, DE: International Reading Association.

Ruddell, R. B., & Unrau, R. J. (1994). Reading as a meaning-construction process: The reader, the text and the teacher. In R. B. Ruddell, M. R. Ruddell, & H. Singer (Eds.), *Theoretical models and processes of reading* (4th ed., pp. 996–1056). Newark, DE: International Reading Association.

Rumelhart, D. E. (1985). Toward an interactive model of reading. In H. Singer, & R. B. Ruddell (Eds.), *Theoretical models and processes of reading* (3rd ed., pp. 722–750). Newark, DE: International Reading Association.

Samuels, S. J. (2002). Reading fluency: Its development and assessment. In A. E. Farstrup & S. J. Samuels (Eds.), *What research has to say about reading instruction* (3rd ed., pp. 166–183). Newark, DE: International Reading Association.

Sanzo, R. (Ed.). (1993). *Fare lingua seconda nella scuola elementare* [Learning and teaching a second language at primary school]. Milan: Instituto Geografico De Agostini.

Savova, L. P., & Alexandrova, B. (1986). *Instructor's resource manual in English for grades 1–4 of the Bulgarian public schools.* Sofia, Bulgaria: Narodna Prosveta.

Savova, L. P., & Alexandrova, B. (1991). *Learn and play with us* (2nd ed.). Sofia, Bulgaria: Prosveta.

Scarbrough, D. R. (1976). Practical theory in the training of teachers of EFL. *ELT Journal, 30,* 103–109.

Schurr, S., Lewis, S., LaMorte, K., & Shewey, K. (1996). *Signaling student success: Thematic learning stations and integrated units.* Columbus, OH: National Middle School Association.

Scott, W. A., & Ytreberg, L. H. (1993). *Teaching English to children.* New York: Longman.

Scott, W. A., & Ytreberg, L. H. (2001). *Teaching English to children* (14th ed.). Essex, England: Longman.

Secretaría de Educación Pública. (1993). *Plan y programas de estudios* [National study plan and programs]. Mexico City, Mexico: Author.

Shum, S., & Tinker Sachs, G. (1999). What do EFL primary pupils' oral retelling show? In V. Crew, V. Berry, & J. Hung (Eds.), *Exploring diversity in the language curriculum* (pp. 227–246). Hong Kong: Hong Kong Institute of Education.

Singleton, D. (1989). *Language acquisition: The age factor*. Clevedon, England: Multilingual Matters.

Slaughter, J. P. (1993). *Beyond storybooks: Young children and the shared book experience*. Newark, DE: International Reading Association.

Smith, K. (1999). Why do we want to assess young learners? How do we do it? Who does it? In C. Milsud & G. Mallia (Eds), *Ways and measurements* (pp. 140–155). Msida, Malta: World Academic.

South Korea Ministry of Education. (1995). *The English curriculum for elementary schools*. Seoul, Korea: Author.

South Korea Ministry of Education. (1996). *Proposal for employing elementary school English teachers*. Seoul, Korea: Author.

South Korea Ministry of Education. (1997). *New policy of teaching English in elementary schools*. Seoul, Korea: Author.

Stahl, R. J. (1994). *The essential elements of cooperative learning in the classroom*. Bloomington, IN: ERIC Clearinghouse for Social Studies/Social Science Education. (ERIC Document Reproduction Service No. ED370881)

Stake, R. E. (1995). *The art of case study research*. Thousand Oaks, CA: Sage.

Swain, M. (1981). Time and timing in bilingual education. *Language Learning, 31,* 1–15.

Taeschner, T. (1993). *Insegnare la lingua straniera con il Format* [Teaching foreign languages through FORMAT]. Rome: Anicia.

Taeschner, T., Ploij, F. X., Etxeberria, F., Arzamendi, J., Garagorri, X., & O'Hanlon, C. (1997). *The adventures of hocus and lotus*. Milan: Franco Angeli.

Thornton, B. (2001, November). *What's so special about primary teaching?* Workshop presented at the Fifth International INGED—Anadolu Conference, Eskisehir, Turkey.

Thornton, B., Burch, R., & McCloskey, M. L. (1999, October). *"May I take your order, please?" An ecological approach to language development*. Paper presented at the EgypTesol 1999 Annual Convention, Cairo, Egypt.

Tierney, R. J., Readence, J. E., & Dishner, E. K. (1995). *Reading strategies and practices*. Needham Heights, MA: Allyn & Bacon.

Tinker Sachs, G. (2001, June). *Reading in English as a favourite pastime. Who, what, where and when*. Paper presented at the Critical Perspectives on Literacy Conference, Hong Kong.

Tinker Sachs, G., & Leung, A. (2001). Phonological awareness in beginning EFL primary pupils. In C. L. Chern, M. L. Liaw, & V. T. C. Shen (Eds.), *ESOL literacy in the Asia-Pacific region* (pp. 1–18). Taipei: Taiwan Reading Association.

Tinker Sachs, G., & Mahon, T. (1997). Reading in English as a foreign language: Primary students' oral reading behaviour and comprehension. *Perspectives, 9*(2), 78–109.

Tinker Sachs, G., & Mahon, T. (1998). Translating vision into reality through a collaborative approach to teacher development. *Perspectives, 10*(1), 170–227.

Titone, R. (1990). Dix thèses sur l'enseignement précoce des langues étrangères [Ten theses on the early teaching of foreign languages]. In R. Titone (Ed.), *La lingua straniera* [The foreign language]. Milan: Fabbri.

Titone, R. (1993). Apprendimento precoce di una L2: Bilinguismo e sviluppo metalinguistico [L2 early language learning: Bilingualism and metacognitive development]. *RILA, 3.* Rome: Bulzoni.

Torres, R. M. (1996). Without the reform of teacher education there will be no reform of education. *Prospects, 6,* 447–468.

Toth, M. (1995). *Heinemann children's games*. London: Heinemann.

Toulemonde, B. (1999a, June 17). *Enseignement des langues vivantes étrangères* [Teaching foreign languages]. Retrieved September 25, 2005, from http://www.education.gouv.fr /botexte/bo990624/MENE9901329C.htm

Toulemonde, B. (1999b, June 11). *Enseignements élémentaire et secondaire: Enseignement des langues vivantes étrangères* [Elementary and secondary school teaching: Teaching foreign languages]. *Bulletin Officiel de l'Education Nationale, 25*. Retrieved November 9, 2005, from http://www.education.gouv.fr/bo/1999/25/ensel.htm

Toulemonde, B. (1999c, November 11). *Langues vivantes étrangères—Orientations pédagogiques pour la mise en úuvre au CM1 et CM2* [Foreign languages—Pedagogical guidelines for implementation in 4th and 5th grades]. *Bulletin Officiel de l'Education Nationale, 40*. Retrieved September 25, 2005, from http://www.cndp.fr/ecole/langues/pdf/bo40_11111999.pdf

Translanguage in Europe: Content and language integrated learning (TIE-CLIL). (2004, December 12). Retrieved February 23, 2004, from http://www.tieclil.org

Tsui, A. B. M. (1996). Reticence and anxiety in second language learning. In K. M. Bailey & D. Nunan (Eds.), *Voices from the language classroom* (pp. 145–167). New York: Cambridge University Press.

Tucker, G.R. (1999). *A global perspective on bilingualism and bilingual education*. Washington, DC: Center for Applied Linguistics. Retrieved April 26, 2005, from http://www.cal.org/resources/digest/digestglobal.html

University of Cambridge. (n.d.). *ESOL examinations: YLE (Cambridge Young Learners English Tests)*. Retrieved November 16, 2005, from http://www.cambridgeesol.org/exams/yle.htm

Ur, P. (1996). *A course in language teaching: Practice and theory*. Cambridge, England: Cambridge University Press.

Vale, D. (1995). *Teaching children English: A training course for teachers of English to children*. Cambridge, England: Cambridge University Press.

Veenman, S., Tulder, V., & Voeten, M. (1994). The impact of in-service training on teacher behavior. *Teaching and Teacher Education, 10*, 303–317.

Walker, M. (1989). *Addison-Wesley kids 1*. Boston: Addison-Wesley.

Watson, D. J. (1994). Whole language: Why bother? *The Reading Teacher, 47*, 600–607.

Wilson, A. M., & Berne, J. (1999). Teacher learning and the acquisition of professional knowledge: An examination of research on contemporary professional development. In A. Iran-Nejad & P. D. Pearson (Eds.), *Review of research in education* (Vol. 24, pp. 173–209). Washington, DC: American Educational Research Association.

Wong, W. S. Y., & Pang, M. Y. M. (2000). An analysis of the primary English curriculum: Mismatches and implications. In Y. C. Cheng, K. W. Chow, & K. T. Tsui (Eds.), *School curriculum change and development in Hong Kong* (pp. 295–310). Hong Kong: Hong Kong Institute of Education.

Wood, D. (1988). *How children think and learn* (2nd. ed.). Malden, MA: Blackwell.

Wright, A. (1995). *Storytelling with children*. London: Oxford University Press.

Wright, D. (1989). English from the very first year of primary school. *English Teaching Forum, 22*(1), 29–30.

Yin, R. K. (1994). *Case study research: Design and methods* (2nd ed.). Thousand Oaks, CA: Sage.

Zohry, I. A. (2002). Creating and using low-tech teaching aids. In El Naggar, Z., Fadel, R., Hanna, R., McCloskey, M. L., & Thornton, B. (Eds.), *Spotlight on primary English education resources (SPEER)*. Washington, DC: Academy for Educational Development.

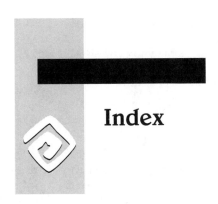

Index

Page numbers followed by an *f, t,* or *n* indicate figures, tables, or footnotes.

Q

 R

Also Available From TESOL

Academic Writing Programs
Ilona Leki, Editor

Action Research
Julian Edge, Editor

Bilingual Education
Donna Christian and Fred Genesee, Editors

Bridges to the Classroom: ESL Cases for Teacher Exploration
Joy Egbert and Gina Mikel Petrie

CALL Essentials
Joy Egbert

Communities of Supportive Professionals
Tim Murphey and Kazuyoshi Sato, Editors

Community Partnerships
Elsa Auerbach, Editor

Content-Based Instruction in Primary and Secondary School Settings
Dorit Kaufman and JoAnn Crandall, Editors

Distance-Learning Programs
Lynn Henrichsen, Editor

ESOL Tests and Testing
Stephen Stoynoff and Carol A. Chapelle

Gender and English Language Learners
Bonny Norton and Aneta Pavlenko, Editors

Grammar Teaching in Teacher Education
Dilin Liu and Peter Master, Editors

Interaction and Language Learning
Jill Burton and Charles Clennell, Editors

Internet for English Teaching
Mark Warschauer, Heidi Shetzer, and Christine Meloni

Journal Writing
Jill Burton and Michael Carroll, Editors

Literature in Language Teaching and Learning
Amos Paran, Editor

Mainstreaming
Effie Cochran, Editor

Planning and Teaching Creatively within a Required Curriculum for School-Age Learners
Penny McKay, Editor

PreK–12 English Language Proficiency Standards
Teachers of English to Speakers of Other Languages, Inc.

Professional Development of International Teaching Assistants
Dorit Kaufman and Barbara Brownworth, Editors

Teacher Education
Karen E. Johnson, Editor

Teaching English From a Global Perspective
Anne Burns, Editor

Technology-Enhanced Learning Environments
Elizabeth Hanson-Smith, Editor

For more information, contact
Teachers of English to Speakers of Other Languages, Inc.
700 South Washington Street, Suite 200
Alexandria, Virginia 22314 USA
Toll Free: 888-547-3369 • **Fax on Demand:** 800-329-4469
Publications Order Line: 888-891-0041
or 301-638-4427 or 4428
9am to 5pm, EST
publications@tesol.org • http://www.tesol.org/
Order online at www.tesol.org

T E S O L